FASHION HANDICRAFTS

Golden Hands Books

Marshall Cavendish
London and New York

Published by Marshall Cavendish Publications Limited
58 Old Compton Street
London W1V 5PA

©Marshall Cavendish Limited 1970–71–72–73

This material was specially prepared for
Findus Ltd. by the Promotional Publications Section
of Marshall Cavendish Publications Ltd. It was
first published by Marshall Cavendish Limited in *Golden
Hands, Golden Hands Monthly, Embroidery—50 New
Designs, 25 Leisure Fashions to Sew* and *All You Can
Sew for the Home,* and by Marshall Cavendish Publications
Limited in the *Golden Hands Book of Macramé.*

This volume first published 1975

Printed by Morrison & Gibb, Edinburgh, Scotland

ISBN 0 85685 092 6

This volume is not to be sold in
the USA, Canada or the Philippines

Introduction

Step into style the inexpensive and creative way. Let this book show you exciting ways of bringing new glamour to your wardrobe and luxurious comfort and colour into your home. From the hundreds of step-by-step instructions you can make unusual and striking clothes and attractive and practical items for the home.

The easy-to-follow patterns will appeal to both beginner and expert. The six handicrafts covered are Fashion Sewing, Knitting, Crochet, Home Sewing, Embroidery and Macramé. Learn to knit a bright and trendy sweater which will turn heads, or try your hand at crochet by creating a stunning beach outfit. Or, if you're looking for new ideas for gifts, delightful macramé designs are given for beautiful hanging lampshades, eye-catching watch-straps and bright Persian pattern hand bags.

If last year's wardrobe looks drab and dreary to you, or if you want to add new sparkle and style to your home, then this book was designed with you in mind. Pick the handicraft of your choice—or master new ones!—through the straight-forward instructions and the hundreds of drawings which will be your guide to a smarter and more fashionable you.

Contents

FASHION HANDICRAFTS

p. 1 and **15** John Carter, design by
Brenda Naylor; **p.9** Roger Charity,
design by Paula Reaston; **p.12** Roger
Charity, design by Brenda Naylor;
p.14 John Carter, design by Brenda
Naylor; **p.18** John Carter, design by
Kelly Flynn; **p.20** John Carter, design by
Janet Smith; **p.23** and **p.26** John Carter;
p.33 and **48** John Carter; **p.41** Camera
Press; **p.42** Beta Pictures; **p.46** Beta
Pictures; **p.50** John Carter, design by
Patricia Roberts; **p.52** Beta Pictures;
p.54 Beta Pictures; **p.56** Beta Pictures;
p.58 Camera Press; **p.60** Beta Pictures;
p.62 Beta Pictures; **p.65** and **74** Peter
Pugh-Cook; **p.73** Camera Press; **p.76** John
Carter, design by Liz Blackwell; **p,78** Beta
Pictures; **p.80** John Carter, design by
Liz Blackwell; **p.82** Tony Horth, design
by Jean Litchfield; **p.84** Camera Press;
p.85 Phillip Gallard, design by Liz
Blackwell; **p.88** John Carter, design by
Patricia Panvalkar; **p.90** Jim Williams;
p.92 Beta Pictures, Chris Lewis; **p.96** John
Carter; **p.97** and **118** Chris Lewis, design by
Suzy Ives; **p.106** Sanderson Triad,
design by Angela Fishburn; **p.110** by
Joyce Kirkland; **p.112** Dawn Marsden,
design by Angela Fishburn; **p.114** Chris
Lewis; **p.116** Chris Lewis, design by
Anna Griffiths; **p.123** Suzy Ives; **p.125** Chris
Lewis, design by Anna Griffiths; **p.128** Alan
Dunns; **p.129** and **152** Chris Lewis, design
by Patty Knox; **p.135** Simis Press Service;
p.138 illustrations by Barbara Firth;
p.140 Camera Press; **p.142** Roger Charity;
p.144 Camera Press; **p.146** Beta Pictures;
p.148 Beta Pictures; **p.150** Roger Charity,
design by Angela Walters; **p.157** Camera
Press;
Macramé consultant: Kit Pyman;
authenticator, Ena Milton;
Photographers: Michael Murray, Malcolm
Aird, John Carter, Roger Charity, Richard
Clapp, Phillip Gallard, Chris Lewis, Peter
Rand, Peter Watkins.
Designers: Mavis Bee, Germaine
Brotherton, Jennifer Cordell, Marjorie
Craske, Audrey Hersch, Lilian Hughes,
Kit Pyman, Lilian Temple, Hilary Turnbull.

FASHION SEWING

To make this long caftan (or short version) see page 15

Crash Course Learn to sew

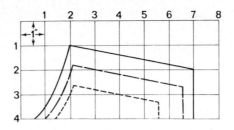

Contents

A. Sewing requirements

You will need the following:
Sewing machine: straight stitch or with a useful zigzag. Hand needles: size 8 for usual dress making, size 9 for sewing fine fabrics, size 7 for heavier fabrics and heavier sewing, such as stitching on buttons. Machine needles: a range of sizes for various fabrics. Pins: steel. Scissors: sharp cutting shears, small dressmaking scissors. Tailor's chalk. Tape measure. Thimble. Set square and yardstick for making patterns. Iron. Ironing board.

B. Choosing the pattern size

Before making patterns note the following measurements:
Bust, waist, hips, width of back, upper arm, sleeve length, back length from nape to waist. Allow tape to run closely over body without measuring tightly. Also take waist to hem measurement.
When deciding on size of pattern choose according to your bust measurement. If your hips are larger than the pattern measurements it is a simple matter to add extra seam allowance to the skirt seams.

Table of sizes

Size	32	34	36	38
Bust	32	34	36	38 inches
Waist	25	26½	28	30 inches
Hips	34½	36	38	40 inches

C. The patterns

How to read the graphs

Patterns on graphs are all given in either two or three sizes. Follow the straight line, broken line or dotted line, according to the size you need. In some graphs the different sizes are indicated by coloured lines.
☐ Each square represents one inch square.

Key to sizes

Largest size	———————
Middle size	— — — — —
Smallest size	- - - - - - -

Seam allowances

These are not included on graphs. Before cutting out fabric add ¾ inch for seams, 3 inches for hems of dresses, 2 inches for hems of trousers and jackets and jerkins, 1½ inches for sleeve hems.
If the pattern measurement is too small for you at the hips allow extra at side seams.

Ease

If you check the pattern pieces you will find they are larger than the measurements given. This is because they have 'ease' built in for movement, so that the garment feels comfortable to wear, not skin tight. The amount of ease differs with the type and purpose of the garment and weight of fabric used.

Making a pattern from a graph

Use a pencil and graph paper. (Graph paper specially for dressmaking is available at many large department stores.) Alternatively you can use large sheets of paper and draw them up accurately into 1-inch squares, using a set square and yardstick.
On each pattern piece count the number of squares across the top and down one side (for example the one here measures 8 inches by 4 inches). Cut a piece of graph paper exactly to this size, just count the squares and translate them into inches.
Starting at one corner, number the lines along top and down side then number your paper similarly. To copy pattern, say for a bodice, start from top left hand corner of diagram, count squares to lower point of neck line and mark on same line on paper. Take note of distance of upper point of neck from side and top of paper, mark and connect the two points to copy the neck curve. Draw remainder of pattern to scale similarly. Copy all pattern pieces in the same way. Identify every pattern piece – back, front skirt and so on, marking centre front, centre back, darts, fronts of sleeve, edges to be placed on a fold and any other details.

D. Altering pattern lengths

To alter the length of a bodice, skirt, sleeve or trouser leg, find a point about one third of the way up from lower edge and draw a horizontal line across pattern. To deduct length, fold away surplus at this point. To add, cut through pattern and insert necessary amount of extra paper. Never add or deduct at hem of a flared garment as this will alter shape of flare.

E. Making a facing pattern

Where possible the inner facing line has been indicated by a dotted line. In this case make a pattern to cover area between outer edge and dotted line, see shaded section in illustration. Always fold away any neck darts before making facing pattern.
If there is no dotted line and pattern calls for a facing, lay edge to be faced on a piece of paper, pencil round outside edges of front neck and centre front. Measure 2 inches for facing width and make a line of pencil dots parallel to edges. Join dots to make facing outline. Repeat for back. Make armhole facing pattern in the same way.
Where facing has to be made to join a folded-back front facing, fold pattern along fold line and make pattern of remaining section.

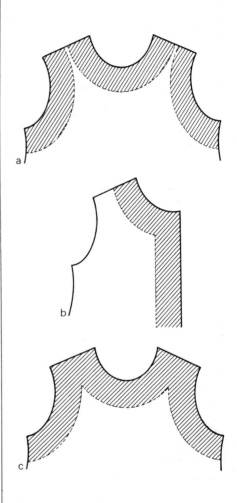

a Neck and armhole facing
b Combined neck and front facing
c Combined neck and armhole facing

F. Cutting out

If fabric has become creased, press carefully. Following the given fabric layout, leave the fabric folded, selvedges together, or fold as illustrated if different. Place pattern pieces on the fabric, following the layout, placing patterns on fold where indicated. Be careful with one-way fabrics where pattern or pile run in one direction; pattern pieces must all run in one direction. Where there is an arrow on the fabric, this arrow must be placed on the grain of the fabric; if on the lengthways grain, arrow must run parallel to selvedges. Where no arrow is marked, the graph squares should be used as a guide. Pin pattern pieces round edges, leaving enough room between the pieces for seam and hem allowances. Do not add seam allowance to inner edge of facings. Mark seam and hem allowances with sharpened tailor's chalk. Mark darts and other details with tailor's tacks.

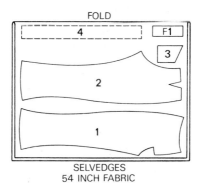

FOLD

SELVEDGES
54 INCH FABRIC

Broken line of layout indicates single fabric only.

G. Preparing for fitting

Place cut out pieces on a flat surface. Pin and tack darts. Pin and tack front to back along side and shoulder seam lines, right sides of fabric together, raw edges level, leaving centre front or centre back seam open so that garment is easily slipped on and off. Pin and tack skirt seams, gather skirt to correct size with running stitch if necessary. Pin and tack bodice and skirt together. Try on garment. Pin opening to close.

Making alterations

If you have to let out or take in at sides do so equally to each side. Never cut away any surplus until you are absolutely sure the fit is right.
If neck or armholes are strained, carefully snip seam allowance at intervals until it lies flat and mark new seam line. Check the shoulder seam. Sloping shoulders may need to be taken in at outer edge and square shoulders let out at outer edge. If alterations have been made to shoulder line, neck and armholes must be carefully re-marked from pattern.
When you are satisfied with the alterations start stitching the garment.

H. Second fitting

Tack sleeve seams and tack sleeves into armholes, making sure they are inserted right way round. Check position of armhole seam on shoulder and adjust if necessary. Check sleeve and hem lengths and see that hems are straight. Adjust position of pockets or other details.
Mark any adjustments before unpicking any tacking.

Working details

Contents

A. Seams and darts

Before stitching try out stitch length and tension on a double scrap of fabric. It is most important to use a sharp needle, and the right thickness for the fabric.
Aim to run straight lines into curves gradually. Start at top of side seams, stitching just outside tacking lines.
Begin at base of dart and stitch just outside tacking lines, tapering gradually towards point. Secure threads at point with a knot.

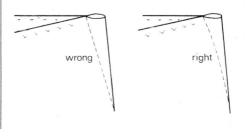

B. Pressing

Pressing means fixing a certain shape and pressing as you work is essential for a good final result. Use a lifting and pressing movement, adjusting pressure according to fabric you are using. Woollens and linens require heavy pressure. Rayons, silks and man-made fabrics need only light pressure. If using a damp cloth for steam pressing, do not keep iron in same place until cloth is dry, but lift and press repeatedly until all steam has gone.

Seams. First press along stitching line with seam allowances together to blend stitches. Open seam with tip of iron and press. To avoid impression on right side of fabric either press over a seam roll or you can slip a piece of brown paper under the seam edges. Armhole seams are pressed together towards sleeve. Waist seams are pressed together towards bodice.
Darts. Darts can be pressed together, flat or open. Press shoulder and waist line darts towards centre, press underarm darts downwards. To press a dart flat tack centre fold of dart to seam line as shown, then press flat. On heavy fabrics darts should be pressed open; slash dart to within ½ inch of point and press open over press pad.

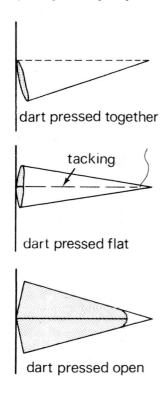

dart pressed together

tacking

dart pressed flat

dart pressed open

Aids to good pressing

Pressing pad. This is invaluable for pressing darts as they can be gently moulded on the pad. Also good for pressing armhole seams.
Seam roll. Good for sleeve seams and for pressing seams open as it prevents the seam edges from making impressions in the fabric. To make a seam roll either cover a wooden rod with blanket, sewing the edge with herringbone stitch, or make a tight roll of blanket, again sewing the edge with herringbone stitch.

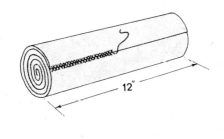

12″

Pressing cloths. A cotton pressing cloth used dry or wet as needed. A fine wool cloth is used to prevent shine when top pressing.

C. Finishing the seam

After seam has been pressed open oversew or use zigzag machine stitch for neatening. Armhole and waist seam allowances are oversewn together. Do not pull stitches too tight. Snip into curves to release any tightness.

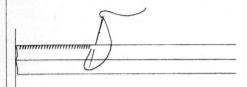

Layering seam allowances

Thick seam allowances as found in outer edges of collar, neck edges, cuffs, should be layered and clipped if necessary. Corners should be trimmed diagonally. To layer a seam allowance trim each seam edge to different widths.

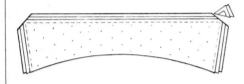

Topstitching

Used for decoration. Use a fairly large stitch setting. For a more definite effect topstitch in buttonhole twist. You will need a thick machine needle for this thread. Work a row of machine topstitching each side of seam, on outside of garment. Topstitch parallel to edge on collars, cuffs or pockets. If worked by hand use a $\frac{1}{4}$ inch running stitch.

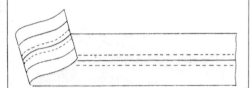

Use these two special seam techniques for neatening and strengthening:

Flat fell seam

Stitch seam in usual way. Trim one seam allowance to $\frac{5}{8}$ inch and the other to $\frac{3}{16}$ inch. Press seam allowances to one side with wider seam allowance on top. Turn under edge of upper seam allowance so it is level with trimmed seam. Pin and tack over trimmed seam edge. Stitch close to fold.

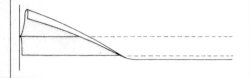

French seam

With wrong sides facing, pin and stitch seam $\frac{3}{8}$ inch from seam line in the seam allowance. Trim seam allowance and lightly press stitched seam towards front of garment. Turn garment inside out. Working on wrong side, pin, tack and stitch along original seam line, encasing raw edges in seam.

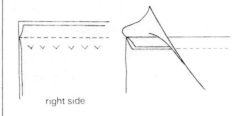

right side

D. Facings

Stitch back and front neck facings at shoulder seams. Press. With right sides together lay facings in position on garment with neck edges level, shoulder seams matching. Pin and tack. Working with facings uppermost stitch in place. Stitch armhole facings also at underarm seam then attach in same way.

Trim, layer and snip seam allowance. Turn to right side. Edgetack round seam edge to ensure a good line and press. Remove tacking.

Understitching. On garments designed for hard wear, facings can be understitched to seam allowances. Press both seam allowances towards facing and stitch on right side of facing just outside seam line, through all thicknesses of allowances and facing. Turn facings to inside of garment, press in position. Lightly sew facing edges to seam allowances only.

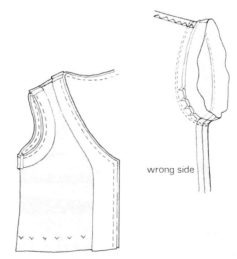

wrong side

Stay tape. On edges such as a low neck line or faced armhole edge, where interfacing has not been used and you think the seam might stretch, it is a wise precaution to stitch a narrow tape (not wider than $\frac{1}{4}$ inch) in with the seam. To do this first tack tape centrally

to seam line on wrong side of garment, then proceed with facing as before, stitching the tape in with the seam.

E. Setting in sleeves

Pin, tack and stitch sleeve seams. Press seam open. If there is any fullness around top of sleeve cap, this must be evenly distributed. Make a line of running stitches around cap of sleeve, just outside seam line. Draw in gathering thread until sleeve fits armhole, fastening gathering thread over a pin for adjustment. Unless sleeve is puffed try to shrink away fullness by pressing over a pressing pad or end of sleeve board, using steam on woollen fabrics, but making sure that fabric does not mark. Pin sleeve into armhole, right sides facing, matching seams, and notches, if any. Tack and stitch in place, working with sleeve uppermost.

F. Sleeve with a cuff
Opening

There are several methods for making an opening at the lower edge of a cuffed sleeve. The method used in this book is a slashed opening.

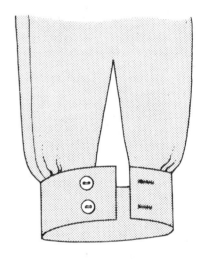

Slashed opening: Make a facing for opening with piece of fabric $2\frac{1}{2}$ inches by 4 inches (for a 3 inch long opening). Neaten one end and the two long edges. Place facing to sleeve centrally along opening, right sides together, and stitch from markings at lower edge tapering to a point 3 inches in. Slash carefully to point without cutting stitching. Turn right side out and press.

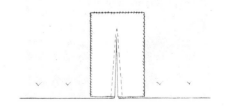

Making cuffs

Once opening has been neatened stitch sleeve seam. Press. Gather lower edge of sleeve with two rows of long machine stitches. Tack interfacing to wrong side of one half of each cuff and catch stitch along fold line. The interfaced section will go to the top of the cuff. (For cuffs with two pieces interface a complete section. Place one interfaced section to one plain section, right sides together, and stitch along one long edge.) Tack interfaced cuff edge to sleeve, right sides together, adjusting gathers to fit and allowing 1 inch wrap on the back edge of the slashed opening. Stitch. Fold cuff lengthways, right sides together, and stitch across ends and along wrap. Layer seam allowances. Turn right side out and press seam allowances into cuff. Turn in remaining edge of cuff and slip stitch in place over seam line.

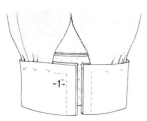

G. Putting in a zipper

Prepare opening by tacking seams together along seam line. Press open carefully. Remove tacking. Open zipper to bottom and lay it in opening so that seam edges just cover zipper teeth on both sides. Tack zipper into position. To make sure that seams lie perfectly flat, close zipper before you machine it in. Start stitching about $\frac{3}{8}$ inch down from seam edge on one side, stitch down until level with end of zipper. Turn work and stitch towards seam. Pivot work on needle and return on other side in same way. Remove tacking. Press gently wrong side up. Nylon zippers should have only the lightest touch.

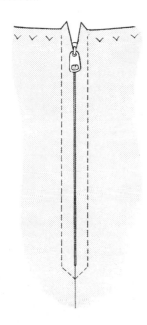

H. Making a collar
Collar without facings

With right sides facing and raw edges level, pin collar and under collar together. Tack and stitch round outer edges, leaving neck edge open. Remove tacking. Layer seam allowances and trim seam allowance across corners. Turn to right side. Edge tack along stitched edges so that both pieces lie flat. Press lightly. Place collar to neck edge, underside to garment, tack and stitch under collar only. Press collar seam allowances upwards, turn under remaining edge and slip stitch over previous stitching line.

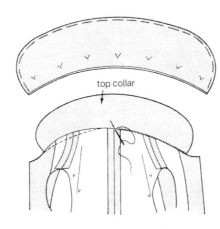

top collar

Collar with neck facings

Prepare collar as above. Place collar to neck edge, under side to right of garment. Tack along neck edge, through all layers. Stitch neck facings to front facings. Position facing to neck edge, right sides together, so that collar is sandwiched between garment and facing. Stitch, snip and layer seam allowances. Turn facing to inside and press.

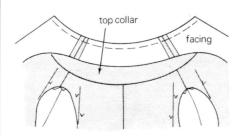

top collar

facing

I. Buttonholes
Bound buttonhole

1. Measure out buttonhole position and mark (figure 1).

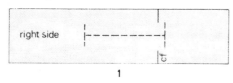

right side

cf

1

2. For each buttonhole cut a strip of fabric on the cross, 2 inches wide and $1\frac{1}{2}$ inches longer than buttonhole length. Working on outside of garment lay strip centrally over buttonhole position, right sides of fabric facing (figure 2).

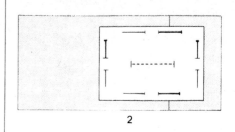

2

3. Working on wrong side of fabric and using a small stitch setting, stitch outline of buttonhole, shaping it into a perfect rectangle (figure 3) running last stitches over first to secure.

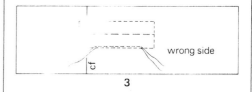

wrong side

cf

3

4. Using sharp pointed scissors, cut into stitched area, taking care not to cut stitches at corners (figure 4).

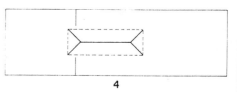

4

5. Pull binding to inside (figure 5). Press seam allowances away from opening.

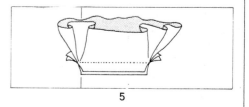

5

6. Turn work to outside and gently roll folded edges of binding so that they meet along centre of buttonhole with equal width to each side (figure 6). Tack along opening.

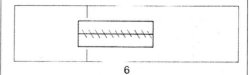

6

7. Turn work to inside and gently pull horizontal edges of binding fabric to make rolls continue evenly beyond opening of buttonhole. Catch them together (figure 7). Press.

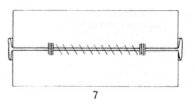

7

8. Turn garment facing over buttonholes. Tack front edge of facing into position. Feel buttonhole through facing fabric and make a cut through facing to length of buttonhole opening. Turn in edges of cut and hem to buttonhole (figure 8).
Make a small bar across each end as shown to strengthen buttonhole.

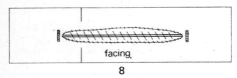

8

Hand-worked buttonhole

1. Mark length of buttonhole; for flat buttons diameter of button plus $\frac{1}{8}$ inch. For thick buttons add $1\frac{1}{2}$ times thickness of button.
2. Using sharp scissors, cut along buttonhole length. Oversew cut edges.
3. Starting with length of thread long enough to complete buttonhole, work buttonhole stitches from left to right along length of buttonhole. Do not pull loops too tight or edge will roll. If the stitches are worked too close together, the edge will cockle. Form a fan of stitches round the end of the buttonhole, keeping centre stitch in line with slit. Continue along top edge of buttonhole. Make small bar across both rows of stitches at end.

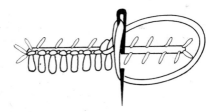

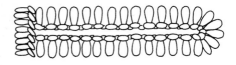

Hand-worked button loops

Use buttonhole twist. Form the loop with three strands of twist, secured with back stitches. With the same thread work blanket stitches firmly along the loop.

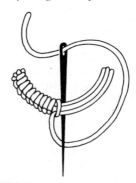

J. Making a stiffened waist band

Cut petersham stiffening to waist measurement plus 2 inches. Cut waist band to length of the petersham stiffening and twice the width, plus seam allowances all round. With right sides facing, tack waist band to skirt waist edge, easing skirt to fit band, and with 2 inches extending at one end for a wrap fastening. With waist band and skirt still right sides facing, position petersham over waist band seam allowance with lower edge just above seam line. Stitch petersham to seam allowances close to lower edge. Fold waist band over top of petersham, turn in seam allowances at ends and along inner edge. Slip stitch inner edge to first seam line and slip stitch ends to close. Fasten waist band with hooks and eyes or a button, as directed.

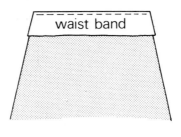

waist band

petersham

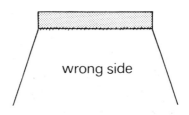

wrong side

K. Interfacing

Interfacing is recommended for more tailored styles and a crisp look. Cut to shape of front neck facing, collar, cuffs as suggested.
Front. Tack in place to wrong side of front of garment, with front edge to fold line or front seam line. Catch stitch lightly down front edge. Stitch facing as normal.
Collar. Tack interfacing to wrong side of one layer of collar and use as top collar, unless otherwise stated.

catch stitch

L. Pleat backing

Tack along pleat line, right sides facing. Stitch top of pleat if required. Cut pleat backing to width of pleat and to length plus hem allowance. Place garment right side down and position backing to pleat right side down. Stitch down both sides to pleat seam allowance to within about 5 inches of hem. Turn up hem of pleat and backing separately. Then continue stitching backing to pleat to hem edge as shown, through all layers. Remove tacking from pleat.

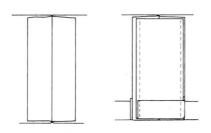

M. Making a hem

Always pin at right angles to hem. Make sure that hem depth is even all round. Working with hem lying flat on table, tack hem about $\frac{1}{2}$ inch from lower edge. Press from wrong side, with hem lying flat on ironing board.

Invisibly hemming a skirt

Prepare as above. Then, if the skirt is flared, use small running stitch to gather in fullness along raw edge by hand. Shrink in fullness. Tack about $\frac{3}{4}$ inch from upper edge. Taking depth of hem in your hand, without creasing it turn over $\frac{1}{4}$ inch of upper edge. Sew invisibly behind hem as shown, taking up very little thread from the skirt and a good deep thread from the hem.

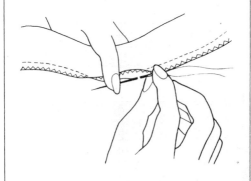

Invisible herringbone

Use same technique as invisible hemming but with herringbone stitch, catching fabric on garment and hem. This method is good for heavier fabrics.

Coat hem

For heavy fabrics work as for invisible hemming but work two rows of stitches to hold the extra weight.

N. Making up and inserting a coat lining

Cut out lining using 36 inch layout but omitting facings. Cut centre back to a fold allowing an extra inch for pleat (for ease of movement). Stitch side, shoulder and sleeve seams. Press. Press in one inch pleat in centre back and secure with cross stitches for three inches from neck edge.

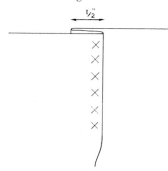

Slip lining into coat, wrong sides facing, matching seam lines; pin along seam lines then pin round edges starting at centre back. Trim away front edge to clear the buttonholes, turn in ½ inch and fell in place from neck to hem. Stitch to armhole seam allowance with running stitch. Slip sleeve lining into sleeve, wrong sides facing. Turn in seam allowance at top of sleeve and fell in place over coat lining. Turn up lower edge and slip stitch in place ½ inch above sleeve hem. Turn up lining hem 1 inch above coat hem and slip stitch in place; the lining should be left separate at hem edge.

O. Bias binding
Commercial bias binding

1. Commercial bias binding has two creases already pressed in. It should be opened out and placed to the edge to be bound with the first crease along the seam line. Stitch, trim seam, press. Turn binding to inside along seam line and slip stitch in place (figures 1 and 2).

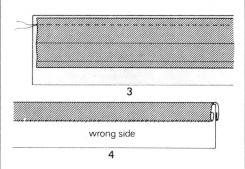

2. Where binding is intended to show, no seam allowance is necessary on edge to be bound. Place binding to fabric, right sides together, raw edges level, and stitch along first crease line of binding. Turn second crease line of binding to inside and slip stitch to seam line (figures 3 and 4).

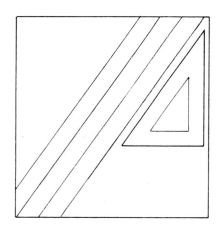

Self binding

This is made from strips of the garment fabric cut on the bias (figure 5). Both above methods of application are suitable for self bias binding except, of course, you do not have creases to guide you. Where edge is bound cut strips four times width of finished binding width.

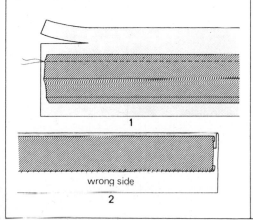

5a Marking the bias strips

5b Joining the bias strips

Mitring a corner

To mitre a corner for method 2, carefully mark the inner corner of the binding. Stitch binding up to this corner on one side. Keeping the binding in line with the outer edge of the garment fold the binding as shown. Stitch other side of corner. Fold binding over to inside arranging top side into neat fold. On the reverse side turn in and tack seam allowance and arrange mitre into neat fold and slip stitch.

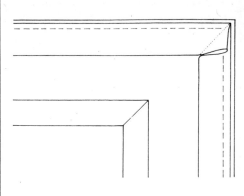

P. Fabrics
Working with jersey

Marking pattern detail: Use a soft thread such as a No. 50 tacking thread. Sharp thread can cut jersey stitches.

Stitching: Reduce pressure on presser foot of machine as jersey tends to spread. Use finest needle size and pure silk thread. Engage shallowest zigzag stitch and stitch length setting of 12 to 14 stitches per inch. Gently stretch seams when stitching to give maximum elasticity. Seams which have to bear strain should be stitched over twice.

Seam finishes: Unnecessary.

Darts: Slash along centre and press open.

Making hem: Use invisible herringbone stitch for extra strength and 'give'.

Fur fabric

Cutting out: Fur fabric has a woven or knitted backing. In either case lay the fabric, pile side down, and cut one layer at a time, keeping pattern pieces on straight grain of backing. Mark round pattern pieces with tailor's chalk and cut backing with sharp blade, taking care not to cut the pile. Keep pile running downwards.

Stitching: Stitch with strong needle and a thread with elasticity, such as a silk or a synthetic thread. Experiment on scraps for stitch tension. Separate hairs of pile before stitching. When stitched use a pin to pull out pile along seam line and trim away pile on seam allowances. Press with cool iron.

After care: Fur fabrics are made from a variety of man-made or natural fibres. Be sure to ask about after care when buying and carefully follow manufacturers instructions. Experiment on scraps for pressing.

P.V.C.

Cutting out: As pins leave holes in PVC keep patterns in position with transparent adhesive tape.

Stitching: Hold seam allowances together with paper clips when stitching seams. Stitch with a fine needle and a fairly large stitch. If you have difficulty in topstitching the fabric a roller foot can be used on the machine or simply dust the surface with talcum powder. Press seams open on wrong side with damp cloth and iron at a coolish setting or with a dry iron over brown paper. PVC does not fray so the seam edges are not finished off.

Stitch library

Herringbone stitch

Work from left to right, taking a small stitch in hem, then a one-thread stitch in the fabric.

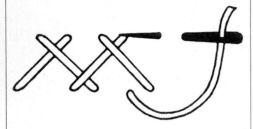

Blanket stitch

The thread loops underneath needle which lies vertically in the fabric. Make a button loop or bar for a hook by working over a foundation of tacking stitches.

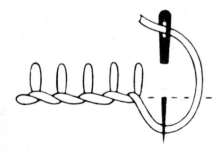

Buttonhole stitch

This gives a tighter, more durable knot than blanket stitch.

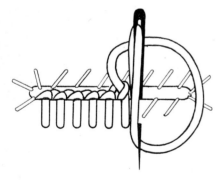

Catch stitch

Used to catch one fabric to another where bulk is to be avoided. Lift one thread of fabric with each stitch so as to be invisible on right side. Do not pull stitches tight.

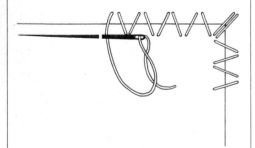

Slip stitch

Gives an invisible finish. Its strength, which is not great, is determined by closeness of the stitches. Use a fine needle. Edge of garment should first be turned in. Work from right to left, picking up one thread of garment and passing along fold of hem for $\frac{1}{4}$ to $\frac{1}{2}$ inch.

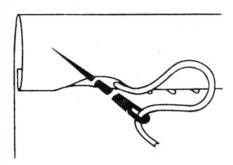

Felling stitch

A form of hemming one piece of fabric by its edge to another piece. Edge can be folded or left raw.

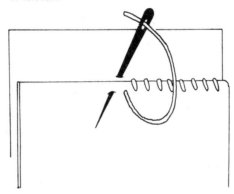

Running stitch

Weave needle in and out of fabric before pulling through. Several stitches can be made on needle at same time. Draw up stitches if gathers are required.

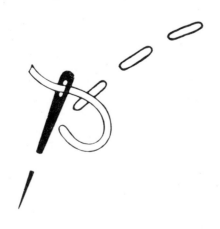

Back stitch

A very firm stitch worked by taking needle and thread back one stitch on side facing you, inserting needle just in front of preceding stitch.

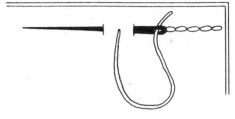

Tailor's tacks

Thread needle with tacking cotton, pulling it through so ends meet and cotton is doubled. Make stitches $\frac{1}{2}$ inch long, leaving loop about size of your finger tip on every other stitch. To separate layers after garment is cut out, pull gently apart and cut through tacks.

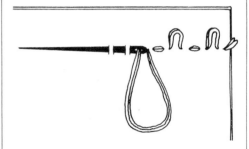

Draw stitch

Used to close two folds of material together. Slip the needle through the top fold for $\frac{1}{4}$ inch. Then, directly under the end of the first stitch, slip the needle through the lower fold for $\frac{1}{4}$ inch.

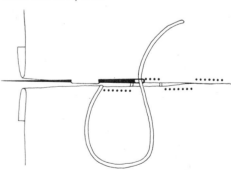

Prick stitch

A version of back stitch, worked over a single grain of fabric, forming a tiny surface stitch.

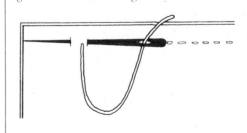

Scalloped skirt

Make this beautifully cut gored skirt in a fabric which drapes well such as crepe, jersey or a lightweight wool. The skirt is shaped in eight curved gores which form a soft hem line of large scallops.

Team it with a classic jumper for daytime wear, or dress it up with a pretty blouse for evenings.

Measurements

The pattern and instructions given here are to fit size 10. The pattern can easily be adapted to fit larger sizes by adding $\frac{1}{8}$ inch to the waist and seam edges and $\frac{1}{2}$ inch to the hem for each size larger required. The skirt measures 43 inches from the waistline to the lower edge of the hem.

Requirements and notions
You will need:

☐ $6\frac{1}{2}$ yards 36 inch wide fabric for all sizes
☐ $\frac{1}{8}$ yard 36 inch wide woven interfacing for waistband
☐ 14 inch zip fastener
☐ sewing cotton to match fabric
☐ 1 inch squared paper for drafting patterns

Making the pattern

Draw up the pattern to scale from the graph pattern given here. Each square on the graph represents 1 square inch.
Note: the pattern has no seam allowances, so add $\frac{5}{8}$ inch to all edges when cutting out.
Cut eight sections in fabric to make the skirt.

Making the skirt

1. With right sides together, matching points A to B and points C to D (leaving an opening on one seam for inserting the zip), tack and stitch the eight skirt sections together. Clip seams on curves where necessary. Press all the seams open.

2. Turn and tack the seam allowance on the opening to the wrong side and press. Insert the zip fastener following the instructions given on the zipper packet.

3. Tack the interfacing to the wrong side of the waistband and catch stitch it down to the fold line.

4. With right sides together, tack and stitch the interfaced edge of the waistband to the skirt waist. Trim the interfacing close to the stitching, trim and grade the seam. Press the seam up towards the waistband.

5. With right sides together, fold the waistband on the fold line and stitch the ends as shown. Clip the seam to the stitching as shown. Trim and grade the seam and clip across the corners.

6. Turn the waistband right side out. Tack round the fold and side edges. Press the band edges. Turn under the seam allowance on the waistband and hem to the stitching line.

7. Neaten the hem edge by turning under $\frac{1}{4}$ inch and stitching close to the fold edge. Press on the wrong side. Turn a narrow hem to the wrong side of the skirt and stitch. Press.

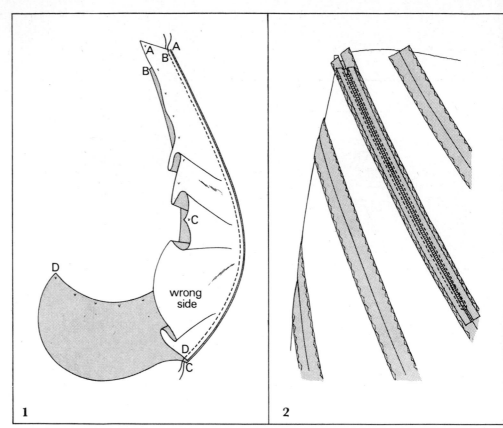

1
2

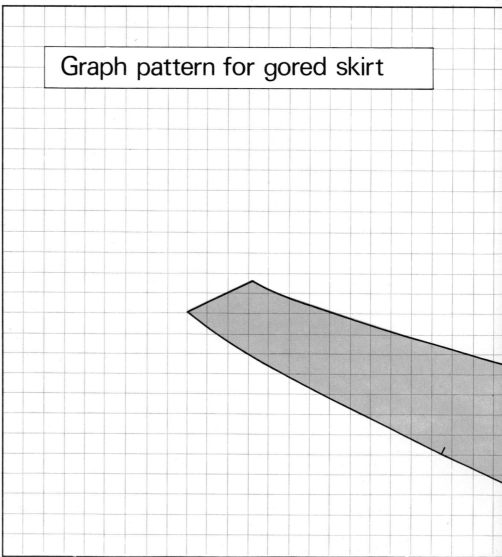

Graph pattern for gored skirt

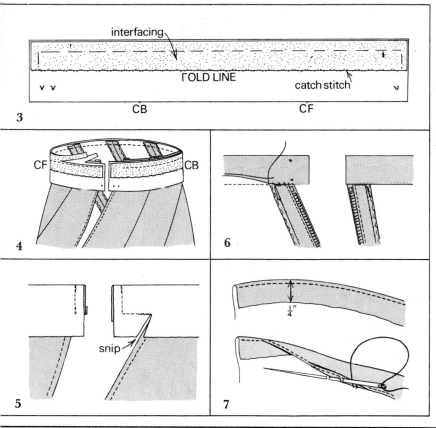

interfacing

FOLD LINE

catch stitch

CB   CF

3

4 CF   CB

6

5 snip

7 ¼"

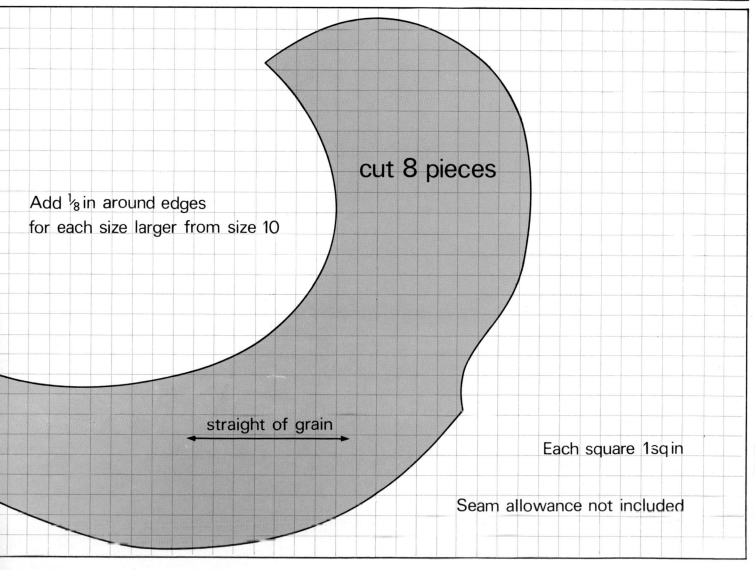

cut 8 pieces

Add ⅛ in around edges
for each size larger from size 10

straight of grain

Each square 1 sq in

Seam allowance not included

Sunny two-piece

Choose a firm, crease-resisting cotton seersucker for this holiday two-piece and you'll have an adaptable, trouble-free addition to your wardrobe, ideal for both the beach and casual parties. Wear the skirt and halter top together or team the top with plain coloured trousers or skirts.

You will need:

☐ Paper for the pattern
☐ 3½ yards 36 inch wide fabric
☐ ¾ inch wide elastic to the length of your midriff measurement just under the bust plus 1 inch
☐ 4 Newey's Poppa fasteners, small size
☐ ¼ yard 1 inch wide petersham stiffening
☐ One large hook and eye, and one small hook
☐ Matching thread

Pattern

The pattern will fit up to a size 38 inch bust, 40 inch hip. Seam allowances are included.

Make a pattern for the skirt and halter top on paper as shown (**1b**). The skirt is 42 inches long but can be adjusted to any length required.

Cutting out

Position the pattern pieces on the single fabric as shown in the layout (**1a**). Cut out two skirt pieces (one in reverse), and one top and one lining piece, using the halter top pattern. ½ inch turnings are allowed in the pattern. From single fabric also cut a bias strip (**a**) 2 inches wide for the necktie, and another (**b**) 3 inches wide for the back elastic casing. Cut a waistband (**c**) 4 inches wide to the length of your waist plus ¾ inch for ease and 1 inch for seams.

Making up

All seams are stitched with a ½ inch seam allowance unless otherwise stated.

The halter top

The midriff strap: To trim the casing for the midriff strap to the correct length, stretch out the elastic to its full extent, measuring along a tape measure, and trim the casing bias to half the extended elastic length.

Fold the strip in half lengthways, right sides facing, and stitch ⅝ inch from the edge. Trim seam allowance and turn to right side.

2. Insert the elastic through the casing, positioning the casing at the centre of the elastic. Stretch the elastic out full, pin the ends of the casing in place, and stitch casing to elastic at each end. By this method the casing will stretch with the elastic.

Overlap the ends of the elastic 1 inch and stitch.

Making the top: 3. Turn in ¼ inch double hems along the side edges of both halter top and lining pieces. Then stitch top to lining along the long waist edges, right sides together. Press seam open.

4. Turn in the point of both ends of the seam so that the folded edge measures 2¼ inches. Trim the turnings to ½ inch and stitch a ¼ inch double hem. The hemmed ends will become the openings to the lower casing which is stitched later.

5. Following the illustration, slip the midriff strap over the lining section as shown. Stitch the halter top to its lining along top edges, right sides together. Press seam open and trim seam allowances.

Turn through to right side and top stitch along top and bottom edges close to seams.

6. Position the midriff elastic so that the uncovered part of the elastic is centred at the centre front of the halter top, out of sight, between the fabric layers.

Stitch the elastic to the lining only, at the centre front, so that it cannot slip out of place when the top is being worn.

Pin and tack 1 inch deep casing along the lower edge of the top to contain the midriff strap. Make sure that the strap is running freely and not caught in with the tacking, then stitch the casing. At the top seam edge pin and tack a ½ inch casing. Stitch.

To make the rouleau for the necktie fold the bias strip (**a**) in half lengthways down the centre, right sides facing. Stitch lengthways. Turn through to right side.

Push in ends and slip stitch to neaten, or knot them firmly and trim. Thread the rouleau through the casing.

Pull the halter top over your head like a sweater. Tie the necktie high or low and arrange the gathers to suit your own figure.

If your bust needs more support, slip a pair of profile forms between top and lining. Tack lightly in place.

The skirt

Stitch the centre back seam, right sides facing. Press seam open.

Pin, tack and stitch darts. Press the front darts towards the front and the back and side darts towards the back.

Pin the skirt round you and adjust the length. Trim the hem allowance to 1½ inches and press. Turn in the raw hem edge narrowly and machine stitch. Finish off the hem.

Turn in each front edge ¾ inch and press. Turn in again ¾ inch and stitch down both edges of the double hem. Gather the top of the skirt to your waist measurement plus ¾ inch. Distribute the gathers evenly.

Pin the skirt waist seam edge to the waistband, right sides together. Position the skirt waist seam 1 inch down from one long edge of the band and with the ½ inch seam allowance at each end of the waistband extending to each side.

Turn in the ends of the waistband ½ inch. Turn in the top edge for 1 inch. Then turn fold over to stitching line. Tack. You now have a finished waistband 1 inch wide with four thicknesses of fabric for support.

Top stitch all round waistband. Attach four Poppa fasteners at 5 inch intervals down the front of the skirt below the waistband.

Waistband tab: Cut a 4½ inch length of 1 inch wide petersham stiffening. Trim the ends into equal points.

7. Cut a piece of skirt fabric 5½ inches by 3 inches and place the petersham to the wrong side ½ inch from one long edge as shown. Tack.

Fold the fabric in half along the upper edge of the petersham, right sides of fabric together. Stitch round both ends, taking care not to stitch through the petersham. Trim and turn to right side.

8. Turn in remaining seam allowances. Machine stitch all round tab close to the edge.

9. Position the tab centrally to the right-hand side of the waistband and stitch in place carefully over the first stitching. Attach two hooks and an eye and hand-work a bar in the position shown to complete the waist edge. (**10**).

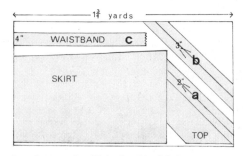

1a. *Layout for 36 inch wide fabric*

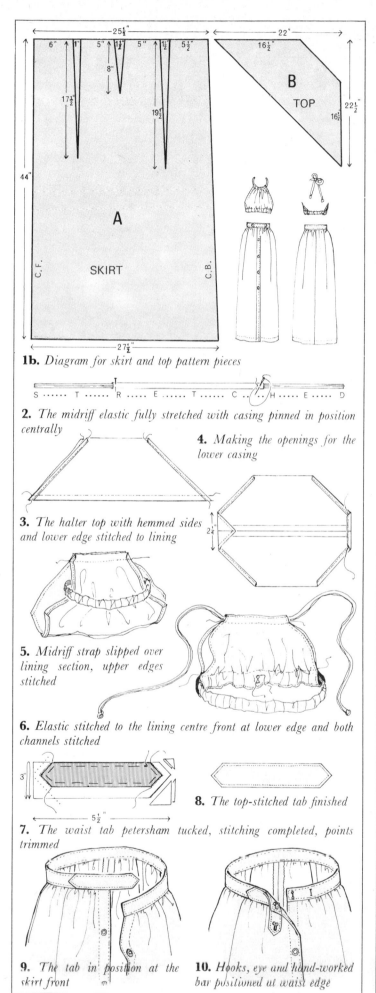

1b. *Diagram for skirt and top pattern pieces*

2. *The midriff elastic fully stretched with casing pinned in position centrally*

4. *Making the openings for the lower casing*

3. *The halter top with hemmed sides and lower edge stitched to lining*

5. *Midriff strap slipped over lining section, upper edges stitched*

6. *Elastic stitched to the lining centre front at lower edge and both channels stitched*

8. *The top-stitched tab finished*

7. *The waist tab petersham tucked, stitching completed, points trimmed*

9. *The tab in position at the skirt front*

10. *Hooks, eye and hand-worked bar positioned at waist edge*

Caftans-long or short

This elegant caftan is quick and simple to make. Wear it full length as a dinner dress or a more casual house robe, or cut it short for a pretty top to wear over trousers or a long skirt.

Measurements

The pattern and instructions given here are to fit a 32½ inch to 38 inch bust size. The back neck to hem measurement for the long version is 59½ inches and for the short version 26½ inches.

Add a 1 inch seam allowance down the centre front and all side edges and a 1 inch hem. On all other edges allow ½ inch.

It is advisable to wash or pre-shrink both fabric and lace before cutting out.

Requirements
For long version
☐ 2¼ yards 54 inch wide wool fabric or 4 yards of 36 inch wide cotton fabric
For short version
☐ 2¼ yards 36 inch wide cotton fabric
For both versions
☐ 1 yard 3 inch wide lace
☐ a size 14 inch collar band or
☐ ⅛ yard of iron-on interfacing
☐ ¼ yard contrast fabric
☐ matching mercerised sewing thread
☐ link button fastening (optional)

Making the caftan

1. Mark the front darts with lines of tacking stitches. Cut the length of lace in half and lay the pieces onto the fronts, overlapping the upper dart line. Tack in position then, using a small back-stitch, hand-stitch down both sides of each piece of lace.

2. With the right sides together stitch the front darts, thus anchoring the lower edges of the lace. Press the darts downwards.

3. With right sides together, stitch the centre front seam starting 7 inches from the neckline. Press seam open, then turn under and press the raw edges to neaten. Top-stitch down both sides of the centre front seam from neck to hem.

4. With right sides together, stitch the shoulder seams. Press the seam towards the back. Turn work to right side and machine two rows of top stitching, the first row $\frac{1}{16}$ inch from the seam and the second row $\frac{1}{8}$ inch away from the first row. Oversew the raw edges to neaten.

5. With right sides together, stitch the side seams from underarm to 21 inches from the bottom. (The short version is seamed right down to the hem.) Press and tack back the 1 inch seam allowances and neaten the raw edges by turning back ⅛ inch and top-stitching. (For fine woollens and heavier fabrics, over-

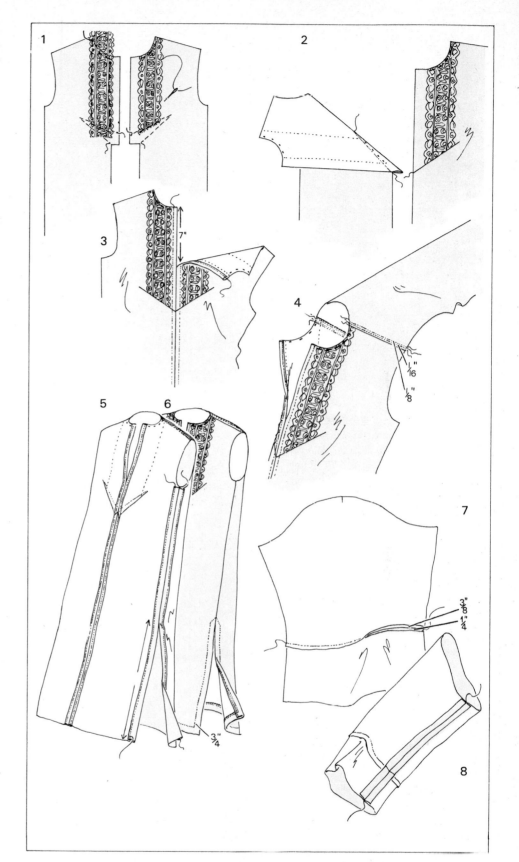

sew the edges to neaten.)

6. Neaten the raw edges of the hem by oversewing. Turn up a 1 inch hem and tack. Top-stitch ¾ inch from the edge round the hem and the side slits.

7. With right sides together, stitch the cuffs to the sleeves. Trim the turnings to ¼ inch for the cuff and ⅜ inch for the sleeve, then press both edges down-

wards away from the armhole edge.

8. With right sides together and the cuff seams matching, stitch the underarm seams. Press seams open.

9. Turn in and press ½ inch seam allowance to the wrong side of the cuff, then fold cuff up and match the underarm seams. Stitch by hand to the previous line of machine stitching. Press cuff edge.

15

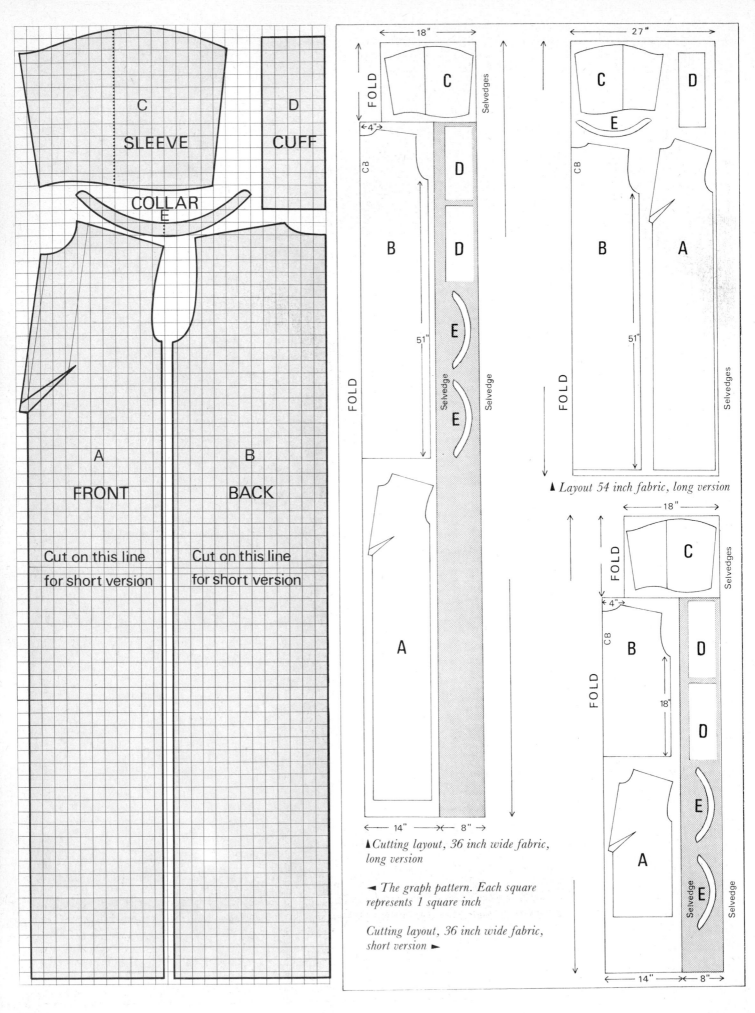

C

SLEEVE

D

CUFF

COLLAR

E

A

FRONT

B

BACK

Cut on this line for short version

Cut on this line for short version

18"

FOLD

C

Selvedges

4"

CB

B

D

D

51"

E

E

Selvedge

Selvedge

A

14"

8"

▲ Cutting layout, 36 inch wide fabric, long version

◄ The graph pattern. Each square represents 1 square inch

Cutting layout, 36 inch wide fabric, short version ►

27"

C

D

E

CB

B

A

51"

FOLD

Selvedges

▲ Layout 54 inch fabric, long version

18"

FOLD

C

Selvedges

4"

CB

B

D

18"

D

FOLD

A

E

E

Selvedge

Selvedge

14"

8"

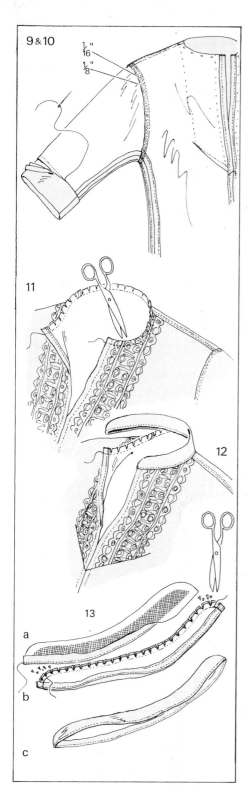

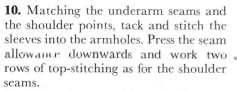

▲ *The caftan cut short to wear as a casual top over trousers or a skirt*

10. Matching the underarm seams and the shoulder points, tack and stitch the sleeves into the armholes. Press the seam allowance downwards and work two rows of top-stitching as for the shoulder seams.

11. Using long machine stitches, sew round the neckline $\frac{1}{2}$ inch from the edge. Clip all round, almost to the stitches.

12. Drop the collar band into place along the line of stitching, sandwiching the clipped edge. Tack and machine top-stitch.

13. If desired, close neck with a linked button fastening.

To make a collar band

Cut the collar band and facing with $\frac{1}{2}$ inch seam allowances. Cut the iron-on interfacing without turnings. The collar band can be made in matching or contrasting fabric.

13a. Position the interfacing centrally on the wrong side of the band and iron in place. Press up and top-stitch the lower edge of the seam allowance.

b. With right sides together, lay the band and facing together and stitch all round the top edge. Fasten off the thread securely at both ends. Layer and clip the seam allowance.

c. Turn band to right side. Turn up the seam allowance of the facing and press. Drop the collar band into place along the line of stitching, sandwiching the clipped edge and tack in position. When stitching the collar band to the neckline, top-stitch entire edge.

strips (d) each 12 inches by 1 inch, for armhole binding, and one strip (e) 6 inches by 1 inch, for pocket binding.

Making up

Binding the armholes. With right sides together, pin and tack armhole binding to each armhole edge, from A to B. Stitch, taking $\frac{1}{4}$ inch seam. Turn binding to wrong side, turn in long raw edge for $\frac{1}{4}$ inch and slip stitch to seam line (figure 1).

Neck casing. Trim armhole binding at the top level with the top of the apron. To make neck casing turn under edge for $\frac{1}{4}$ inch, then turn under again for 1 inch. Stitch close to fold.
Join two short ends of two of the tie strips together, right sides facing, and machine stitch, taking $\frac{1}{2}$ inch seam. Place the long sides of the joined strip together, right side facing, and machine stitch, taking $\frac{1}{4}$ inch seam.
Using a large safety pin attached to one end of strip, turn strip to right side, turn in ends and slip stitch to neaten.
Using a safety pin attached to one end of tie strip, thread the tie through the casing at the top of the apron.
Make the waist tie strip as above, using the two remaining strips of fabric.
To make the waist casing, turn in each long edge of the casing strip $\frac{3}{8}$ inch and press. Position the casing to wrong side of apron, wrong sides facing and tack. Machine stitch casing to apron close to each fold. Remove tacking, then thread the tie strip through.

The pocket
Run a gathering thread through the top of the pocket, $\frac{1}{4}$ inch in. Pull up till top of pocket measures 6 inches. Secure gathering thread and bind top of pocket in the same way as armholes, leaving ends of binding raw. Turn in $\frac{1}{2}$ inch seam allowance on remaining edges of pocket, and tack.
Pin the pocket in position indicated on graph. Tack, then machine stitch down close to the edge, leaving top open.

The frill
Join the frill together down two selvedge edges, right sides together, taking a $\frac{1}{4}$ inch seam. Press seam open. Pin, tack and sew a $\frac{1}{4}$ inch hem along one long edge. Run a gathering thread along the unhemmed long edge, $\frac{1}{4}$ inch in, and pull up till frill fits apron hem. Secure gathering thread, and with right sides together, pin, tack and sew frill to apron. Using seam binding, bind the frill seam to neaten.

☐ 2$\frac{1}{2}$ yards 36 inch wide cotton fabric
☐ Matching thread
☐ 1 yard $\frac{3}{4}$ inch wide matching seam binding

Pretty party pinny

A full-length, frilled, Edwardian-look apron to wear over a long skirt. Wear it just for fashion, or to keep you looking pretty as you dash between your guests and the kitchen.

You will need:
☐ Graph paper with 1 inch squares

The pattern
Using the graph paper, draw up the apron front and pocket pattern pieces to scale. Each square in the diagram represents a 1 inch square. Seam allowances are included.

Cutting out
Following the layout, cut one apron front and one pocket from the cotton fabric. Also cut: one strip (a) 36 inches by 2 inches for the waist casing; four strips (b) each 36 inches by 2 inches, for the ties; two pieces (c) each 36 inches by 10 inches for the frill.
Cutting on the bias, as shown, cut two

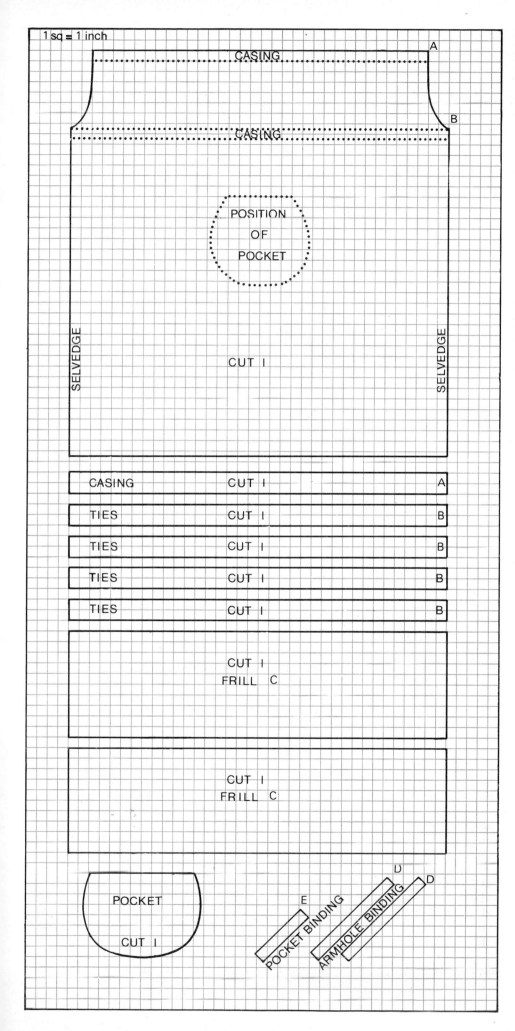

1 sq = 1 inch

CASING .... A

CASING

CASING

POSITION

OF

POCKET

SELVEDGE

CUT I

SELVEDGE

CASING	CUT I		A
TIES	CUT I		B
TIES	CUT I		B
TIES	CUT I		B
TIES	CUT I		B

CUT I

FRILL C

CUT I

FRILL C

POCKET

CUT I

POCKET BINDING E

ARMHOLE BINDING D D

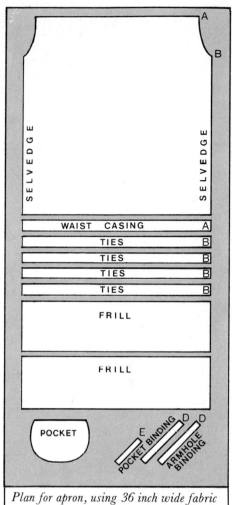

A
B

SELVEDGE   SELVEDGE

WAIST CASING	A
TIES	B
TIES	B
TIES	B
TIES	B

FRILL

FRILL

POCKET

POCKET BINDING E   ARMHOLE BINDING D D

Plan for apron, using 36 inch wide fabric

◄ *Graph for the apron — 1 square = 1 inch*

The apron without the frill, with pockets

Slim-fit trousers

Make these trousers in a dramatic checked fabric.
The trousers are cut on classic lines with straight legs for style and easy movement.

Fabrics and notions

For the trousers in all sizes you will need:
- ☐ 2¾ yards 36 inch wide fabric *or*,
- ☐ 2 yards 54 inch wide fabric

Note. Allow extra material for matching design on checked fabrics. (Between ¼ and ½ yard depending on size of check.)
- ☐ 8 inch zipper
- ☐ One ¾ inch button
- ☐ ⅛ yard 36 inch wide interfacing
- ☐ 2 hook and eye fastenings
- ☐ Matching sewing thread
- ☐ Graph paper for patterns

The pattern

The pattern is given in sizes 25 inch, 26½ inch, 28 inch or 30 inch waist measurement and to fit a 34½ inch, 36 inch, 38 inch or 40 inch hip measurement. Make the back and front trouser and waistband patterns from those on the graph.

The squares on the graph represent 1 inch squares. A seam allowance of ⅝ inch has been allowed on all seams and 2⅝ inches for the hem on the trouser legs.

Cutting out

Lay out the pattern on the fabric as shown, matching the notches to the check of the fabric.

Making up

Darts

1. With right sides together, tack and stitch the front waist darts. Press the darts towards the centre front.

2. With right sides together, tack and stitch the back waist darts. Press the darts towards the centre back.

Seams

3. With right sides together, matching

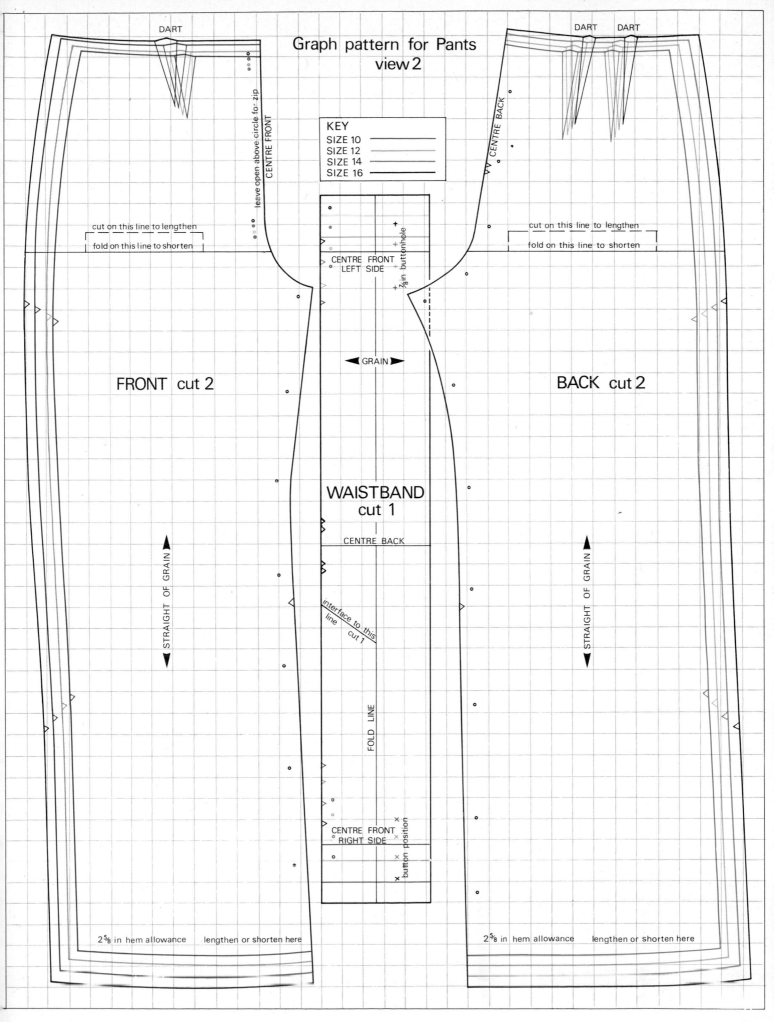

Graph pattern for Pants
view 2

KEY
SIZE 10 ─────
SIZE 12 ─────
SIZE 14 ─────
SIZE 16 ─────

DART

CENTRE FRONT

leave open above circle for zip

cut on this line to lengthen

fold on this line to shorten

CENTRE FRONT LEFT SIDE

◄ GRAIN ►

FRONT cut 2

WAISTBAND
cut 1

CENTRE BACK

interface to this line
cut 1

FOLD LINE

CENTRE FRONT RIGHT SIDE

button position

STRAIGHT OF GRAIN

DART   DART

CENTRE BACK

cut on this line to lengthen

fold on this line to shorten

⅞ in buttonhole

BACK cut 2

STRAIGHT OF GRAIN

2⅝ in hem allowance   lengthen or shorten here

2⅝ in hem allowance   lengthen or shorten here

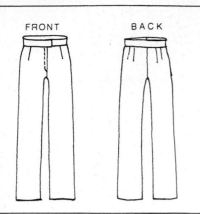

notches, tack and stitch the inside leg seam and the side seam. Press the seams open.

Crotch

4. With right sides together, matching notches and inside leg seam, tack and stitch the crotch seam to small circle. Clip the curved edges and press the seam open.

5. Turn and tack the seam allowance of the right front to the wrong side and press. Place the zipper face down to the left front opening. Tack and stitch in place using the zipper foot on the machine.

6. Tack and stitch the right front to the zipper as shown. If desired, edge stitch the seam close to the zipper teeth on the left-hand side as shown.

7. Tack the interfacing to the wrong side of the waistband and catch stitch it down to the fold line.

8. With right sides together, matching notches, tack and stitch the waistband to the trouser waist. Trim the interfacing close to stitching and trim and grade the seam. Press the seam up towards the waistband.

9. With right sides together, fold the waistband on the fold line and stitch the ends as shown. Clip the seam at centre front to the stitching as shown. Trim and grade the seam and clip across the corners.

10. Turn the waistband to the inside tacked edges. Tack and press. Turn under the seam allowance and hem to the stitching line.

11. Try on the trousers and mark the hem. Tack round the folded edge. Trim the hem to an even width all round. Neaten the raw edge of the hem with hand oversewing or machine stitch. Sew the hem with invisible hemming stitch.

12. Work a hand- or machine-made buttonhole in the left front waistband in the position indicated on the pattern. Stitch the button on to the right front waistband on the under band. Stitch on the hooks and eyes at the waistband opening as shown.

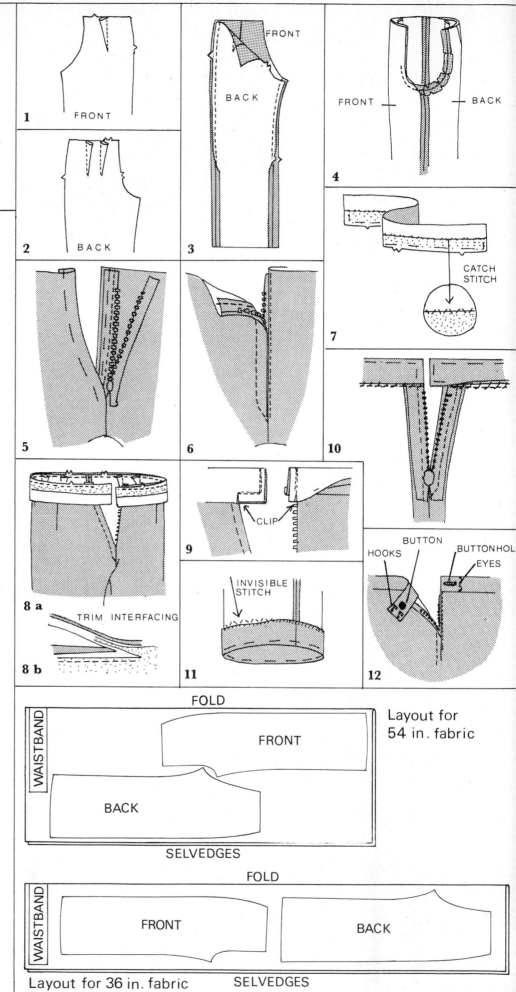

Bias cut skirt

This flared skirt has been cut on the bias of the fabric for a good fit and smooth lines. Here it is made in an even weave check, but it would look equally attractive made in a plain fabric without an obvious diagonal weave or nap.

And; as a perfect complement to the skirt, make up this delightful, full-sleeved shirt blouse in a toning silk. Turn to page 24 for complete graph pattern and instructions.

Graph pattern for skirt

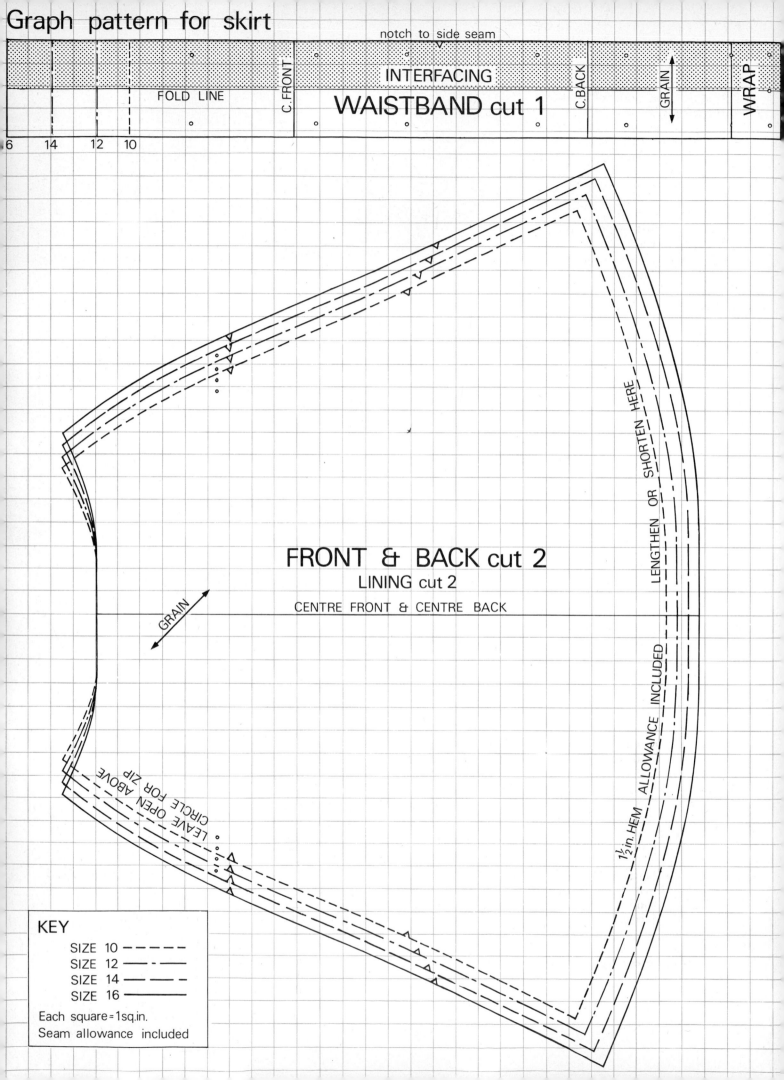

notch to side seam

FOLD LINE

C. FRONT

INTERFACING

WAISTBAND cut 1

C. BACK

GRAIN

WRAP

6   14   12   10

LENGTHEN OR SHORTEN HERE

FRONT & BACK cut 2

LINING cut 2

CENTRE FRONT & CENTRE BACK

GRAIN

1½ in. HEM ALLOWANCE INCLUDED

LEAVE OPEN ABOVE
CIRCLE FOR ZIP

KEY

SIZE 10 – – – –
SIZE 12 – · – · –
SIZE 14 — – — –
SIZE 16 ————

Each square = 1 sq. in.
Seam allowance included

Measurements

The instructions given here are for a skirt to fit sizes 10, 12, 14 and 16.

Requirements

- ☐ 2 yards 54 inch wide woven linen, heavy weight cotton, wool or wool mixture fabric without nap for all sizes
- ☐ 54 inch wide lining: sizes 10 and 12, 1½ yards; sizes 14 and 16, 1⅝ yards
- ☐ ⅛ yard 36 inch wide woven interfacing for all sizes
- ☐ 7 inch zip fastener
- ☐ 2 hooks and eyes
- ☐ matching sewing thread

Making the skirt

Side seams and zip fastening

1. With right sides together, matching notches, tack and stitch the left side seam up to the circle. Press seam open. Insert the zip in the opening on the left side, following the instructions on the zipper packet.

With right sides together, matching notches, tack and stitch the entire right side seam. To neaten seam edges, overcast by hand or machine. Press seam open.

Lining

2. Make up the lining in the same way as the skirt, omitting the zip.

With wrong sides together, matching side seams, tack the lining to the skirt at the waist line.

Slip stitch the lining to the zipper tape at zip opening.

Waistband

3. Tack the interfacing to the wrong side of the waistband along the notched edge. Catch stitch the interfacing along the fold edge. Turn and tack the seam allowance to the inside on the unnotched edge inside and press flat.

4. With right sides together, matching the notch to the side seam, pin the waistband to the skirt. Stitch through all thicknesses.

Trim the interfacing close to the stitching line. Trim and grade the seam and press it up towards the waistband.

5. With right sides together, stitch the ends of the waistband as shown. Trim the seam and cut across the corners.

6. Turn the waistband to the inside and tack along the folded edge. Slip stitch the waist band to the stitching line. Press.

7. Sew hooks and eyes to the waistband as shown.

Hem

8. Hang the skirt up and leave it over-

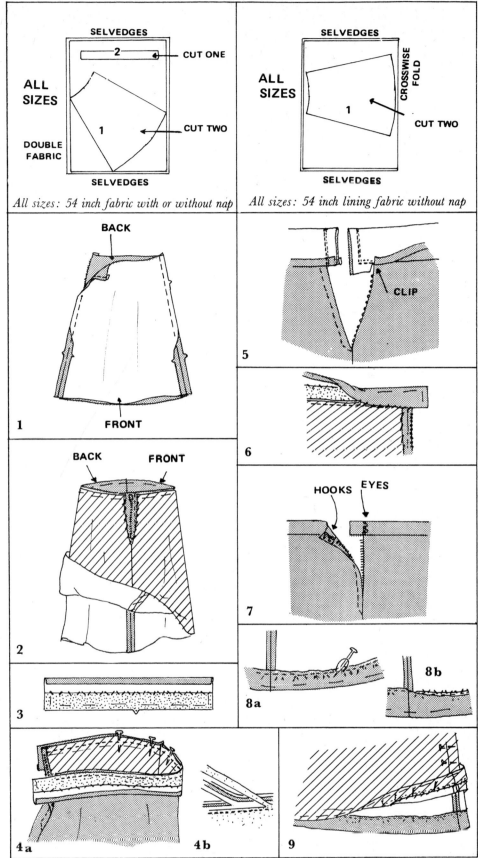

All sizes: 54 inch fabric with or without nap

All sizes: 54 inch lining fabric without nap

night to allow the flare in the skirt to drop. Try the skirt on and mark the hem line. Tack the folded edge. Trim the hem to an even width all round. Finish raw edge with oversewing. Machine gather at the raw edge, pull up the thread to shrink the fullness out. Sew hem with invisible hemming stitch. Press the folded edge of the hem.

Lining hem

9. Make the lining hem 1 inch shorter than the skirt. Tack the folded edge. Pleat the fullness of the hem. Neaten the raw edge by machine. Slip stitch the hem up.

Classic in silk

This beautifully cut shirt blouse has been specially designed to team up with the bias cut skirt featured on page 23. However, the design is so versatile that it would look equally attractive worn casually with trousers or dressed up for evening wear with a long skirt.

The blouse shown here is made in a fine, plain silk, but other soft light fabrics would also be suitable. Printed fabrics which require matching of pattern need extra care in cutting out.

Fabrics and notions

- [ ] 36 inch wide fabric, with or without nap: $3\frac{5}{8}$ yards for sizes 10 and 12; $3\frac{3}{4}$ yards for sizes 14 and 16
- [ ] interfacing, $\frac{1}{2}$ yard for all sizes
- [ ] 17 buttons measuring $\frac{3}{8}$ inch across
- [ ] matching sewing thread
- [ ] graph paper for patterns

The pattern

The pattern is for sizes 10, 12, 14 and 16. Draw up the pattern pieces from the graph. The squares on the graph represent 1 square inch. A seam allowance of $\frac{5}{8}$ inch is included on all edges.

Making up

Front

1. Tack the interfacing to the wrong side of the front, having the edge level with the fold line. Catch stitch the interfacing in position along the fold line. Neaten the raw edge of the facing. Fold the facing on the fold line to the inside. Tack and press the folded edge.

Seams

2. With right sides together, matching notches, tack and stitch the side backs to the back and the side fronts to the fronts, easing between the upper notches. Clip the curved edges and press the seams open.

3. With right sides together, matching notches, tack and stitch the shoulder and side seams. Clip the curves and press the seams open.

Collar

4. Tack the interfacing to the wrong side of the collar. With right sides together, matching notches, tack and stitch the upper and under collars together around the unnotched edges. Grade the seam and clip across the corners.

Turn the collar to the right side, tack around all stitched edges. Press flat.

5. With right sides together, matching notches, pin and tack the interfaced edge of the collar to the blouse neck edge, leaving the upper collar free.

Stitch the entire neck seam. Grade the seam and press towards the collar.

Turn the seam allowance on the upper collar to the inside. Hem to stitching line and press. Top-stitch round the collar edge if desired.

Sleeve opening

6. Cut two pieces of fabric measuring 3 inches square. With right sides together, pin and tack the pieces to the sleeves centrally over the slash line. Stitch $\frac{1}{4}$ inch away from the slash line to the circle as shown. Slash to the circle as shown. Turn the piece to the inside. Tack around all edges and press flat.

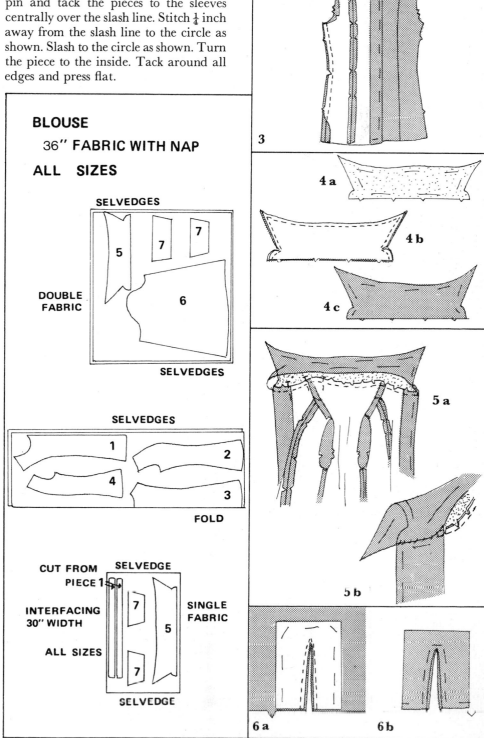

BLOUSE

36″ FABRIC WITH NAP

ALL SIZES

SELVEDGES

5 7 7

DOUBLE FABRIC

6

SELVEDGES

SELVEDGES

1 2 4 3

FOLD

CUT FROM PIECE 1

SELVEDGE

INTERFACING 30″ WIDTH

ALL SIZES

7 7 7

5

SINGLE FABRIC

SELVEDGE

1 2 3 4 a 4 b 4 c 5 a 5 b 6 a 6 b

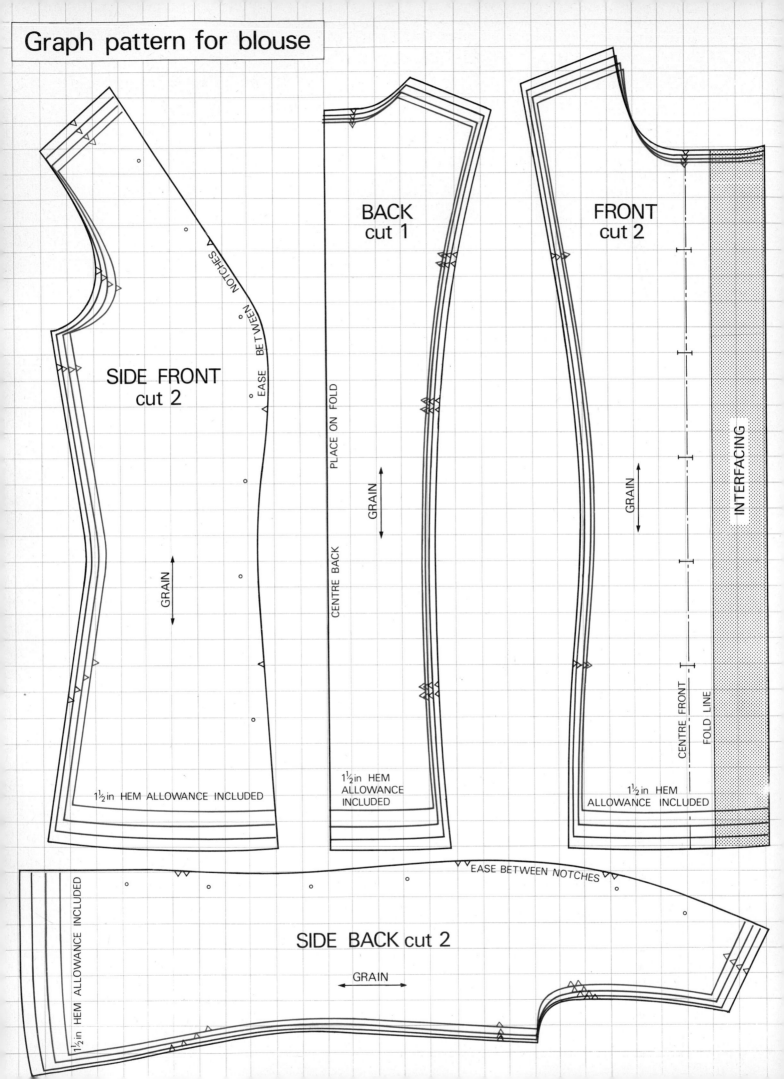

Graph pattern for blouse

SIDE FRONT cut 2

EASE BETWEEN NOTCHES

GRAIN

1½in HEM ALLOWANCE INCLUDED

BACK cut 1

PLACE ON FOLD

CENTRE BACK

GRAIN

1½in HEM ALLOWANCE INCLUDED

FRONT cut 2

GRAIN

INTERFACING

CENTRE FRONT

FOLD LINE

1½in HEM ALLOWANCE INCLUDED

SIDE BACK cut 2

EASE BETWEEN NOTCHES

GRAIN

1½in HEM ALLOWANCE INCLUDED

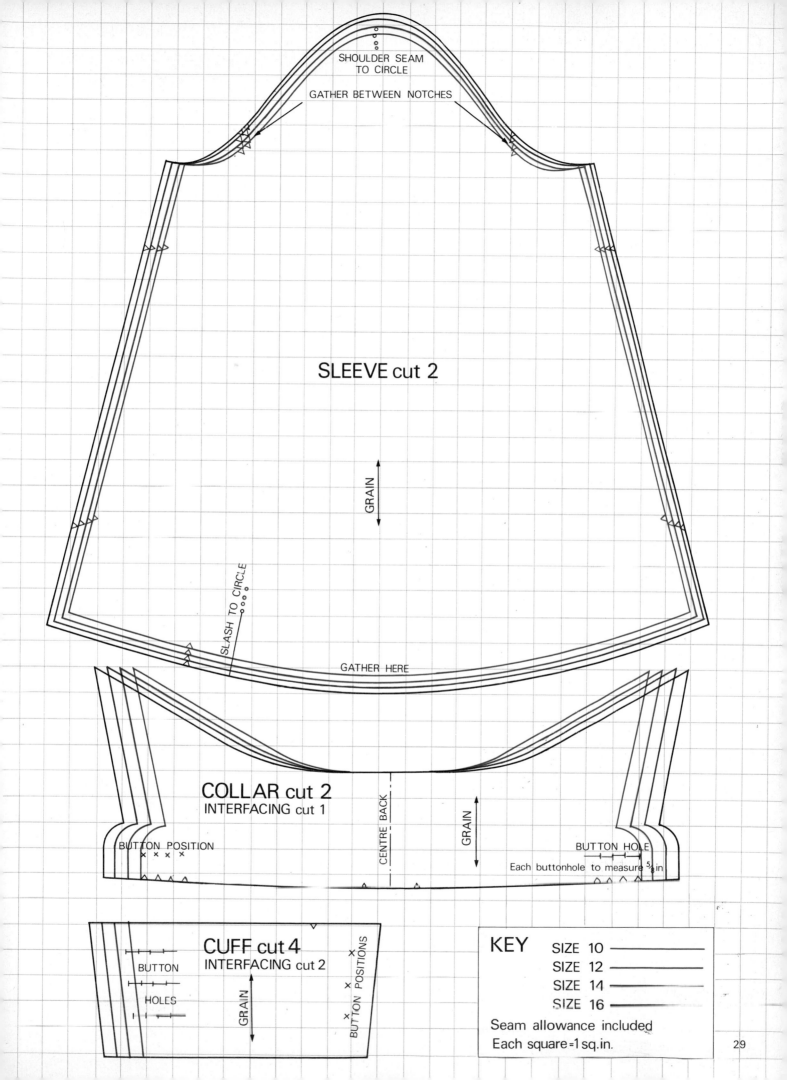

SHOULDER SEAM
TO CIRCLE

GATHER BETWEEN NOTCHES

SLEEVE cut 2

GRAIN

SLASH TO CIRCLE

GATHER HERE

COLLAR cut 2
INTERFACING cut 1

CENTRE BACK

GRAIN

BUTTON POSITION

BUTTON HOLE

Each buttonhole to measure $\frac{5}{8}$ in

CUFF cut 4
INTERFACING cut 2

BUTTON

HOLES

GRAIN

BUTTON POSITIONS

KEY

SIZE 10 ——————
SIZE 12 ——————
SIZE 14 ——————
SIZE 16 ——————

Seam allowance included
Each square = 1 sq. in.

29

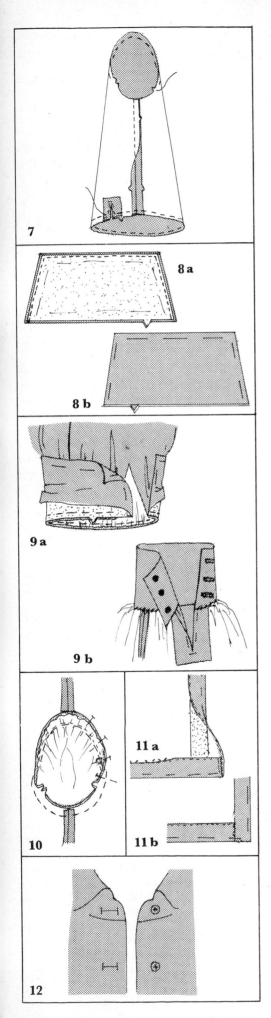

Sleeve

7. With right sides together, matching notches, tack and stitch the underarm seam. Press open. Run a row of gathers between the notches on the sleeve head and around the lower edge of the sleeve as shown.

Cuff

8. Tack the interfacing to the wrong side of the cuff. With right sides together, matching notches, tack and stitch the cuffs together around the unnotched edges. Grade the seam and turn the cuff to the right side. Tack around the stitched edges and press flat.

9. With right sides together, matching notches and the edge of the cuff to the sleeve, draw the gathers up to fit the cuff. Tack and stitch the interfaced side of the cuff to the sleeve, leaving the other side of the cuff free. Grade the seam and press it up towards the cuff. Turn the seam allowance on the unstitched cuff to the inside, and hem to the stitching line. Top-stitch round cuff edges if desired. Mark four buttonholes, each $\frac{1}{2}$ inch wide and evenly spaced, on the cuff, working $\frac{1}{2}$ inch in from the lower edge of the cuff.

Work hand or machine stitched buttonholes and sew the buttons into position.

Setting in the sleeve

10. With right sides together, matching notches and underarm seam, pin the sleeve to the armhole, drawing the gathers up evenly to fit the armhole. Tack and stitch with the sleeve uppermost. Trim the seam and clip the curves. Neaten edge and press the seam towards the sleeve.

Hem

11. Turn the facing out, turn up the hem and tack along the fold line. Neaten the raw edge of the hem with machine overcasting. Stitch the hem with invisible hemming stitch.

Turn the facing to the inside and slip stitch to the hem. Press flat.

Buttonholes and buttons

12. On the collar, mark a $\frac{1}{2}$ inch buttonhole $\frac{3}{4}$ inch in from the edge. Mark a further 8 buttonholes down the right front, $\frac{3}{4}$ inch in from the fold line.

Work hand or machine stitched buttonholes. Sew the buttons to the centre front on the left side under the buttonholes.

YOUNG IDEAS

Who doesn't need an extra skirt in her wardrobe—and these pages show the reader with absolutely no sewing experience how to make one in colourful felt in only an hour or so. Just gather the materials needed and surprise yourself with the results.

You will need:

- [ ] 1⅛yds of felt (usually 70-72ins wide, but it must be at least 40ins wide for this skirt)
- [ ] 3ins of Velcro to match the skirt
- [ ] ¾yd of petersham ribbon (to strengthen the waist-band)
- [ ] 3 squares of felt, in different colours for the motifs
- [ ] Thread to match the skirt
- [ ] 2 hooks and eyes
- [ ] Scissors
- [ ] Needle and dressmaking pins
- [ ] Long ruler (about 3ft long) or its equivalent (a length of wood would do)
- [ ] 1 piece of string about 23ins long
- [ ] Felt pen or chalk in contrasting colour

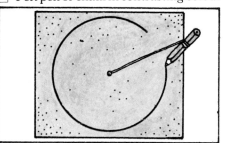

1. Drawing a circle
Spread the felt out on the floor. Pin one end of the piece of string in the centre of the felt. Tie a pencil to the other end of the string. Hold the pinned end down and gently stretch the string until the pencil is as far away from the centre of the felt as it will go. You will find that, as you move the pencil, the point draws a circle.

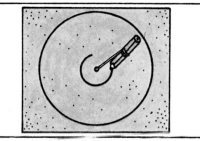

2. To make the waist hole
Untie the pencil and tie it on the string again, this time 4 inches from the centre. Draw another circle for the waist. Diagram 2 shows both circles drawn.

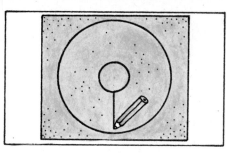

3. To make the back opening
Unpin the string from the felt. Mark the place with a pencil. Lay the long ruler, or whatever you are using for a straight edge, from the marked centre to the edge of the larger circle. Draw along this line (call it line A-B).

4. Cutting out the skirt
Cut round the edge of the big circle. Cut out the small circle in the centre. Cut up line A-B for the back opening.

5. Trying on for fit
Now try the skirt on. Hold it round you with the back opening in front, so that you can see how much overlap there is. Remember, a blouse or jumper might have to be tucked in, so don't make the waist fit too tightly. If there is more than an inch overlap, lay the skirt out flat again on the floor and cut a strip of felt off along the straight line A-B, so that the waist line fits. If the waist seems too tight, cut a tiny strip off the edge of the smaller circle. Be sure to cut a very small amount, because even ¼ inch off will make the waist much bigger. Keep trying the skirt on until it fits.

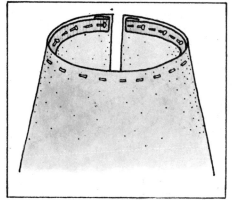

6. Putting in the waist-band
The petersham strip now goes inside the waist of the skirt to keep it firm. Cut a piece to your waist measurement plus 1 inch. Pin it to the felt, turning both ends under as you pin. Then tack and remove the pins. Sew the petersham ribbon to the skirt, *making the stitches*

about ⅛in down from the waist edge. Use back stitch if you are hand sewing or, better still, machine stitch. Oversew the ends to neaten the ribbon.

7. Sewing in the fastening
Pull the Velcro apart into two strips. Place one half of the Velcro on the right side of the felt along the centre back opening (line A-B), just below the waist-band, and pin. Place the other half in the matching position inside the skirt, making sure that both halves meet exactly when pressed together; now firmly oversew all round the edges of the Velcro.

Sew the hooks and eyes onto the waist-band. Put the back edges of the skirt so that one side overlaps the other and the Velcro strips are closed together. Now make the centre back seam by sewing down from the bottom of the Velcro fastening to the edge of the skirt, stitching about ¼ inch from the cut edge. You can use either running stitches for this seam, or machine stitch.

8. Decorating the skirt
Trace the motifs (drawing overleaf) and cut them out for patterns. Pin them onto the pieces of coloured felt and cut them out. Stick these onto the skirt with Copydex, using only a small amount. Place the motif in position carefully as Copydex will leave white marks on felt if too much is used, and put something heavy on top until it is dry. Alternatively, make small, neat stitches all round the shapes, using thread to match the motif.

To vary the skirt, any number of different shapes can be traced from pictures – flowers, faces, designs – and used instead of those motifs given.

*One word of caution in caring for this skirt: felt will not wash and must therefore be dry cleaned.

EASY~MAKE SKIRT

KNITTING

To knit this soft
Angora sweater see page 48

Crash Course Learn to knit

Methods

There are two types of knitting, 'flat' and 'in the round'. Flat knitting is worked backwards and forwards using two needles. Round knitting is useful for items such as socks, gloves and certain types of sweaters and is worked with a set of four needles, pointed at both ends.

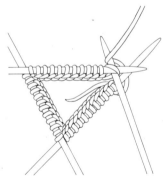

Alternatively, there are long flexible needles known as circular needles and these are used on larger items in the round to make them seamless. Circular needles can also be used for flat knitting working backwards and forwards in rows.

Needles

Needles are manufactured in varying sizes to combine with the different thicknesses of yarns and to create different tensions. The range is wide from very fine needles to those measuring one inch in diameter.

Tension

This refers to the number of stitches and rows to the inch. Unless the same tension is obtained as that worked by the designer of the original garment, then obviously the garment will not fit. It is always advisable before embarking on a project to work a tension sample at least a minimum of four inches square. If there are too many stitches to the inch, change to a larger size of needle until the correct number is obtained. Conversely, if too few stitches

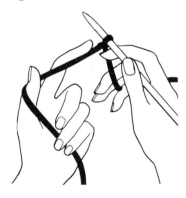

are being made, adjust to a smaller needle until the correct tension is acquired. Even half a stitch too many or too few, although seemingly little, will amount to nine stitches too many or too few on the back of a thirty-four inch sweater. This would mean the completed garment would be two inches too large or too small.

Substituting yarns

Each design has been worked out for the knitting yarn which is stated, but if you wish to substitute another do so only if you are absolutely sure that the same tension can be obtained. Not even two different double knitting wools will knit up exactly the same and the yardage on the different makes of the yarns will mean that you will need a different quantity.

Casting on

There are several methods of casting on, each with its own appropriate use. The following are the most often used.

Thumb method

This is worked using only one needle. It is an excellent way to begin most garments since it gives an elastic, hard-wearing edge. Make a slip loop in the yarn about three feet from the end. This length varies with the number of stitches required but one yard will cast on about one hundred stitches. Alternatively, take a guide from the width of the piece of knitting multiplied by three.

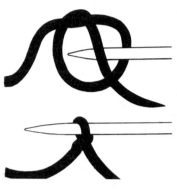

Slip the loop onto the needle, which should be held in the right hand.

Working with the short length of yarn in the left hand, pass this round the left thumb.

Insert the point of the needle under the loop on the thumb and hook forward the long end of yarn from the ball.

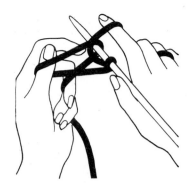

Wind the yarn under and over the needle and draw through the loop, leaving stitch on needle.

Tighten stitch on needle, noting that yarn is round the thumb ready for the next stitch.

Repeat actions 3 to 5 for the required number of stitches.

Two needle method

This method, sometimes known as the English cable version, is necessary when extra stitches are required during the knitting itself, for instance for a buttonhole or pocket, although it can also be used at the beginning of a garment.

Make a slip loop in the yarn three inches from the end. It is not necessary to estimate the yarn required as the stitches are worked from the ball yarn. Slip the loop onto the left-hand knitting needle.

Insert right-hand needle into the loop holding yarn in the right hand, and wind the yarn under and over the needle.

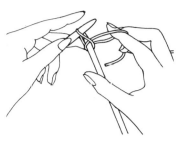

Draw the new loop through the first loop on left-hand needle thus forming a second loop. Pass newly made loop onto the left-hand needle.

Place point of right-hand needle between two loops on the left-hand needle and wind yarn under and over the right-hand needle point and draw this new loop through between the two stitches on the left-hand needle. Slip this loop onto the left-hand needle.

Repeat action 3 between the last two stitches on the left-hand needle until the required number of stitches have been cast on.

Invisible method

This gives the flat hemmed effect of a machine knit garment. It is a flexible, strong finish which can hold ribbon or elastic and is very useful for designs which need casings. Using a contrast yarn which is later removed, and the Thumb method, cast on half the number of stitches required, plus one. Now using the correct yarn, begin the ribbing.

1st row K1, *yfwd, K1, rep from * to end.
2nd row K1, *yfwd, sl 1, ybk, K1, rep from * to end.
3rd row Sl 1, *ybk, K1, yfwd, sl 1, rep from * to end.

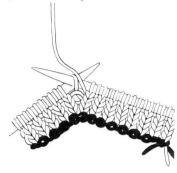

Repeat second and third rows once more.
6th row K1, *P1, K1, rep from * to end.
7th row P1, *K1, P1, rep from * to end.

Continue in rib for the required depth. Unpick contrast yarn. The ribs should appear to run right round the edge.

Knit stitch

Take the needle with the cast on stitches in the left hand, the other needle in the right hand. Insert the right-hand needle point through the first stitch on the left-hand needle from front to back.

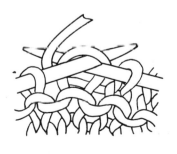

Keeping the yarn behind the needles, pass the yarn round the point of the right-hand needle so that it forms a loop.

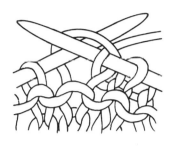

Draw this loop through the stitch on the left-hand needle, so forming a new loop on the right-hand needle.

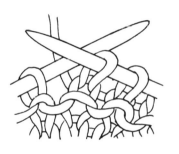

Allow the stitch on the left-hand needle to slip off. Repeat this action until a loop has been drawn through each stitch on the left-hand needle and placed on the right-hand needle.

This completes one row. To work the next row, change the needle holding the stitches to the left hand and the free needle to the right hand.

Repeat the same process as for the first row.

Purl stitch

Take the needle with the cast on stitches in the left hand, the other needle in the right hand. Insert the right-hand needle point through the first stitch on the left-hand needle from back to front.

Keeping the yarn at the front of the needles, pass the yarn round the point of the right-hand needle to form a loop.

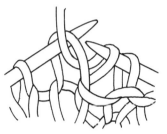

Draw this loop through the stitch on the left-hand needle, thus forming a new loop on the right-hand needle.

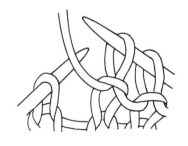

Allow the stitch on the left-hand needle to slip off.

Repeat this action with each stitch along the row until all the stitches on the left-hand needle have been passed over to the right-hand needle.

This completes one row. To work the next row, change the needle holding the stitches to the left hand and the free needle to the right hand. Repeat the process as for the first row.

35

Lifting dropped stitches

On stocking stitch, insert a crochet hook into the dropped stitch with the knit side of the work facing. Lift the first thread above the stitch onto the hook tip and hold it in the hook curve as you slowly draw the hook back until the first stitch slips off the tip, leaving the lifted thread as the new stitch. Repeat this until all the threads have been lifted, then return the stitch to the needle.

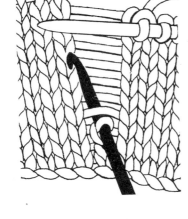

If the purl side is the right side, lift the stitch on the wrong or knit side.

Casting off

To cast off on a knit row, knit into each of the first two stitches. Then, * with the left-hand needle point, lift the first stitch over the second stitch, leaving only one stitch on the right-hand needle.

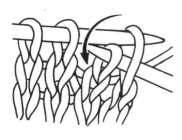

Knit the next stitch, repeat from * until one stitch remains. Cut the yarn and draw it through the last stitch, pulling tight.

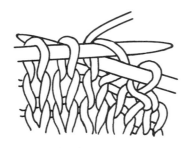

On a purl row, each stitch is purled before being cast off. To cast off on a patterned or ribbed row, each stitch is lifted over the next in the same way having first knitted the stitches as in the patterning.

Garter stitch

This consists of working every row in knit stitches. Because the wrong side of a knit row forms purl stitches, this gives a ridge of purl stitches on every second row on both sides of the work.

Stocking stitch

By working a knit row alternately with a purl row, the ridges of the purl stitches form on the same side of the work and the right side gives a smooth fabric.

Ribbing

To form a ribbed pattern both knit and purl stitches are combined on the same row. This can be done by simple alternating of one knit, one purl stitch, or two knit, two purl stitches, although it can be worked in more unusual combinations repeated systematically. On the next row, the knit stitches become purl stitches and the purl stitches knit stitches.

The slipped stitch

The slipped stitch is so called because it is transferred from the left-hand needle to the right-hand needle without being worked. The yarn is carried either behind or in front of the stitch. It is used in

several different ways – decreasing, making a fold for a pleat or facing, to form lacy patterns and to form a texture on the surface of the knitting.

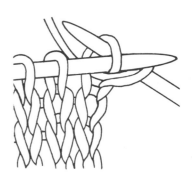

Slip stitch knitwise on a knit row. Hold the yarn behind the work as if to knit the stitch. Insert the right-hand needle point into the stitch from front to back, as in the knit stitch, and slip it onto the right-hand needle.

Slip stitch purlwise on a knit row. Hold the yarn behind the work as if to knit the stitch. Insert the right-hand needle point into the stitch from back to front, as in a purl stitch, and slip it onto the right-hand needle.

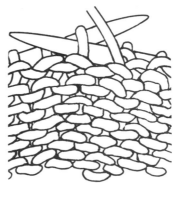

Slip stitch purlwise on a purl row. Hold the yarn at the front of the work as if to purl the stitch. Insert the right-hand needle point from back to front as if to form a purl stitch, and slip it onto the right-hand needle. It is important to remember that when decreasing by slipping a stitch on a knit row, the stitch must be slipped knitwise, otherwise

it will become crossed. On a purl row, the stitch must be slipped purlwise. However, if the slipped stitch does not form a decrease, it must be slipped purlwise on a knit row to prevent it being crossed when purled on the following row.

Increasing

The shape of the work is determined by increasing or decreasing. The simplest way is to knit twice into the same stitch. Knit or purl the stitch in the usual way, but do not slip the stitch off the needle.

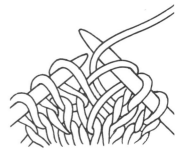

Instead, place the point of the right-hand needle into the back of the stitch and knit or purl into the stitch again. Slip both these stitches onto the right-hand needle, thus making two stitches out of one.

To increase invisibly. Insert the right-hand needle into the front of the stitch below that on the left-hand needle and knit a new stitch. If the increase is on purl work then purl the new stitch. The next stitch on the row being worked is then knitted or purled.

To increase between stitches on knit work. Using the right-hand needle, pick up the yarn which lies between the stitch just worked and the next one, and place it on the left-hand needle. Knit into the back of this loop. This twists and tightens the loops so that no hole is formed. Slip the loop off the left-hand needle.

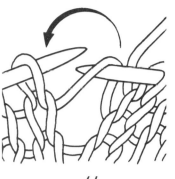

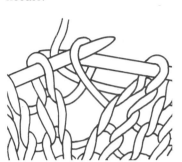

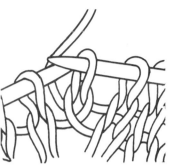

To increase between stitches on purl work. Pick the loop up and purl into it from the back.

Multiple increase at the beginning of a row. Cast on the number of stitches required by the two-needle method and work across the entire row (cast on stitches and knitted stitches) in the usual manner.

Multiple increase at the end of a row. Reverse the work after completing the row and cast on.

Increasing between two knit stitches. Bring the yarn forward as if to purl then taking it back over the right-hand needle ready to knit the next stitch.

Increasing between two purl stitches. A similar method can be used to the one previously given by taking yarn over and round needle before purling next stitch.

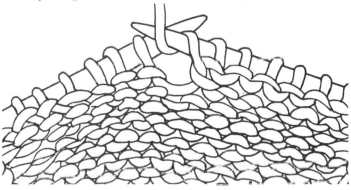

To make a stitch between a purl and a knit stitch. This is particularly useful on ribbed work. The yarn is already in position to the front and the next stitch is knitted in the usual way, the yarn taken over the needle.

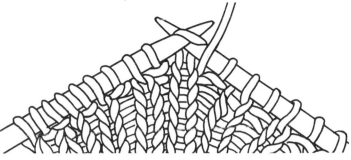

To make a stitch between a knit and a purl stitch. Bring the yarn forward and once completely round the needle before purling into the next stitch to be worked.

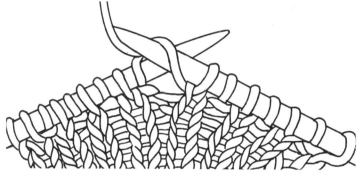

Decreasing

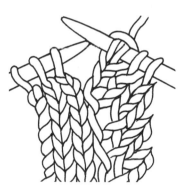

The simplest method of decreasing is to knit or purl two stitches together. This is sometimes worked into the back of the stitches, depending on the fabric pattern.

Another method of decreasing is to slip one stitch, knit the next one and then slip the slipped stitch off the needle over the knitted one.

Multiple decreases. These are worked by casting off, maintaining the continuity of the pattern by knitting knit stitches and purling purl stitches before slipping one over the other.

This part of the knitting crash course covers the techniques of working with different colour yarns, marking, measuring, picking up stitches, making up details and a list of abbreviations.

Working with several colours

Stranding. The colour which is not in use is taken across the back of the work while the colour in use is being worked. It is important not to pull the yarn too tightly or the work will pucker and the garment will not be sufficiently elastic when worn.

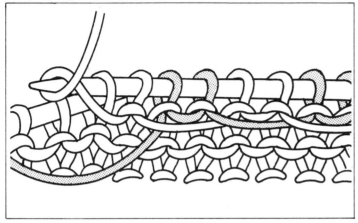

Weaving. This method needs more care, but is worth the extra attention for the professional finish it gives, especially if a colour is out of use across a fairly large number of stitches.

The principle is to weave the colour not in use under the colour being used. This is done by taking the colour in use under the out-of-work strand before working into the next stitch.

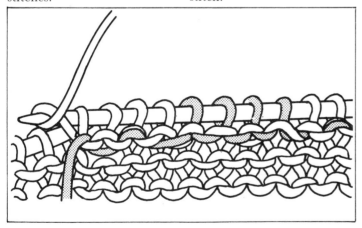

Marker threads

Sometimes it is necessary to mark a particular point in the work to use as a visual guide later. A short length of contrasting yarn is threaded through the stitch, and tied in place so that it does not come out accidentally. Once it has served its purpose, simply pull the strand out.

Measuring

Always lay knitting on a flat surface for accuracy. Always use a rigid rule and not a tape measure. Never measure round curves but measure the depth of, for example, an armhole on a straight line. In the same way a sleeve should be measured up the centre of the work and not along the shaped edge.

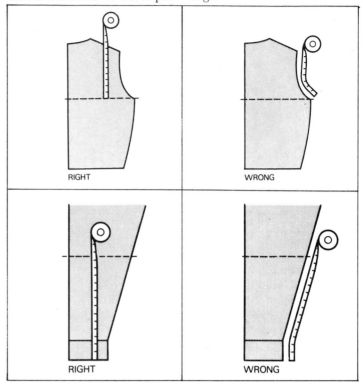

Picking up stitches

As a general rule, when picking up stitches along a side edge, one stitch should be picked up for every two rows. However, whether the stitches are being picked up along the ends of rows or along a cast-off edge, it saves time to divide the length up with equally spaced marker pins. The number of stitches to be picked up can then be spaced evenly right along the length of the work. To pick up stitches, insert the needle into the fabric edge, wrap the yarn round the needle and draw the loop through. This can be done with a crochet hook and the stitches then moved to the knitting needle.

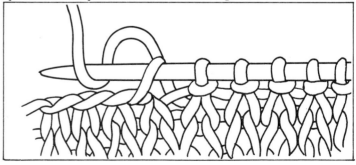

Invisible casting off

This method has all the advantages of invisible cast-on edges and is worked on a K1, P1 rib over an odd number of stitches.

Work the ribbing as normally until only two more rows are required to give the correct finished depth, and ending with a WS row.

1st row K1, *yfwd, sl 1, ybk, K1, rep from * to end.
2nd row Sl 1, *ybk, K1, yfwd, sl 1, rep from * to end. Rep these two rows once more. Break off yarn leaving an end not less than three times the length of the cast-off edge. Thread into a blunt-ended needle and hold in the right hand, the needle with the

stitches in the left.

Insert needle into first knit stitch as if to purl it and pull yarn through, then into next purl stitch as if to knit it and pull yarn through leaving both stitches on the knitting needle.

* Insert needle into first knit stitch as if to knit it, pull yarn through and slip stitch off needle.

Pass needle in front of next purl stitch and into following knit stitch as if to purl it. Pull

lost. Seams should be sewn with a blunt-ended needle using either a back stitch

seam or overcasting stitches. Alternatively, work a crocheted slip stitch along the seam.

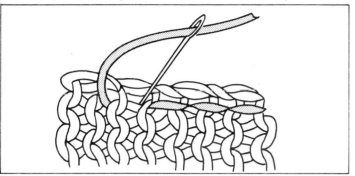

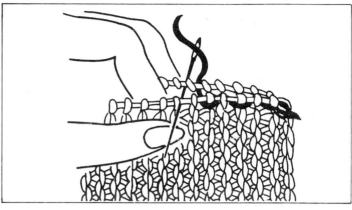

yarn through.

Insert needle into purl stitch at end of row as if to purl it and slip stitch off knitting needle.

Pass needle behind next stitch and into following purl stitch as if to knit it. Pull yarn through. Rep from * until all stitches have been worked off.

Making up

The finishing of a garment is just as important as the working of it. First check whether the yarn can be pressed or not. Many man-made fibres stretch to a high degree and lose their texture when pressed.

Darn in all ends of yarn

securely. Place each piece of knitting, right side down, on an ironing pad and pin evenly round the edges. Always use rustless pins and never stretch the knitting. Once the pieces are pinned out, check the measurements against those given in the instructions. Adjust if necessary. Wring out a clean white cloth or a piece of old sheeting in warm water, and place it over the top of the work. With a warm iron press evenly but not heavily on the surface by pressing the iron down and lifting it up without moving along the surface. Ribbing should never be pressed or the elasticity of the stitch is

For a flat seam, such as that on ribbing, pass the threaded needle through the edge stitch on the right-hand side directly across to the edge stitch on the left-hand side and pull the yarn through. Turn the needle and work through the next stitch on the left-hand side directly across to the edge stitch on the right-hand side, again pulling the yarn through. Continue in this way.

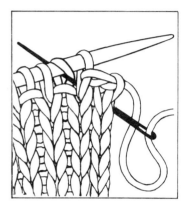

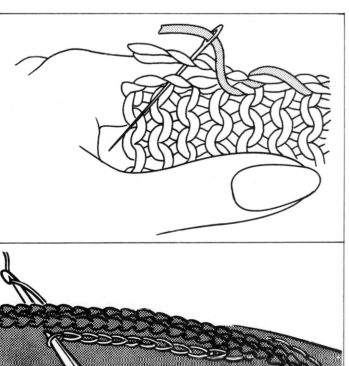

Abbreviations used in Golden Hands

alt	alternate	sl 1P	slip one purlwise
beg	beginning	st(s)	stitch(es)
dec	decrease	st st	stocking stitch
grm(s)	gramme(s)	tbl	through back of
g st	garter stitch		loop(s)
in	inch(es)	tog	together
inc	increase	WS	wrong side
K	knit	ybk	yarn backward
KB	knit into back of	yfwd	yarn forward
	stitch	yon	yarn over needle
M1K	make one knitwise	yrn	yarn round needle
M1P	make one purlwise		

An asterisk (*) shown in a pattern row denotes that the stitches shown after this sign must be repeated from that point.

Square brackets [ ] denote instructions for larger sizes in the pattern.

Round brackets ( ) denote that this section of the pattern is to be worked for all sizes.

No.	number	
P	purl	
patt	pattern	
PB	purl into back of	
	stitch	
psso	pass slip stitch	
	over	
rem	remaining	
rep	repeat	
RS	right side	
sl 1	slip one knitwise	

Quick Check

Use this handy inches/centimetres rule to measure your work as you knit.

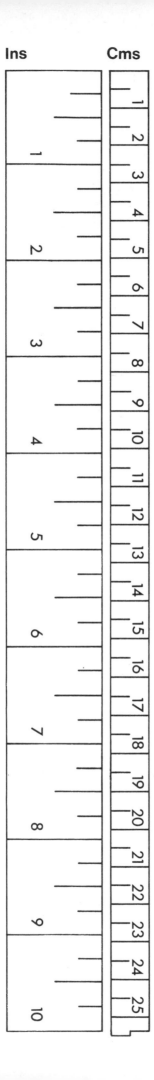

Ins **Cms**

**Yarns
and
Metrication**

When purchasing yarns it is advisable to check with your stockist as to the weight of the balls since they now vary due to the introduction of the metric system.

Metrication has been adopted by most manufacturers now, but some large stocks of wool in standard ounces will take some time to run out, so this confused situation will be with us for some time.

Useful weights in grams (g) and kilograms (kg):

1oz=28.35g
4oz=113.4g
8oz=226.8g
1lb=454g

25g=0.9oz
50g=1.8oz
1kg/1000g=2.2lb

Knitting yarn quantities (to convert either way):

1oz=25g+3.35g
For 3oz buy 4 balls of 25g
For 7oz buy 8 balls
For 12oz buy 14 balls
For 16oz buy 18 balls
For 20oz buy 23 balls

40

Shoulder hugger

This soft green shawl is simple to knit in fine wool crepe. The fringing adds a delicate touch.

Size
40in square, excluding fringe

Tension for this design
7 sts and 9 rows to 1in over st st worked on No. 10 needles

Materials shown here
Ladyship Siesta Crepe
20 1oz balls

One pair No. 10 needles
One No. 3·00 (ISR) crochet hook

Main section

Using No. 10 needles, cast on 280 sts.

Work in st st for 40in.

Cast off.

Edging

Using No. 3·00 hook and with RS facing, beg at a corner, work dc all round shawl, join with ss to first st.

2nd round *7ch, miss 4dc, 1dc in next dc, rep from * all round, ending with ss in first of 7ch.

3rd round Ss to 4th of 7ch, *7ch, 1dc in next loop, rep from * all round, ending with ss to first of 7ch.

Fasten off.

To make up

Press work under a damp cloth, using a warm iron. Cut yarn into 14in lengths and taking 3 strands tog, knot into each loop all round the shawl. Trim fringe.

cheers for the red white and blue

Red white and blue—the clearest, cleanest way with colours—and a quartet of eye-catching knitted tops.

Sleeveless cardigan

Sizes

To fit 34[36:38]in bust
Length to shoulder, 25[25½:26]in
The figures in brackets [] refer to the 36 and 38in sizes respectively

> **Tension for all these designs**
> 6 sts and 8 rows to 1in over st st worked on No.9 needles

Materials shown here

Wendy Double Knitting Nylonised
12[13:14] balls main shade, A
2 balls each of B and C
One pair No.9 needles
Set of 4 No.10 needles pointed at both ends
One No.10 circular Twin-Pin
5 buttons

Back

Using No.9 needles and A, cast on 107[115:123] sts.
1st row K1, *P1, K1, rep from * to end.
2nd row P1, *K1, P1, rep from * to end.
Rep these 2 rows twice more.
Commence patt.
1st row P1, K1, *P3, K1, rep from * to last st, P1.

2nd row K1, P1, *K3, P1, rep from * to last st, K1.
These two rows form patt.
Continue in patt until work measures 18in from beg, ending with a WS row.

Shape armholes

Cast off at beg of next and every row 4 sts twice, 3 sts 4 times, 2 sts 2[2:4] times.
Dec one st at each end of next and following 3[4:4] alt rows then at each end of every following 8th row 4[5: 5] times. 67[71:75] sts.
Continue without shaping until armholes measure 7[7½: 8]in from beg, ending with a RS row.

Shape neck

Next row Patt 14[15:16], cast off 39[41:43] sts, patt to end.
Next row Patt to end.
Cast off 3 sts at beg of next and following 2[1:0] alt rows, then 2 sts at beg of following 0[1:3] alt rows.
Cast off rem 5 sts.
With RS of work facing, rejoin yarn to rem sts and complete to match first side, reversing shapings.

Left front

Using No.9 needles and A, cast on 55[59:63] sts. Work 6 rows K1, P1 rib as given for Back.
Continue in patt as given for Back until work measures 13½in from beg, ending with a WS row.

Shape front edge

1st row Patt to last 3 sts, K2 tog, P1.
2nd row K1, P1, patt to end.
3rd row Patt to last 2 sts, K1, P1.
4th row K1, P2 tog, patt to end.
5th row As 3rd.
6th row As 2nd.
Rep last 6 rows until work measures same as Back to underarm, ending with a WS row.

Shape armhole

Continue dec at front edge on every 3rd row as before, *at the same time* cast off at beg of next and every alt row 4 sts once, 3 sts twice and 2 sts 1[1:2] times, ending with a WS row.
Dec one st at beg of next 4[5:5] alt rows, then at beg of every 8th row 4[5:5] times.
Continue to dec at front edge only on every 3rd row until 5 sts rem.
Continue without shaping until the armhole measures the same as Back up to the shoulder, ending with a WS row. Cast off.

Right front

Work as given for left Front, reversing all the shaping throughout.

Pockets

Using No.9 needles and A, cast on 23 sts.
Work in patt as given for Back, casting on 2 sts at beg of 2nd and following 3 rows, then one st at beg of next 2 rows. 33 sts.
Continue without shaping until 38 rows have been worked from beg, ending with a WS row.
Change to No.10 needles.
Break off A and join in B.
K 1 row.
Work 4 rows K1, P1 rib.
Break off B and join in C.
P 1 row.
Work 3 rows K1, P1 rib.
Cast off in rib.

Front band

Join shoulder seams.
Using No.10 Twin-Pin and B, with RS of work facing, K up 112 sts up right front edge to beg of front shaping, 84[88:92] sts to shoulder, 49[53:57] sts across back neck, 84[88:92] sts down left front to beg of shaping and 112 sts down left front to lower edge. 441[453:465] sts.
Work 3 rows K1, P1 rib.
Next row (buttonhole row) Rib 13 *cast off 3 sts, rib 21, rep from * 3 times more, cast off 3 sts, rib to end.
Break off B and join in C.
Next row P to end, casting on 3 sts above those cast off in previous row.
Work 3 rows rib. Cast off in rib.

Armbands

Using set of 4 No.10 needles and B, with RS facing, K up 117[125:133] sts round armhole.
Work as given for front band, omitting buttonholes.

To make up

Press each piece lightly under a damp cloth with a warm iron. Join side seams. Sew on pockets. Press seams. Sew on buttons.

Pullover and tie

Sizes

To fit 32[34:36]in bust
Length to shoulder, 21½[22: 22½]in
The figures in brackets [] refer to the 34 and 36in sizes respectively

Materials shown here

Wendy Double Knitting Nylonised
Pullover. 7[8:9] balls main shade, A
2 balls each of two contrast colours, B and C
Tie. 1 ball each of A, B and C
One pair No.9 needles
One pair No.10 needles
Set of 4 No.10 needles pointed at both ends
One No.10 circular Twin-Pin
One No.3·00 (ISR) crochet hook

Pullover back

Using No.10 needles and A, cast on 105[111:117] sts.
1st row K1, *P1, K1, rep from * to end.
2nd row P1, *K1, P1, rep from * to end.
Rep these 2 rows for 6in, ending with a 2nd row.
Change to No.9 needles.
Beg with a P row, continue in reversed st st until work measures 13in from beg, ending with a K row.

Shape armholes

Cast off at beg of next and every row 5 sts twice, 4 sts twice and 2 sts 4 times.
Dec one st at each end of next and following 3 alt rows, then every 4th row 6[7:8]

▲ *Left: the sleeveless cardigan which buttons up; Right: the pullover which has a crochet tie to match*

Neckband

Using No.10 Twin-Pin and B, cast on 42[44:46] sts, K up 54[58:62] sts down left front neck, K centre front st from holder, K up 54[58:62] sts up right front neck, cast on 42[44:46] sts and K up 64[68:72] sts round back neck. 257[273:289] sts.

Next round Work in K1, P1 rib to 2 sts before centre front st, K2 tog, P1, sl 1, K1, psso, and rib to end of round.

Rep this round 3 times more.

Break off B and join in C. Continue dec at centre front on every round, K 1 round then rib 4 rounds.

Break off C and join in A. Continue dec at centre front on every round, K 1 round then rib 3 rounds.

Cast off in rib, still dec at centre front.

Armbands

Using No.10 needles and B, with RS facing, K up 145 [155:165] sts round armhole. Work as given for neckband, omitting dec.

Tie

Using No.3·00 crochet hook and B, make 19ch.

1st row Into 2nd ch from hook, work 1dc, 1dc into each ch to end. Turn. 18dc.

Continue in dc, work 4 rows B, 4 rows A and 4 rows C throughout, until 22 rows in all have been worked.

Continue in stripes, dec 1st at each end of next and every following 22nd row until 6 sts rem.

With A only work 24 rows straight, then inc one st at each end of next and every following 30th row until 12 sts rem.

Continue straight until work measures 47in from beg. Fasten off.

To make up

Pullover. Press each piece under a damp cloth with a warm iron. Join side seams. Press seams.

Tie. Press as given for pullover.

---

times. 59[63:67] sts.

Continue without shaping until armholes measure 7[7½:8]in from beg, ending with a P row.

Shape neck

Next row K18 [19:20], cast off 23[25:27] sts, K to end. Complete this side first.

Next row P.

Cast off at beg of next and every alt row 4 sts 4 times and 2[3:4] sts once.

With RS facing, rejoin yarn to rem sts and complete to match first side, reversing shaping.

Pullover front

Work as given for Back until Front measures 10in from the beginning, ending with a K row.

Divide for neck

Next row P52[55:58], turn and leave rem sts on holder.

Next row K.

Next row P to last 2 sts, P2 tog.

Continue dec at front edge on every alt row until work measures same as Back to underarm, ending with a K row.

Shape armhole

Continue dec at front edge on every alt row, *at the same time* cast off at beg of next and every alt row 5 sts once, 4 sts once and 2 sts twice, then dec one st at armhole edge on following 4 alt rows.

Continue dec at neck edge on every alt row, *at the same time* continue dec at armhole edge on every following 4th row until 2 sts rem. Cast off.

With RS facing, leave first centre st on holder, rejoin yarn to rem sts and P to end. Complete to match first side, reversing shaping.

▲ *Left: the sleeveless jacket which has double breasted buttons and four pockets; Right: a simple pullover shown here with a purchased belt*

Sleeveless jacket

Sizes

To fit 34[36:38] in bust
Length to shoulder, 19[19½:
20]in
The figures in brackets []
refer to the 36 and 38in sizes
respectively

Materials shown here

Wendy Double Knitting
Nylonised
9[10:11] balls main shade, A
2 balls each of two colours
which contrast with the main
shade, B and C
One pair No.9 needles
One pair No.10 needles
One No.10 circular Twin-Pin
6 buttons 3 press studs

Back

Using No.10 needles and A,
cast on 110[116:122] sts.
Beg with a P row, work 1in
reversed st st.
Change to No.9 needles.
Continue in reversed st st
until work measures 13in
from beg, ending with a K
row.

Shape armholes

Cast off at beg of next and
every row 5 sts twice, 3 sts
twice and 2 sts 6 times.
Dec one st at each end of
next and following 2[3:4] alt
rows, then at each end of
every 4th row 5 times.
66[70:74] sts.
Continue without shaping
until armholes measure
7[7½:8]in from beg, ending
with a P row.

Shape neck

Next row K14[15:16], cast
off 38[40:42], K to end.
Complete this side first.
Next row P.
Cast off at beg of next and

following alt rows 3 sts 3
times and 5[6:7] sts once.
RS facing, rejoin yarn to
rem sts and complete as
first side, reversing shaping.

Left front

Using No.9 needles and A,
cast on 29 sts for lower
pocket lining.
Beg with a P row, work 20
rows reversed st st. Leave sts
on holder.
Using No.9 needles and A,
cast on 19 sts for upper
pocket lining. Beg with a P
row, work 16 rows reversed

st st. Leave sts on holder.
Using No.10 needles and A, cast on 67[71:75] sts.
Beg with a P row, work 1in reversed st st.
Change to No.9 needles.
Continue in reversed st st for a further 3in, ending with a K row.

Place lower pocket
Next row P11[13:15], slip next 29 sts on holder and leave for pocket top, P across sts of lower pocket lining, P to end.
Continue in reversed st st until work measures 29 rows less than Back to underarm, ending with a P row.

Shape front edge
Cast off at beg of next and every alt row 3 sts twice and 2 sts 3 times.

Place upper pocket
Next row P11[13:15], slip next 19 sts onto holder and leave for pocket top, P across lining sts, P to end.
Cast off 2 sts at beg of next and following 4 alt rows, then one st at beg of following 4 alt rows.
Work 2 rows, ending with a K row.

Shape armhole
Continue to dec one st at front edge on next and every following 3rd row, *at the same time* cast off at beg of next and every alt row 5 sts once, 3 sts once and 2 sts 3 times, ending with a K row.
Dec one st at beg of next and following 3[4:5] alt rows, then every 4th row 5 times.
Continue to dec at front edge only until 5[6:7] sts rem.
Continue without shaping until armhole measures same as Back to shoulder, ending with a K row. Cast off.
Mark positions for 3 sets of buttons on left front, first two to come 2in above cast on edge and last two to come ½in below beg of front shaping, with 3rd set half way between.

Right front

Make pocket linings as given for left Front.

Using No.10 needles and A, cast on 67[71:75] sts.
Beg with a P row, work 1in reversed st st.
Change to No.9 needles.
Continue in reversed st st for 1in, ending with a K row.
Next row (buttonhole row) P2, cast off 3 sts, P to end.
Next row K to end, casting on 3 sts above those cast off.
Continue in reversed st st until work measures 4in from beg, ending with a K row.

Place lower pocket
Next row P27[29:31], slip next 29 sts onto holder and leave for pocket top, P across sts of lining, P to end.
Complete to match left Front, reversing all shaping and making buttonholes at markers.

Front band
Join shoulder seams.
Using No.10 Twin-Pin and B, with RS of work facing K up 68 sts along right front edge beg 1in above cast on edge to allow for hem, K up 95[99:103] sts up shaped front edge, 53[55:57] sts across back neck, 95[99:103] sts down shaped front edge of left front and 68 sts down left front, ending 1in above cast on edge. 379[389:399] sts.
Beg 1st row with P1, work 4 rows K1, P1 rib.
Break off B and join in C.
P 1 row.
Rib 3 rows. Cast off in rib.

Armband

Using No.10 needles and B, with RS facing, K up 109 [117:125] sts round armhole. Work as given for front band.

Pocket tops

Using No.10 needles and B, with RS facing, work across sts on holders for pocket tops as given for front band.

To make up

Press each piece under a damp cloth with a warm iron. Join side seams. Sew down pocket linings and tops. Press seams. Sew on 3 buttons to correspond with buttonholes, then sew 3 press studs to left front edge to fasten under right front edge and sew 3 buttons to right front.

Slip-over

Sizes
To fit 32[34:36]in bust
Length to shoulder, 22[22½:23]in
The figures in brackets [] refer to the 34 and 36in sizes respectively

Materials shown here
Wendy Double Knitting Nylonised
7[8:9] balls main shade, A
1 ball each of two contrast colours, B and C
One pair No.9 needles
One pair No.10 needles
One No.10 circular Twin-Pin

Back

Using No.10 needles and C, cast on 105[111:117] sts.
1st row K1, *P1, K1, rep from * to end.
2nd row P1, *K1, P1, rep from * to end.
Rep these 2 rows once more.
Break off C and join in B.
K 1 row, then rib 4 rows.
Break off C and join in A.
P 1 row, then rib 38 rows.
Change to No.9 needles.
Beg with a P row, continue in reversed st st until work measures 13in from beg, ending with a K row.

Shape armholes
Cast off at beg of next and every row 5 sts twice, 3 sts twice and 2 sts 4 times.
Dec one st at each end of next and following 4[5:6] alt rows, ending with a K row.
Dec one st at each end of next and every following 4th row 5 times in all. 63[67:71] sts.
Continue without shaping until armholes measure 9[9½:10]in from beg, ending with a P row.

Shape neck
Next row K14[15:16], cast off 35[37:39] sts, K to end.
Complete this side first.
Next row P.
Cast off 3 sts at beg of

next and following 0[1:2] alt rows and 2 sts at beg of following 3[2:1] alt rows.
Cast off rem 5 sts.
RS facing, rejoin yarn to rem sts and complete as first side, reversing shaping.

Front

Work as given for Back until armhole shaping is completed.
Continue straight until armholes measure 4½[5:5½]in from beg, ending with a P row.

Shape neck
Next row K26[27:28], cast off 11[13:15] sts, K to end.
Complete this side first.
Next row P.
Cast off at beg of next and every alt row 5 sts once, 3 sts once and 2 sts twice, ending with a K row.
Dec one st at beg of next and following 8[9:10] alt rows.
Continue on rem 5 sts until armhole measures same as Back to shoulder, ending with a K row. Cast off.
RS facing, rejoin yarn to rem sts and complete as first side, reversing shaping.

Neckband

Join shoulder seams.
Using No.10 Twin-Pin and B, with RS facing, K up 93[97:101] sts round front neck and 47[51:55] sts round back neck. 140[148:156] sts.
Work 4 rounds K1, P1 rib.
Break off B and join in C.
K 1 round, then rib 3 rounds.
Cast off in rib.

Armbands

Using No.10 needles and B, with RS facing, K up 143 [151:159] sts round armhole.
Beg with a 2nd row work 4 rows rib as given for Back.
Break off B and join in C.
P 1 row, then rib 3 rows.
Cast off in rib.

To make up

Press each piece under a damp cloth with a warm iron. Join side seams. Press seams.

Stripes and spots

Guaranteed to make you feel cheerful, this zingy sweater is striped and spotted for a bright effect.

Sizes

To fit 32[34:36] in bust
Length to shoulder, 22½[23:23½]in
Sleeve seam, 18in, adjustable
The figures in brackets [ ] refer to the 34 and 36in bust sizes respectively

> **Tension for this design**
> 7 sts and 9 rows to 1in over st st worked on No. 10 needles

Materials shown here

Hayfield Fourmost 4 ply
9[10:11] balls main shade, A, white
3[4:4] balls each contrast colour, B and C, red and navy
One pair No. 10 needles
One pair No. 12 needles

Back

Using No. 12 needles and A, cast on 122[130:138] sts.
Beg with a K row, work 7 rows st st.
Next row K all sts tbl to form hemline.
Change to No. 10 needles.
Beg with a K row, work 6 rows st st.
Continue in st st and work (4 rows C, 4 rows B, 4 rows A) 3 times then 4 rows C, 4 rows B, *at the same time* dec one st at each end of next and every following 6th row until 106[114:122] sts rem, ending with a P row.

Commence spot patt

Next row K2 A, *K2 C, K2 A, rep from * to end.
Using A and beg with a P row, work 2 rows st st.
Next row P2 B, *P2 A, P2 B, rep from * to end.
Using A and beg with a K row, work 4 rows st st, dec one st at each end of first of these 4 rows.
Next row K1 A, *K2 C, K2 A, rep from * to last 3 sts, K2 C, K1 A.
Using A and beg with a P row, work 2 rows st st, dec one st at each end of 2nd of these 2 rows. 102[110:118] sts.
Next row P2 A, *P2 B, P2 A, rep from * to end.
Using A and beg with a K row, work 4 rows st st.
Keeping spot patt correct, continue without shaping until work measures 7½in from hemline, ending with a P row.
Continue in spot patt, inc one st at each end of next and every following 8th row until there are 118[126:134] sts.
Continue without shaping until work measures 16in from hemline, ending with a P row.

Shape armholes

Keeping patt correct, cast off at beg of next and every row 3 sts 4 times and 2 sts 4 times.
Dec one st at each end of next and following 5[6:7] alt rows. 86[92:98] sts.
Continue without shaping until armholes measure 6½[7:7½]in from beg, ending with a P row.

Shape neck and shoulders

Next row Patt 28[30:32] sts, turn and leave rem sts on holder.
Next row Cast off 3 sts, patt to end.
Next row Cast off 5[5:6] sts, patt to end.
Rep last 2 rows twice more.
Work one row. Cast off rem 4[6:5] sts.

With RS facing, leave first 30[32:34] sts on holder for centre back neck, rejoin yarn to rem sts and patt to end.
Complete to match first side, reversing shaping.

Front

Work as given for Back until front measures 13in from hemline, ending with a P row. Mark centre of work with coloured thread.

Divide for neck

Next row Patt to centre of work, turn and leave rem sts on holder.
Complete this side first.
Continue in patt still inc at side edge on every 8th row until 8 inc in all have been worked, *at the same time* dec one st at neck edge on every alt row 5 times, then on every 4th row until work measures same as Back to underarm, ending with a P row.

Shape armhole

Still dec at front edge on every 4th row, cast off at armhole edge on next and every alt row 3 sts twice, 2 sts twice and one st 6[7:8] times.
Continue to dec at neck edge only on every 4th row until 19[21:23] sts rem.
Continue without shaping until armhole measures same as Back to shoulder, ending with a P row.

Shape shoulder

Cast off at beg of next and every alt row 5[5:6] sts 3 times and 4[6:5] sts once.
With RS facing, rejoin yarn to rem sts and patt to end.
Complete to match first side, reversing shaping.

Sleeves

Using No. 12 needles and A, cast on 53[56:59] sts.
Beg with a K row, work 7 rows st st.
Next row K all sts tbl to form hemline.
Change to No. 10 needles.
Beg with a K row, continue in st st, working (4 rows A, 4 rows C, 4 rows B)

throughout, *at the same time* inc one st at each end of every 10th row until there are 79[83:87] sts.
Continue without shaping until sleeve measures 18in from hemline, or required length to underarm, ending with a P row.

Shape top

Cast off 3 sts at beg of next 4 rows.
Dec one st at each end of. . next and every alt row until 29 sts rem, ending with a P row.
Cast off at beg of next and every row 2 sts 4 times, 3 sts 4 times and 9 sts once.

Neckband

Join right shoulder seam.
Using No. 12 needles, A and with RS facing, K up 70[73:76] sts down left front neck, K up loop between sts at centre front and K tbl, K up 70[73:76] sts up right front neck and 12 sts down right back neck, K across sts on holder for centre back neck then K up 12 sts up left back neck. 195[203:211] sts.
Next row P.
Next row K to 2 sts before centre front, K2 tog, K1, sl 1, K1, psso, K to end.
Rep last 2 rows once more, then still dec in this way on every alt row work 4 rows B, 4 rows C.
Continue using A only.
Next row P.
Next row K to centre front st, K up 1, K1, K up 1, K to end.
Rep last 2 rows 5 times more.
Cast off loosely.

To make up

Press each piece under a damp cloth with a warm iron.
Join left shoulder and neckband seam. Fold neckband in half to wrong side and slip stitch in place. Set in sleeves.
Join side and sleeve seams.
Turn up hem at lower edge and sleeves and slip stitch in place.
Press seams.

The luxury look

This dainty angora blouse has a luxurious and expensive feel to it. It looks good teamed with a silky shirt, but can also be worn on its own.

Sizes

To fit 32[34:36:38]in bust
Length to shoulder, 18¾[19: 19½:19¾]in
The figures in brackets [ ] refer to the 34, 36 and 38in sizes respectively

---

Tension for this design
7 sts and 9 rows to 1in over st st worked on No. 10 needles

Materials shown here

Patons Fuzzy Wuzzy
7[8:8:9] balls
One pair No. 10 needles
One pair No. 12 needles
7 buttons

Back

Using No. 12 needles, cast on 95[101:107:113] sts.
1st row K2, *P1, K1, rep from * to last st, K1.
2nd row *K1, P1, rep from * to last st, K1.
Rep 1st and 2nd rows 16 times more.
Change to No. 10 needles.
Continue in st st.
Beg with a K row, work 4 rows st st.

Shape sides

Inc one st at each end of next and every following 6th row until there are 115[121: 127:133] sts.
Continue without shaping until work measures 12[12: 12½:12½]in from beg, ending with a P row.

Shape armholes

Cast off 5[5:7:7] sts at beg of next 2 rows.
Dec one st at each end of every row until 95[97:99: 105] sts rem, then at each end of every alt row until 85[87:89:93] sts rem.
Continue without shaping until armholes measure 6¾[7: 7:7¼]in from beg, ending with a P row.

Shape shoulders and back neck

Next row Cast off 4[4:5:5] sts, K17[17:17:18] sts, cast off 43[45:45:47] sts, K to end.
Complete this side first.
1st row Cast off 4[4:5:5] sts, P to last 2 sts, P2 tog.
2nd row K2 tog, K to end.
3rd row Cast off 4 sts, P to last 2 sts, P2 tog.
Rep 2nd and 3rd rows once more.
Work 1 row. Cast off rem 4[4:4:5] sts.
With WS facing, rejoin yarn to rem sts.
1st row P2 tog, P to end.
2nd row Cast off 4 sts, K to last 2 sts, K2 tog.
Rep 1st and 2nd rows once more, then 1st row once.
Cast off rem 4[4:4:5] sts.

Left front

Using No. 12 needles, cast on 45[49:51:55] sts.
Work 34 rows rib as given for Back.
Change to No. 10 needles.
Beg with a K row, continue in st st, dec one st in centre of first row on 34in size only. 45[48:51:55] sts.
Work 4 rows.

Shape side

Inc one st at side edge on next and every following 6th row until there are 55[59:61: 65] sts.
Continue without shaping until work measures same as Back to underarm, ending at side edge.

Shape armhole

Cast off 5[5:7:7] sts at beg of next row.
Work 1 row.
Dec one st at armhole edge on every row until 45[46:47: 49] sts rem, then at each end of every alt row until 40[41: 42:44] sts rem.
Continue without shaping until armhole measures 2½[2¾:2¾:3]in from beg, ending at centre front edge.

Shape neck

Next row Cast off 6[7:7:8] sts, work to end.
Dec one st at neck edge on every row until 23[23:24:25] sts rem, then on every alt row until 16[16:17:18] sts rem.
Continue without shaping until armhole measures same as Back to shoulder, ending at armhole edge.

Shape shoulder

Cast off at beg of next and every alt row 4[4:5:5] sts once, 4 sts twice and 4[4:4: 5] sts once.

Right front

Work as given for Left front, reversing all shaping.

Sleeves

Using No. 12 needles, cast on 111[111:121:121] sts.
Work 5 rows g st.
Change to No. 10 needles.
Commence patt.
1st row K1, *yfwd, K3, sl 1, K2 tog, psso, K3, yfwd, K1, rep from * to end.
2nd row P.
3rd row P1, *K1, yfwd, K2, sl 1, K2 tog, psso, K2, yfwd, K1, P1, rep from * to end.
4th row K1, *P9, K1, rep from * to end.
5th row P1, *K2, yfwd, K1, sl 1, K2 tog, psso, K1, yfwd, K2, P1, rep from * to end.
6th row As 4th.
7th row P1, *K3, yfwd, sl 1, K2 tog, psso, yfwd, K3, P1, rep from * to end.
8th row P.
These 8 rows form patt.
Keeping patt correct, dec one st at each end of next 10 rows.

Cast off 5 sts at beg of next 14 rows.
Cast off rem 21[21:31:31] sts.

Neck border

Join shoulder seams.
Using No. 12 needles and with RS facing, K up 43[44: 44:45] sts along right front neck, 59[61:61:63] sts along back neck edge and 43[44: 44:45] sts down left front neck edge.
1st row *K1, P1, rep from * to last st, K1.
2nd row K2, *P1, K1, rep from * to last st, K1.
Rep 1st and 2nd rows 3 times more, then 1st row once. Cast off in rib.

Right front border

Using No. 12 needles, cast on 8 sts.
Next row K2, (K into front then into back of next st, K1) 3 times. 11 sts.
Beg with a 2nd row, work in rib as given for Neck border. Work 2 rows.
Next row (buttonhole row) Rib 4 sts, cast off 2 sts, rib to end.
Next row Rib to end, casting on 2 sts above those cast off in previous row.
Work 22 rows rib.
Make buttonhole as before on next 2 rows.
Make 5 more buttonholes with 22 rows between each.
Work 4 rows after last buttonhole has been completed.
Cast off firmly in rib.

Left front border

Work as given for Right front border, omitting buttonholes.

To make up

Press each piece lightly under a damp cloth with a warm iron.
Join side seams. Set in sleeves, gathering sleeves slightly on each side of shoulder seam, noting that the whole of the sleeve is sewn into armhole including first 8 rows.
Sew borders to fronts. Press seams. Sew on buttons.

Pink, white, blue – and pretty

You'll find this pretty bat-wing sweater with its big, full sleeves very easy to make – it only requires the simplest of shaping. The sweater was designed by Patricia Roberts, who chose the pastel sugared-almond shades of pink, blue and white. The fluffy angora wool she used is a perfect complement to the soft lines of the garment.

Sizes
To fit bust 32[34:36]in
Length from cuff to cuff, 53½[54½:55½]in
Length to shoulder, 18[18½:18¾]in
The figures in brackets [] refer to the 34 and 36in sizes respectively

Tension for this design
8 sts and 10 rows to 1 in over st st worked on No. 12 needles

Materials shown here
Patons Fuzzy-Wuzzy 15[16:17] ½oz balls main colour A, white
Patons Cameo Crepe 2 1oz balls colour B, blue
2 1oz balls colour C, pink
One pair No. 12 needles
One pair No. 13 needles

Right side

Using No. 13 needles and A, beg at sleeve edge and cast on 64[68:68] sts.
Work 24 rows straight in K2, P2 rib.
Continue in rib, inc one st at each end of next and every following 8th row, eight times in all. 80[84:84] sts.
Work 7 rows without shaping.
Next row Inc 1[K2:inc 1], *pick up the loop between the needles, slip it onto the left-hand needle and K tbl – called pick up 1 –, K1, rep from * ending last rep pick up 1, K1[3:1]. 160[164:168] sts.
Change to No. 12 needles
Work 3 rows st st, beg with a P row.
Continue in st st, working patt as follows and joining in and breaking off contrast colours as required.
1st row K2[4:2] sts C, *4 sts A, 4 sts C, rep from * ending last rep 2[4:2] sts C.
2nd row P2[4:2] sts C, *4 sts A, 4 sts C, rep from * ending last rep 2[4:2] sts C.
3rd row As 1st.
4th row P2[4:2] sts A, *4 sts C, 4 sts A, rep from * ending last rep 2[4:2] sts A.
5th row K2[4:2] sts A, *4 sts C, 4 sts A, rep from * ending last rep 2[4:2] sts A.
6th row As 4th.

7th–9th rows As 1st–3rd.
10th and 11th rows Work in A only.
12th and 13th rows Work in C only.
14th and 15th rows Work in A only.
16th row P4[6:4] sts A, *using B P1, turn, K twice into this st, turn, P these 2 sts tog tbl – called bobble 1 –, P7 sts A, rep from * ending last rep 3[5:3] sts A.
17th–19th rows Work in A only.
20th row P8[2:8] sts A, *using B bobble 1, P7 sts A, rep from * ending last rep 7[1:7] sts A.
21st–23rd rows Work in A only.
24th–27th rows As 16th–19th.
28th and 29th rows Work in B only.
30th–32nd rows Work in A only.
These 32 rows form patt. Rep them twice more then work first 10 rows once, marking each end of the last row with a coloured thread.
Continue in patt for a further 46[50:54] rows.**

Divide for neck
Next row Work across 74[78:82] sts. Place these sts on a holder, cast off 10 sts, work across rem 76 sts.
Continue on these sts.

Back
Continue in patt for 29 rows more. Cast off.

Front
Rejoin wool at inner edge of sts on holder.
Continuing in patt, dec one st at neck on each of next 72[76:80] rows. Fasten off rem 2 sts as if they were one.

Left side

Work as given for Right side, working only 45[49:54] rows at **.

Back ribbing

Join centre back seam.
Using No. 13 needles and A, with RS facing pick up and K114[120:128] sts between marker threads.

Work 88 rows K2, P2 rib.
Cast off loosely in rib.

Front ribbing

Using No. 13 needles and A, with RS facing pick up and K112[120:128] sts from right front after marker thread.
Work 88 rows K2, P2 rib.
Cast off loosely in rib.

Neck edging

Using No. 13 needles and B, cast on 6 sts.
1st row Inc 1, K3, dec 1.
2nd row P.
Rep these 2 rows until edging measures same as neck.
Sew in place, casting off only when correct length is obtained.

Collar

Using No. 12 needles and A, cast on 122 sts.
Work 8 rows K2, P2 rib, beg RS rows with K2 and WS rows with P2.
Continue in rib and keeping edges correct, inc one st at each end of next and following 10th rows 4 times in all. 130 sts.
Continue without shaping for 9 rows more. Cast off loosely in rib.

Edging

Using No. 13 needles and B, with RS facing pick up and K40 sts from straight edge of collar, 130 sts from cast-off edge and 40 sts from other straight edge. 210 sts.
1st row Inc purlwise in every st. 420 sts.
Next row K.
Using No. 12 needle, cast off knitwise.

To make up

Press all st st pieces on WS under a damp cloth with a warm iron.
Slip stitch lower edge of left front in position behind right front.
Press seams.
Join sleeve and side seams.
Sew cast-on edge of collar in place on WS at base of edging so that it rolls over the edging to RS.

The inside-out coat

This lightweight, hooded coat in two-colour stripes uses the reverse side of the fabric for an unusual effect. Team it with trousers or work additional button-holes and wear it as a button-through coat-dress.

Sizes

To fit 34[36:38]in bust
  36[38:40]in hips
Length to shoulder,
40[40½:41]in
Sleeve seam, 17in
The figures in brackets [] refer to the 36 and 38in bust sizes respectively

---

Tension for this design
7 sts and 9 rows to 1in over reversed st st worked on No. 10 needles

---

Materials shown here

Patons Cameo Crepe
8[9:10] 50 grm balls main shade, A, pink
6[7:8] 50 grm balls contrast colour B, white
One pair No. 10 needles
One pair No. 12 needles
6 buttons

Back

Using No. 10 needles and A, cast on 150[156:162] sts.
Commence striped patt using separate balls of A and B where necessary.
Using A and beg with a P row, work 6 rows reversed st st, then work (1 row B, 1 row A) twice, then 6 rows B. These 16 rows form patt and are rep throughout.
Continue in patt until work measures 6in from beg, ending with a K row.

Shape sides

Dec one st at each end of next and every following 8th row until 120[126:132] sts rem, then at each end of every following 6th row until 110[116:122] sts rem.
Continue without shaping until work measures 24½in from beg, ending with a K row.
Inc one st at each end of next and every following 6th row until there are 126[132:138] sts.
Continue without shaping until work measures 34in from beg or required length to underarm, allowing 1in for hem and ending with a K row.

Shape armholes

Cast off at beg of next and every row 4 sts twice and 2 sts 4 times.
Dec one st at each end of next and following 3[4:5] alt rows. 102[106:110] sts.
Continue without shaping until armholes measure 7[7½:8]in from beg, ending with a K row.

Shape shoulders

Cast off at beg of next and every row 8 sts 6 times and 8[9:10] sts twice.
Cast off rem 38[40:42] sts.

Right front

Using No. 10 needles and A, cast on 75[79:83] sts.
Work in patt as given for Back until work measures 6in from beg, ending with a K row.

Shape side

Dec one st at end of next and every following 8th row until 60[64:68] sts rem, then at end of every following 6th row until 55[59:63] sts rem.
Continue without shaping until work measures 24½in from beg, ending with a K row.
Inc one st at end of next and every following 6th row until there are 63[67:71] sts.
Continue without shaping until work measures same as Back to underarm, ending with a P row.

Shape armhole

Cast off at beg of next and every alt row 4 sts once and 2 sts twice.
Dec one st at armhole edge on next and following 3[4:5] alt rows. 51[54:57] sts.
Continue without shaping until armhole measures 5¾[6¼:6¾]in from beg, ending with a K row.

Shape neck

Cast off at beg of next and every alt row 10[12:14] sts once and 3 sts 3 times. 32[33:34] sts.
Continue without shaping until armhole measures same as Back to shoulder, ending with a P row.

Shape shoulder

Cast off at beg of next and every alt row 8 sts 3 times and 8[9:10] sts once.

Left front

Work as given for Right front, reversing all shaping.

Sleeves

Using No. 10 needles and A, cast on 58[61:64] sts.
Work in patt as given for Back for 2½in.
Continue in patt, inc one st at each end of next and every following 8th row until there are 88[91:94] sts.
Continue without shaping until sleeve measures 18in from beg or required length to underarm, allowing 1in for hem and ending with a K row and same patt as for Back.

Shape top

Cast off at beg of next and every row 4 sts twice and 2 sts 4 times.
Dec one st at each end of next and following 9[10:11] alt rows. 52[53:54] sts.
Cast off at beg of next and every row 2 sts 8 times, 3 sts 4 times and 4 sts twice.
Cast off rem 16[17:18] sts.

Hood

Using No. 10 needles and A, cast on 136 sts.
Work in patt as given for Back for 13in, ending with a K row.
Cast off loosely or leave sts to graft tog.

Border

Mark positions for 6 buttonholes on Right front edge, first to come just below neck edge with 5 more at intervals of 6in.
Join shoulder seams. Fold Hood in half and join top edge, then sew cast on edge to neck edge.
Using No. 12 needles and A, cast on 21 sts.
1st row K1, *yfwd, sl 1P, ybk, K1, rep from * to end.
2nd row Yfwd, sl 1P, *ybk, K1, yfwd, sl 1P, rep from * to end.
Rep these 2 rows until border comes level with first buttonhole position, allowing 1in for hem, ending with a 2nd row.
Next row (buttonhole row) Patt 7 sts, cast off 7 sts, patt to end.
Next row Patt 7 sts, cast on 7 sts, patt to end.
Continue in patt, making 5 more buttonholes as markers are reached, until border fits round front edges, ending with a 1st row.
Cast off K2 tog all along the row.

To make up

Press each piece under a damp cloth with a warm iron. Set in sleeves. Join side and sleeve seams.
Turn up 1in hem at lower edge and sleeve edges and slip stitch in place.
Sew on border. Press all seams. Sew on buttons.

Stripy twosome

These gaily-striped outfits with bibbed tops make a charming, matching set for brother and sister. An interesting feature is the practical top pocket with button-down flap.

Sizes
To fit 24[26]in chest
Skirt. Length from shoulder, 24[26]in
Trousers. Inside leg, 19[20½]in
Outside leg from waist, 27[29]in

Tension for this design
5½ sts and 7½ rows to 1in over st st worked on No. 8 needles

Materials shown here
Patons Trident Double Knitting
Skirt. 2[3] 50grm balls main shade, A, blue
1[1] ball each in contrast colours B, C and D, green, navy and white
Trousers. 3[4] balls main shade, A
1[1] ball each in contrast colours B, C and D
One pair No. 8 needles
One No. 3·50 (ISR) crochet hook
3 buttons

Skirt back

Using No. 8 needles and A, cast on 87[93] sts.
Work in g st as follows:
(6 rows A, 2 rows D, 6 rows C, 2 rows D, 6 rows B, 2 rows D) twice, *at the same time* dec one st at each end of 17th[25th] row and every following 8th row. 48 rows.
Using A, continue in st st, beg with a K row, dec one st at each end of next and every following 8th row until 65[71] sts rem.
Continue without shaping until 56[64] rows st st have been completed, ending with a P row.
Continue in g st, working 2 rows D, 6 rows A, 2 rows D, 6 rows C, 2 rows D, 6 rows B, 2 rows D, 5 rows A**.
Cast off in A.

Skirt front

Work as given for Skirt Back to **
Next row Using A, K.
Continue in g st, working 2 rows D, 6 rows C, 2 rows D, 6 rows B, 2 rows D, 6 rows A, 2 rows D, 6 rows C, 2 rows D, 6 rows B, 2 rows D, *at the same time* dec one st at each end of every alt row 8[14] times in all, then at each end of every 3rd row 9[5] times. 31[33] sts.
***Continue in A.
Next row (P1, K1) 3 times, P1, K17[19], P1, (K1, P1) 3 times.
Next row (P1, K1) 3 times, P19[21], (K1, P1) 3 times.
Rep last 2 rows 10[12] times more.
Next row Moss st (P1, K1 beg every row P1) over 7 sts, cast off 17[19] sts, moss st to end.
Continue on these last 7 sts in moss st for 16½[17½]in, or length required, ending with a WS row.
Next row (buttonhole) Moss st 2 sts, cast off 3 sts, moss st to end.
Next row Moss st 2 sts, cast

on 3 sts over those cast off on previous row, moss st to end.
Work 3 rows in moss st.
Cast off in moss st.
Rejoin yarn to rem 7 sts and complete to correspond with first side.

Pocket lining and flap

Using No. 8 needles and A, cast on 17[19] sts.
Beg with a K row, work in st st for 21[25] rows.
Next row K to mark turning line.
Beg with a K row, continue in st st.
Work 2 rows without shaping.
Cast off 2 sts at beg of each of next 2 rows.
Next row (buttonhole) Cast off 2 sts, K3[4], cast off 3 sts, K to end.
Next row Cast off 2 sts, P3[4], cast on 3 sts over those cast off on previous row, P to end.
Cast off 2 sts at beg of each of next 2 rows.
Cast off rem 5[7] sts.

Trousers back

Right leg
Using No. 8 needles and A, cast on 40[43] sts.
Work in g st as follows:
6 rows A, 2 rows D, 6 rows C, 2 rows D, 6 rows B, 2 rows D.
Using A, continue in st st, beg with a K row.
Dec one st at each end of 15th[19th] row and every following 28th[30th] row until 32[35] sts rem.
Work 14[16] rows without shaping, ending with a K row.
Cast on 2 sts at beg of next row.
Inc one st at same edge on following 6 alt rows, ending with a K row. 40[43] sts.
Cast off 2 sts at beg of next and following 2 alt rows.
Dec one st at same edge on following 2 alt rows, ending with a K row. 32[35] sts.
Break off yarn and leave sts on holder.

Second leg
Work as given for First Leg,

reversing shapings and ending with a K row.
Next row P31[34], P next st tog with first st of First Leg, P to end. 63[69] sts.
Continue in st st for 33[37] rows more, ending with a K row**.
Shape back. P53[57], turn.
Next row K43[45], turn.
Next row P33[33], turn.
Next row K23[21], turn.
Next row P across all sts.
Continue in g st, working 2 rows D, 6 rows A, 2 rows D, 6 rows C, 2 rows D, 6 rows B, 2 rows D, 1 row A.
Using A, cast off.

Trousers front

Work as for Trousers Back to **.
P 1 row.
Continue in g st, working (2 rows D, 6 rows A, 2 rows D, 6 rows C, 2 rows D, 6 rows B) twice, 2 rows D, *at the same time* cast off at beg of 27th and every following row 3 sts 2[4] times, 2 sts 4[6] times, and one st 18[12] times. 31[33] sts.
Continue as for Skirt Front from *** to end.

Pocket lining and flap

Work as given for Skirt pocket lining and flap.

To make up

Press work lightly under a damp cloth, using a warm iron.
Skirt. Join side seams.
Using No. 3·50 hook and A, work row of dc round pocket flap.
With WS facing, sew pocket lining inside bib top so that the flap folds over to the outside.
If required, a row of dc can be worked round shoulder straps and back edges.
Sew 2 buttons to back waist and 3rd button to front of pocket to correspond with buttonholes.
Press all seams.
Trousers. Join leg seams.
Join side seams.
Complete as given for Skirt.

Classic crew neck

A heavily textured pattern gives a rugged masculine look to this classic sweater for a man.

Sizes
To fit 38[40:42]in chest
Length to shoulder, 26[27: 28]in, adjustable
Sleeve seam, 17½[18:18½]in, adjustable
The figures in brackets [ ] refer to the 40 and 42in sizes respectively

Materials shown here
Patons Fiona
30[32:34] balls
One pair No. 6 needles
One pair No. 8 needles
Set of 4 No. 8 needles pointed at both ends
NB Yarn is used double throughout

Back

Using No. 8 needles and 2 strands of yarn, cast on 90[90:98] sts.
1st row K2, *P2, K2, rep from * to end.
2nd row P2, *K2, P2, rep from * to end.
Rep these 2 rows for 2in, ending with a 2nd row.
Change to No. 6 needles.
Commence patt.
1st row K2, *P6, K2, rep from * to end.

2nd row P2, *K6, P2, rep from * to end.
3rd row As 2nd.
4th row As 1st.
5th row As 1st.
6th row As 2nd.
7th row K.
8th row P.
9th row P4, *K2, P6, rep from * to last 6 sts, K2, P4.
10th row K4, *P2, K6, rep from * to last 6 sts, P2, K4.
11th row As 10th.
12th and 13th rows As 9th.
14th row As 10th.
15th row K.
16th row P.
These 16 rows form patt. Continue in patt until work measures 18[18½:19]in from beg, or required length to underarm ending with a WS row.

Shape armholes
Keeping patt correct, cast off 4[2:4] sts at beg of next 2 rows. 82[86:90] sts.
**Cast off 2 sts at beg of next 4 rows.
K2 tog at each end of next and every alt row until 66[68:70] sts rem.**
Continue without shaping until armholes measure 8[8½: 9]in from beg, ending with a WS row.

Shape neck and shoulders
Next row Patt 26[27:27], turn and leave rem sts on holder.
Next row Cast off 3 sts, patt to end.
Next row Cast off 4 sts, patt to end.
Rep last 2 rows twice more.

Work 1 row. Cast off rem 5[6:6] sts.
With RS facing, slip first 14[14:16] sts on holder and leave for back neck, rejoin yarn to rem sts and patt to end.
Complete to match first side, reversing shaping.

Front

Using No. 8 needles and 2 strands of yarn, cast on 90[98:98] sts.
Work as given for Back until work measures same as Back to underarm, ending with a WS row.

With RS facing, slip first 8[8:10] sts on holder and leave for centre neck, rejoin yarn to rem sts and patt to end.
Complete to match first side, reversing shaping.

Sleeves

Using No. 8 needles and 2 strands of yarn, cast on 42[42:50] sts.
Work in rib as given for Back for 2in, ending with a 2nd row.
Change to No. 6 needles.
Continue in patt as given for Back inc one st at each end of 9th [1st:9th] and every following 10th row until there are 62[66:70] sts.
Continue without shaping until sleeve measures 17½[18:18½]in from beg, or required length to underarm ending with a WS row.

Shape top
Cast off 4 sts at beg of next 2 rows.
Dec one st at each end of next and every alt row until 26 sts rem.
Cast off at beg of next and every row 2 sts 6 times and 3 sts twice.
Cast off rem 8 sts.

Neckband

Join shoulder seams.
Using set of 4 No. 8 needles, 2 strands of yarn and with RS facing, K up 13 sts down side of back neck, K across back neck sts, K up 13 sts up other side of back neck and 24 sts down side of front neck, K across front neck sts, then K up 24 sts up other side of front neck. 96[96:100] sts.
Continue in rounds of K2, P2 rib for 3in.
Cast off loosely in rib.

To make up

Sew in sleeves.
Join side and sleeve seams.
Fold neckband in half to WS and slip stitch in place.
Press seams very lightly under a damp cloth with a cool iron, taking care not to flatten patt.

Shape armholes
Cast off 4[6:4] sts at beg of next 2 rows. 82[86:90] sts.
Work as given for Back from ** to **.
Continue without shaping until armholes measure 6[6½:7]in from beg, ending with a WS row.

Shape neck
Next row Patt 29[30:30], turn and leave rem sts on holder.
Cast off at beg of next and every alt row 3 sts twice and 2 sts twice.
K2 tog at neck edge on next and following alt row.

Continue without shaping until armhole measures same as Back to shoulder, ending with a WS row.

Shape shoulder
Cast off at beg of next and every alt row 4 sts 3 times and 5[6:6] sts once.

Family of sweaters

Here is a collection of sturdy sweaters for the whole family, worked in two widths of ribbing. Neat saddle top shoulders and polo collars guarantee comfort and warmth.

Sizes

Children. 24[27:30] in chest
Length to shoulder, 13[15:17]in adjustable
Sleeve seam, 11[12½:14]in adjustable
Adult. 34[36:38:40]in bust/chest
Length to shoulder, 27[28:29:30]in adjustable
Sleeve seam, 17[17½:18:18½]in adjustable
The figures in brackets [ ] refer to the 27, 30, 34, 36, 38 and 40in bust/chest sizes respectively

---

Tension for this design
5 sts and 7 rows to 1in over rib slightly stretched, worked on No. 8 needles

---

Materials shown here
Mahony Killowen Double Knitting
6[7:8:10:11:11:12] 50 grm balls
One pair No. 8 needles

Back

Using No. 8 needles, cast on 66[74:82:93:99:105:111] sts.

24, 27 and 30in sizes only
1st row K2, *P2, K2, rep from * to end.
2nd row P2, *K2, P2, rep from * to end.
These 2 rows form patt and are rep throughout.

34, 36, 38 and 40in sizes only
1st row K3, *P3, K3, rep from * to end.
2nd row P3, *K3, P3, rep from * to end.
These 2 rows form patt and are rep throughout.

All sizes
Continue in patt until work measures 8[9¼:10½:19:19½:20:20½]in from beg, ending with a 2nd row.

Shape armholes
Cast off 4[5:6:6:6:6:6] sts at beg of next 2 rows.
**Next row P1[1:1:2:2:2:2], K2 tog, patt to last 3[3:3:4:4:4:4] sts, sl 1, K1, psso, P1[1:1:2:2:2:2].
Next row K1[1:1:2:2:2:2], P1, patt to last 2[2:2:3:3:3:3] sts, P1, K1[1:1:2:2:2:2].**
Keeping edge sts as set on all sizes, continue dec in this way on every 6th row until 46[50:54:65:69:75:79] sts rem, then work 3[3:3:3:1:5:3] rows without shaping after last dec row.

Shape shoulders
Cast off at beg of next and every row 4[4:4:4:4:4:5] sts 4 times and 4[5:6:4:5:5:5] sts 2[2:2:4:4:4:4] times.
Leave rem 22[24:26:33:33:39:39] sts on holder for centre back neck.

Front

Work as given for Back.

Sleeves

Using No. 8 needles, cast on 30[34:38:39:43:47:51] sts.

24, 27 and 30in sizes only
1st row P2, *K2, P2, rep from * to end.
2nd row K2, *P2, K2, rep from * to end.
These 2 rows form sleeve patt.

34, 36, 38 and 40in sizes only
1st row P3[2:1:0], *K3, P3, rep from * to last 6[5:4:3] sts, K3, P3[2:1:0].
2nd row K3[2:1:0], *P3, K3, rep from * to last 6[5:4:3] sts, P3, K3[2:1:0].
These 2 rows form sleeve patt.

All sizes
Continue in patt as now set for all sizes, inc one st at each end of 13th and every following 6th[6th:8th:8th:8th:8th:8th] row until there are 50[54:58:63:67:71:75] sts.
Continue without shaping until sleeve measures 12[13½:15:18:18½:19:19½]in from beg, or required length to underarm plus one inch ending with a WS row.

Shape top
Work from ** to ** as given for Back until 28[26:24:21:21:21:21] sts rem, ending with a WS row.
Cast off 2 sts at beg of next 8[6:4:2:2:2:2] rows. 12[14:16:17:17:17:17] sts.
Continue in rib on rem sts for length of shoulder, ending with a WS row.
Leave sts on holder.

Neckband

Note that when RS is facing, centre 2[2:2:3:3:3:3] sts of each sleeve should be K[P:K:P:K:P:K] and centre 2[2:2:3:3:3:3] sts of back and front neck should be K[K:K:P:K:P:K] to ensure that rib for each size is kept correct on neckband.
Using No. 8 needles and with RS facing, beg with left sleeve top and work in rib as set for all sizes across all sts on holder, working 2 sts tog at each seam and inc one st at end of back neck sts. 66[74:82:98:98:110:110] sts.
Continue in rib as set for each size for 4[5:6:8:8:8:8]in.
Cast off loosely in rib.

To make up

Sew saddle top of sleeves to shoulder and join neckband seam.
Sew sleeve seam leaving one inch open before top shaping. Sew side seams. Set in sleeves, positioning open part of seam against cast off stitches of armhole. Press seams very lightly under a damp cloth with a warm iron to finish off.

Matched set

Matched-up cardigans in a simple 'window pane' stitch – one buttoned to the neck, one with a V neckline.

Sizes

To fit 34/36 [40/42]in bust/chest
Length to shoulder, 24 [23]in
Sleeve seam, 17½ [18½]in
The figures in brackets [] refer to the 40/42in size only

Tension for this design
6 sts and 8 rows to 1in over st st worked on No. 9 needles

Materials shown here

Ladyship County Double Knitting
20 [22] balls
One pair No. 9 needles
One pair No. 11 needles
One No. 11 circular Twin-Pin
3[5] buttons

Back

Using No. 11 needles, cast on 113 [129] sts.
1st row K1, *P1, K1, rep from * to end.
2nd Row P1, *K1, P1, rep from * to end.
Rep these 2 rows 4 [7] times more.
Change to No. 9 needles. Commence patt.
1st–7th rows K.
8th row (WS) P7 [0], *K3, P13 [18], rep from * 5 times more, K3, P7 [0].
9th row K.
Rep 8th and 9th rows 6 [9] times more, then 8th row once. These 22 [28] rows form patt.
Continue in patt until work measures 17 [15]in from beg, ending with a WS row.

Shape armholes

Keeping patt correct, cast off at beg of next and every row 4 sts twice and 2 sts 4 [6] times.
K2 tog at each end of next and following 3 [5] alt rows. 89 [97] sts.
Continue without shaping until armholes measure 7 [8] in from beg, ending with a WS row.

Shape shoulders

Cast off at beg of next and every row 5 [6] sts 6 times and 6 sts 4 times.
Leave rem 35 [37] sts on holder for back neck.

Left front

Using No. 11 needles, cast on 56 [64] sts.
1st row *K1, P1, rep from * to end.
Rep this row 9[15] times more.
Change to No. 9 needles. Commence patt.
1st–7th rows K.
8th row (WS) K1, *P13 [18], K3, rep from * twice more, P7 [0].
9th row K.
Rep 8th and 9th rows 6 [9] times more, then 8th row once.

Woman's cardigan only

Continue in patt until work measures 13in from beg, ending with a WS row.

Shape front

Next row Patt to last 3 sts, K2 tog, K1.
Work 3 rows without shaping.
Continue to dec in this way on next and every following 4th row until work measures same as Back to underarm, ending with a WS row.

Shape armhole

Continue to dec at front edge as before on every 4th row, *at the same time* cast off 4 sts at beg of next row and 2 sts at beg of following 2 alt rows.
Dec one st at armhole edge on following 4 alt rows.
Continue to dec at front edge only until 27 sts rem.
Continue without shaping until armhole measures same as Back to shoulder, ending with a WS row.

Shape shoulder

Cast off at beg of next and

every alt row 5 sts 3 times and 6 sts twice.

Man's cardigan only

Continue in patt until work measures same as Back to underarm, ending with a WS row.

Shape armhole

Cast off at beg of next and every alt row 4 sts once and 2 sts 3 times.
Dec one st at armhole edge on following 6 alt rows.
Continue without shaping until armhole measures 5in from beg, ending with a RS row.

Shape neck

Cast off at beg of next and every alt row 3 sts twice and 2 sts twice.
K2 tog at neck edge on next and following 7 alt rows.
Continue without shaping until armhole measures same as Back to shoulder, ending with a WS row.

Shape shoulder

Cast off at beg of next and every row 6 sts 4 times.

Right front

Using No. 11 needles, cast on 56 [64] sts.
1st row *P1, K1, rep from * to end.
Rep this row 9 [15] times more.
Change to No. 9 needles. Commence patt.
1st–7th rows K.
8th row (WS) P7 [0], *K3, P13 [18], rep from * twice more, K1.
9th row K.
Rep 8th and 9th rows 6 [9] times more, then 8th row once.
Complete to match left front, reversing shaping.

Sleeves

Using No. 11 needles, cast on 47 [55] sts.
Work 10 [16] rows rib as given for Back, inc 6 [1] sts evenly across last row. 53 [56] sts.
Change to No. 9 needles. Commence patt.

Woman's cardigan only

Next row K.
Next row P9, (K3, P13) twice, K3, P9.
Rep these 2 rows once more.

Both versions

K7 rows.
Next row P9 [16], *K3, P13 [18], rep from * 1[0] times more, K3, P9 [16].
Continue in patt as now set to match Back, inc one st at each end of every 10th [8th]

▲ *Detail of window pane patterning*

row until there are 75 [88] sts.
Continue without shaping until sleeve measures 17½ [18½]in from beg, ending with same patt row as for Back armhole.

Shape top

Cast off at beg of next and every row 4 sts twice and 2 [3] sts 6 [2] times.
(Cast off one st at beg of next 2 rows, then 2 sts at beg of next 2 rows) 7 times.
Cast off 2 sts at beg of next 4 [12] rows.
Cast off rem 5 [8] sts.

Woman's front band

Using No. 11 Twin-Pin and with RS facing, K up 100 sts along right front to beg of shaping, 75 sts to neck, K across back neck sts, K up 175 sts down left front edge. 385 sts.
Beg with 2nd row of rib as given for Back, work 3 rows rib.
Next row (buttonhole row)

▲ *Two cardigans, in a matching stitch for a similar look, with their own distinctive design features*

Rib 9, (cast off 3, rib 39) 3 times, rib to end.
Next row Rib to end, casting on 3 sts above those cast off in previous row. Rib 4 rows. Cast off in rib.

Man's front band

Using No. 11 Twin-Pin and

with RS facing, K up 152 sts along right front edge to neck, K up 115 sts round neck including back neck sts on holder, and K up 152 sts along left front edge. 419 sts. Mark corner st at each side of front neck with thread. Beg with a 2nd row of rib as given for Back, work 5 rows

rib, inc one st at each side of corner sts on first and every alt row.
Next row (buttonhole row) Rib to last 151 sts, (cast off 3, rib 31) 4 times, cast off 3, rib to end.
Next row Rib to end, casting on 3 sts above those cast off in previous row.

Rib 4 more rows, still inc at corners as before.
Cast off in rib.

To make up

Press each piece under a damp cloth with a warm iron. Join seams and press. Sew on buttons.

Two for sports

Colourful horizontal stripes for her, patterned vertical stripes for him. Both garments have saddle top shoulders and a close fit for a warm, sporting look.

Women's jumper

Sizes

To fit 34[36:38]in bust
Length to shoulder, 27[27½: 28]in, adjustable
Sleeve seam, 17[17½:18]in, adjustable
The figures in brackets [] refer to the 36 and 38in sizes respectively

---

Tension for this design
5½ sts and 7 rows to 1in over st st worked on No.8 needles

Materials shown here

Templeton's Double Scotch 14[15:16] balls main shade, A, purple
6[7:8] balls contrast colour, B, red
3[3:4] balls each of contrast colours, C and D, yellow and gold
One pair No.8 needles
One pair No.10 needles
Set of 4 No.10 needles pointed at both ends

Back

Using No.10 needles and A, cast on 99[105:111] sts.
1st row K1, *P1, K1, rep from * to end.
2nd row P1, *K1, P1, rep from * to end.

Rep these 2 rows for 2in, ending with a 2nd row.
Change to No.8 needles.
Continue in K1, P1 rib working the stripes as follows; 4 rows C, 4 rows D, 8 rows B and 6 rows A.
Rep these 22 rows until work measures 20in from beg, or required length to underarm, ending with a WS row.

Shape armholes

Keeping striped patt correct cast off 4 sts at beg of next 2 rows, then 2 sts at beg of next 2 rows.
K2 tog at each end of next and every alt row until 79[83:87] sts rem.
Continue without shaping until armholes measure 6[6½:7]in from beg, ending with a WS row.

Shape shoulders

Cast off at beg of next and every row 7 sts 2[4:6] times and 6 sts 6[4:2] times.
Leave rem 29[31:33] sts on holder for back neck.

Front

Work as given for Back until armholes measure 5[5½:6]in from beg, ending with a WS row.

Shape neck

Next row Rib 34[35:36] sts, turn and leave rem sts on holder.
Complete this side first.
Cast off at beg of next and every alt row 3 sts once and 2 sts 3 times, ending with a WS row.

Shape shoulder

Cast off 7 sts at beg of next and following 0[1:2] alt rows and 6 sts at beg of following 2[1:0] alt rows.
Work 1 row. Cast off rem 6 sts.
With RS facing, slip first 11[13:15] sts onto holder and leave for center neck, rejoin yarn to rem sts and rib to end.
Complete to match first side, reversing shaping.

Sleeves

Using No.10 needles and A, cast on 47[49:51] sts.
Work in rib as given for Back for 3in, ending with a WS row.
Change to No.8 needles.
Using A throughout, continue in rib, inc one st at each end of 7th and every following 6th row until there are 75[79:83] sts.
Continue without shaping until sleeve measures 17[17½: 18]in from beg, or required length to underarm, ending with a WS row.

Shape top

Cast off 4 sts at beg of next 2 rows.
K2 tog at each end of next and every alt row until 35[37:39] sts rem, ending with a WS row.
Cast off 2 sts at beg of next 10 rows. 15[17:19] sts.

Work saddle shoulder

Continue in rib on these sts for length of shoulder, ending with a WS row.
Leave sts on holder.

Neckband

Join saddle tops of Sleeves to back and front shoulders.
Using set of 4 No.10 needles and A, with WS facing rib across sts of back neck and left sleeve, K up 11 sts down side of front neck, rib across front neck sts, K up 11 sts up other side of neck and rib across sts of right sleeve. 92[100:108] sts.
Continue in rounds of K1, P1 rib for 1½in.
Cast off loosely in rib.

To make up

Sew in sleeves. Join side and sleeve seams. Fold neckband in half to WS and slip stitch down. Press seams very lightly under a damp cloth with a warm iron, taking care not to flatten the rib.

▼ *Close-up showing the colour combination used on the woman's jumper*

Man's Sweater

Sizes

To fit 38[40:42]in chest
Length to shoulder, 28½[29:
29½]in, adjustable
Sleeve seam, 18[18½:19]in,
adjustable
The figures in brackets []
refer to the 40 and 42in sizes
respectively

> **Tension for this design**
> 5½ sts and 7 rows to
> 1in over st st worked
> on No.8 needles

Materials shown here

Templeton's Double Scotch
24[26:27] balls
One pair No.8 needles
One pair No.10 needles
Set of 4 No.8 needles pointed
at both ends
Set of 4 No.10 needles
pointed at both ends

Back

Using No.10 needles, cast on
115[121:127] sts.
1st row K1, *P1, K1, rep
from * to end.
2nd row P1, *K1, P1, rep
from * to end.
Rep these 2 rows for 2½in,
ending with a 2nd row and
inc one st at end of last row.
116[122:128] sts.
Change to No.8 needles.
Commence patt.
1st row K3[6:9], *P2, K10,
rep from * to last 5[8:11]
sts, P2, K3[6:9].
2nd row P3[6:9], *K2, P10,
rep from * to last 5[8:11]
sts, K2, P3[6:9].
3rd row K3[6:9], *P2,
(insert needle behind first st
and K 2nd st then K first
st and sl both sts off needle
tog—called TW2L) 5 times,
P2, K10, rep from * to last
17[20:23] sts, P2, (TW2L)
5 times, P2, K3[6:9].
4th row As 2nd.
5th row K3[6:9], *P2, (K
2nd st in usual way then K
first st and sl both sts off
needle tog—called TW2R)
5 times, P2, K10, rep from *
to last 17[20:23] sts, P2,
(TW2L) 5 times, P2, K3[6:9].
Rep 2nd to 5th rows until
work measures 19in from
beg, or required length to
underarm, ending with a WS
row.

Shape armholes

Keeping patt correct, cast
off at beg of next and every
row 5 sts twice, 3 sts twice
and 2 sts twice.
K2 tog at each end of next
and every alt row until
92[96:100] sts rem.
Continue without shaping
until armholes measure
8[8½:9]in from beg,
ending with a WS row.

Shape shoulders

Cast off at beg of next and
every row 7[8:8] sts 6 times
and 8[6:7] sts twice.
Leave rem 34[36:38] sts on
holder for back neck.

Front

Work as given for Back until
armholes measure 6[6½:7]in
from beg, ending with a WS
row.

Shape neck

Next row Patt 39[40:41],
turn and leave rem sts on
holder.
Complete this side first.
Cast off 2 sts at beg of next
and following 2 alt rows,
then K2 tog at neck edge on
next and following 3 alt rows,
ending with a WS row.

Shape shoulder

Cast off at beg of next and
every alt row 7[8:8] sts 3
times and 8[6:7] sts once.
With RS facing, sl first
14[16:18] sts on holder and
leave for centre neck, rejoin
yarn to rem sts and patt to end.
Complete to match first side,
reversing shaping.

Sleeves

Using No.10 needles, cast on
49[51:53] sts.
Work in rib as given for
Back for 2½in, ending with a
2nd row.
Change to No.8 needles.
Beg with a K row, continue
in st st, inc one st at each
end of 7th and every
following 8th row until there
are 77[81:85] sts.
Continue without shaping
until sleeve measures
18[18½:19]in from beg, or
required length to underarm,
ending with a P row.

Shape top

Cast off 5 sts at beg of next
2 rows.
K2 tog at each end of next
and every alt row until 43
sts rem.
Cast off at beg of next and
every row 2 sts 6 times and
3 sts 4 times. 19 sts.

Work saddle shoulder

Continue in st st on these
sts for length of shoulder,
ending with a P row.
Leave sts on holder.

Neckband

Join saddle tops of sleeves
to shoulders.
Using set of 4 No.10 needles
and with RS facing, K across
sts of back neck and left
sleeve, K up 16 sts down
side of front neck, K across
front neck sts, K up 16 sts
up other side of neck and K
across sts of right sleeve.
118[122:126] sts.
Continue in rounds of K1,
P1 rib for 3in.
Change to set of 4 No.8
needles and continue in
rounds of rib for a further
3in. Cast off loosely in rib.

To make up

Press each piece under a
damp cloth with a warm
iron. Sew in sleeves. Join side
and sleeve seams. Press seams.

▼*Close-up of the patterning used on the body of the man's sweater*

CROCHET

To make this stunning
beach outfit see page 74

Crash Course Crochet

How to begin

The materials required are a crochet hook, yarn, a pair of scissors and a large eyed, blunt ended needle.

There are many sizes of hook available ranging from the fine steel hooks for cotton or fine yarns to the larger alloy ones for use with thicker wools. However, to practise it is perhaps easiest to work with a double knitting yarn and No. 4·00 (ISR) crochet hook.

Placing yarn on hook

Crochet works on the principle of one loop being pulled through another and all crochet stitches are simply varying permutations of this.

Start with a slip loop to place the yarn onto the hook. Hold the end of the yarn between the thumb and forefinger of the left hand. Using the right hand, form a loop and hold this in position with the left hand and making the long end of the yarn fall behind the loop.

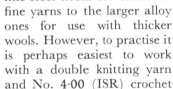

Hold the crochet hook in your right hand with the thumb and forefinger positioned on the flat bar. Insert the hook through the loop and behind the long end, catching it in the curve of the hook. Pull the hook out of the loop, thus

bringing the long end through to form another loop. Keep-

ing this loop on the hook, pull the short end downwards to tighten the loop round the curve of the hook.

Holding the work

The hook is held in the right hand in the same way as a pencil, gripping the flat bar between thumb and forefinger and resting the hook against the second finger.

It is with this finger that the hook is controlled and guided through the loops. The left hand holds the work and controls the yarn.

Pass the long end of the yarn round the little finger, across the palm, through between the second and ring fingers.

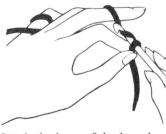

Catch the knot of the loop between thumb and forefinger.

Stitches
Chain. This forms the foundation of crochet work.

Pass the hook under the yarn which lies between the left hand and the hook, catching the yarn in the curve of the hook. This is called 'yarn round hook'. Draw the yarn through the loop already on the hook. This forms one chain stitch which can be repeated indefinitely.

To work a practice sampler, make twenty-two chain.

Turning chain. Because there are varying depths to crochet stitches and they are worked from the top down, at the beginning of a row the hook has to be taken up to the correct level. This is done with chain which then lie up the side of the next stitch and these are called 'turning chain'. The number depends on the stitch to follow.

These chain count as the first stitch of the row and the last one is worked into at the end of the next row.

Treble. For treble three turning chain are required.

Pass the yarn round the hook and insert hook into fourth chain from the hook, yarn round hook and draw loop through (three loops on hook), yarn round hook and draw through two loops (two loops on hook), yarn round hook and draw through two loops (one loop on hook).

On the sampler, working first treble into fourth chain from hook, work one treble into each chain. 20 stitches.

continued on page 60

Working into spaces. When following a pattern it is often necessary to work into a space made on the previous row rather than into a stitch.

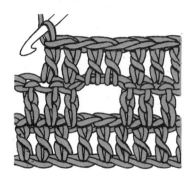

In such cases the hook is inserted into the actual space and not the chain running over the top of it.

On the practice sampler, turn, make three chain and work one treble into each of the next eight treble, make two chain, miss two treble, work one treble into the next treble to the end, finishing with one treble into the third of the three turning chain. Turn, make three chain, work one treble into each of next eight chain, two treble into two-chain space, one treble into each treble to end working last treble into third of three turning chain.

Slip stitch. This stitch is most often used for joining the end of a round to the beginning, fastening in or repositioning the yarn without adding to the dimension of the work. It can also be used to give a firm edge and is the flattest stitch of all.

Insert the hook into the next stitch, yarn round hook and draw loop through the stitch and the loop already on the hook.

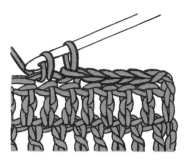

On the practice sampler, turn and work a row of slip stitches across the top of the trebles. Slip stitch requires no turning chain.

Fastening off. Cut the yarn about six inches from the work. Thread the end through the one remaining loop and pull tight. The end can later be darned in.

How to work a Granny square

Although there are several other stitches which will follow, with the information already given here it is possible to work a Granny square. Make 5 chain and join with a slip stitch to form a ring.

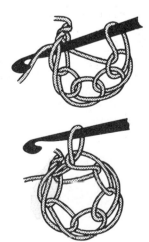

1st round Make 3 chain which will count as the first treble, work 2 treble into the ring, *2 chain, work 3 treble

into the ring, repeat from * twice more, 2 chain, join with a slip stitch into the third of the three chain.

2nd round 2 chain, * work 3 treble, 2 chain and another 3 treble all into the next 2-chain space, one chain, repeat from * 3 times more omitting one chain at the end of the last repeat, join with a slip stitch into the first of the first 2 chain.

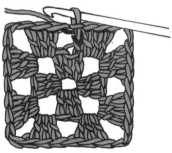

3rd round Work 3 chain to count as first treble, into the chain space immediately to the left of the hook work 2 trebles, *one chain, work 3 treble, 2 chain and 3 treble into the corner 2-chain space, one chain, work 3 treble into next one-chain space, repeat from * twice more, one chain, work 3 treble, 2 chain and 3 treble all into the corner 2-chain space, one chain, join with a slip stitch into the third of 3 chain.

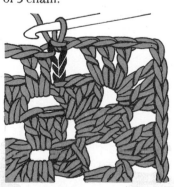

4th round 2 chain, * work 3 treble into next one-chain space, one chain, work 3 treble, 2 chain and 3 treble all into corner, one chain, work 3 treble into next one-chain space, one chain, repeat from

* 3 times more omitting the one chain at the end of the last repeat, join with a slip stitch into the first of first 2 chain.

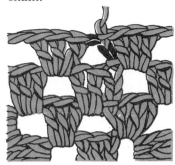

Joining the squares
The squares can be joined either by back stitching together, right sides facing, or by

crocheting. Place two squares right sides together and work a slip stitch through the double thickness, working into the top of the trebles on the last round.

Tension
This refers to the number of stitches and rows to the square inch. If the tension is not correct as given in the instructions, the garment will probably not fit. If by using the number of hook suggested, the tension does not work out accurately, adjust the size of hook as required.

Metrication
Until all patterns and yarn stocks are metric, you may be confused by the weights given. Remember that one ounce is equal to 28.350 grams. Therefore to convert a number of one ounce balls to gram balls, multiply 28.350 by the number of ounces and divide by either 25 or 50 depending on how the brand is balled. For example, 10 ounces equals ten 25g balls or five 50g balls.

Abbreviations

alt = alternate
beg = beginning
ch = chain
gr = group
in = inch
ISR = International Standard range
oz = ounce
patt = pattern
rep = repeat
RS = right side
ss = slip stitch
sp = space
st(s) = stitch(es)
tr = treble
WS = wrong side
yrh = yarn round hook

Stitches

Double crochet. Two turning chain are required.

Insert the hook into the next stitch to the left of the hook, yarn round hook and draw loop through (two loops on hook), yarn round hook and draw through two loops (one loop on hook).

Half treble. Two turning chain are required with this stitch.

Yarn round hook, insert hook into stitch, yarn round hook and draw loop through (three loops on hook), yarn round hook and draw through all three loops (one loop on hook).

Double treble. This stitch requires four turning chain.

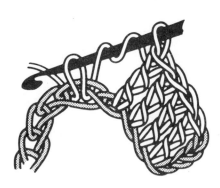

Pass yarn round hook twice, insert hook into next stitch, yarn round hook and pull through (four loops on hook), yarn

round hook and pull through two loops (three loops on hook), yarn round hook and pull through two loops (two loops on hook), yarn round hook and pull through both remaining loops (one loop on hook).

Triple treble. Five turning chain are required.

Pass yarn round hook three times, insert hook into next stitch, yarn round

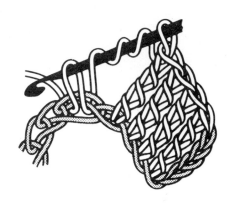

hook and draw through (five loops on hook), yarn round hook and draw through first two loops (four loops on hook), yarn round hook and draw through next two loops (three loops on hook), yarn round hook and draw next two loops (two loops on hook), yarn round hook and draw through remaining two loops (one loop on hook).

Quadruple treble. This stitch requires six turning chain.

Pass the yarn over the hook four times.

Insert hook into next stitch, pass yarn round hook and draw loop through (six loops on hook), pass yarn round hook and draw through the first two loops (five loops on hook), yarn round hook and draw through next two loops (four loops on hook), yarn round hook and draw through next two loops (three loops on hook), yarn round hook and draw through next two loops (two loops on hook), yarn round hook and draw through remaining two loops (one loop on hook).

Picots
Picots can be used within a pattern to give an interesting bobble effect. They are also frequently used to give an attractive edging.

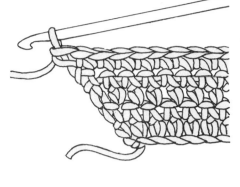

to the one already there and when all the stitches are worked to within the last stage, then the yarn is passed round the hook and pulled through all loops. Occasionally, at the beginning of a row, slip stitch is worked over the top of several stitches and then they are omitted on the next row.

The picot is formed by a chain of three, four or five stitches depending on the size of picot desired, and these are formed into a circle by working a double crochet into the first chain.

Clusters
Sometimes several stitches are worked in a group, usually trebles or double trebles.

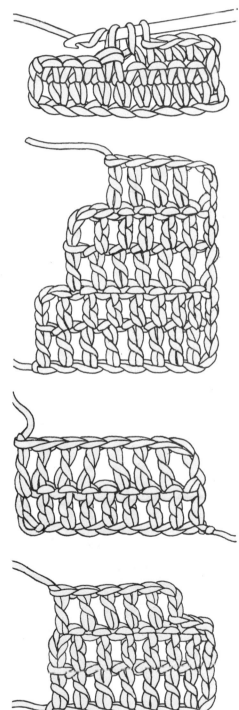

Work three or more of the stitch, each time leaving the last loop of the stitch on the hook. Finally, pass yarn round hook and draw through all loops on the hook.

Increasing
It is usual for specific instructions for increasing to be included in pattern instructions. However, as a general rule, two or more stitches can be worked into the same foundation. Sometimes in an open piece of work additional chain stitches are positioned between groups, and occasionally several chain stitches are added at the end of a row and used as a foundation chain on the next row.

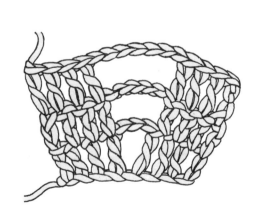

An alternative method is to simply change to a larger hook to give a slightly bigger tension.

Decreasing
As with increasing, instructions are given specifically with individual patterns.

One method is to simply omit a stitch, either at the end of a row or when the resulting space is not too obvious. Sometimes several stitches are worked into one and to do this the last loop of each stitch is left on the hook in addition

As with increasing, by changing the size of the hook, to alter the tension, this time to a smaller one, the overall size of the work is altered.

On the final two pages of your crash course we have included three special forms of crochet which will enable you to make many interesting variations. They are the filet, Tunisian and hairpin crochet techniques.

Joining in new yarn

In crochet, it is better to avoid tying knots when joining in new yarn. Work until about three inches of the yarn is left, lay it across the top of the previous row to the left, lay the beginning of the new yarn with it and work over both ends with the second ball of yarn.

If the join comes when chain is being worked, lay the new thread alongside the first one, the ends pointing in opposite directions, and work with the double thickness until the first thread runs out.

Cover with a damp cloth and leave until the cloth is absolutely dry.

Pieces of crochet can be joined by a crocheted slip stitch (illustrated in the first crochet crash course lesson), by sewing with overcasting stitch for a flat seam or by using a back stitch seam.

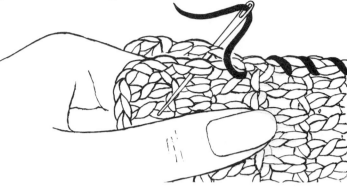

Joining a seam with overcasting

Joining in the new yarn

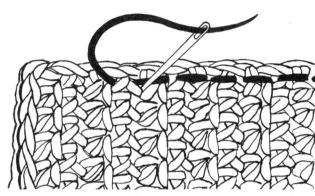

Joining work with a backstitch seam

Joining in new yarn on chain

Blocking out, joining pieces and finishing

Most crochet, especially when it is very open in texture, should be blocked out on completion. Using a clean, flat surface into which you can stick rustless dressmaking pins, pin the piece out to the correct measurements.

Cotton crochet items such as delicate edgings or table cloths and tea cloths often look better for a light stiffening. Use a starch solution (about one desertspoonful to a pint of hot water), or a gum arabic solution. Dab the solution over the article when it is blocked out.

Left-handed workers

When following instructions, read left for right and right for left. Wherever there are diagrams, hold them up in front of a mirror and follow the reversed reflection. Many left-handed people however find that they can learn to crochet in exactly the same way as right-handed people and it is worth trying first.

Filet crochet

In this technique the shapes in the patterning are formed by solid and open squares formed by blocks and spaces.

This type of crochet is always worked in straight rows. The blocks are formed by trebles and the spaces by chain, each space divided from the next one by one treble.

Blocking out a piece of crochet pinning diagonally opposite corners first.

Abbreviations
dc = double crochet
htr = half treble
dtr = double treble
tr tr = triple treble
quad tr = quadruple treble

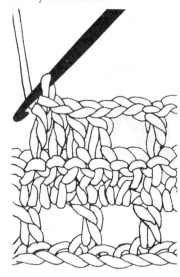

Filet crochet

Very often instructions for filet crochet are given as a chart but whereas in knitting each square would represent one stitch, in filet crochet a square represents a block or space. Each block is a given number of trebles.

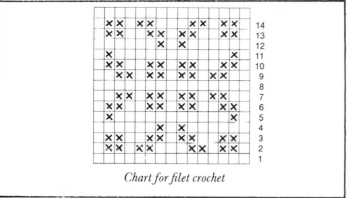

Chart for filet crochet

Tunisian crochet

This form of crochet is a marriage between crochet and knitting and is worked with a crochet hook of a similar length to a knitting needle. The basic principle is to work one row forward and then the next back through the centre of the first loops. This results in a firm texture which can be varied for different effects. As each loop is drawn through the next stitch it is left on the needle until the end of the row.

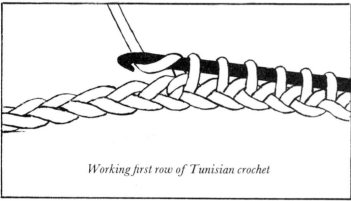

Working first row of Tunisian crochet

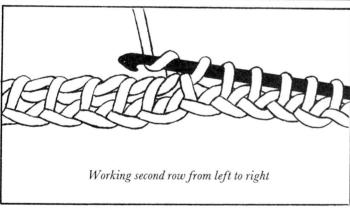

Working second row from left to right

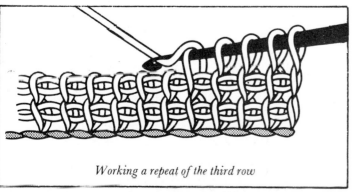

Working a repeat of the third row

1st row Begin with a length of chain. Insert hook into second chain from hook, yarn over hook and draw loop through, insert hook into each chain in same way.

2nd row 1 chain, *yarn over hook, draw through two loops on hook, repeat from * to end.

3rd row 1 chain, *insert hook into vertical loop, yarn over hook and draw yarn through, rep from * to end, insert hook into chain at end of row, draw yarn through. Repeat 2nd and 3rd rows.

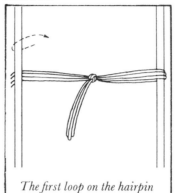

The first loop on the hairpin

Hold the yarn behind the left rod with the index finger and thumb of the left hand and turn the frame towards you from right to left until the right hand rod has reversed to the left side. The yarn will now pass round the other rod and should be held again by the left hand behind the left-hand rod.
*Insert the crochet hook through loop and draw a single thread through so that there are two loops on the hook, yarn round hook and draw through both loops to complete one double crochet. Keeping loop on hook, pass the hook through to the back

Hairpin crochet

This technique is worked on a tool which looks like a very large hairpin and which is sometimes adjustable to varying widths. The knots are formed down the centre with loops to both the prongs of the hairpin. Hairpin crochet makes up in long strips which are then joined together.
Make a slip knot in the yarn and place the loop on the right hand rod or prong. Draw the loop out so that the knot is exactly central.

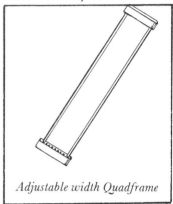

Adjustable width Quadframe

of the frame and turn the frame towards you from right to left as before.
Repeat from * turning the frame after each stitch. The frame is always turned the same way.

Working the centre stitch

Joining the strips of hairpin crochet together

Crochet in circles

Worked as a circle, in four contrasting colours, this unusual 'cobweb' crochet waistcoat goes well over light blouses and tops.

Size
To fit 34/36in bust

> **Tension for this design**
> 4 sts and 2 rows to 1in over tr worked on No. 4·50 hook

Materials shown here
Twilley's Crysette
2 balls main shade A, nutmeg
4 balls contrast colour B, white
2 balls contrast colour C, red
2 balls contrast colour D, pink
One No. 4·50 (ISR) crochet hook

Main section

NB Garment is worked in one piece, beg at centre back. Using No. 4·50 hook and A, make 6ch. Join with ss to first ch to form circle.
1st round 3ch to count as first tr, 13tr into circle, join with ss to 3rd of 3ch. 14 sts.
2nd round 3ch to count as first tr, 1tr into same place, 2tr into each tr to end, join with ss to 3rd of 3ch. 28 sts.
3rd round 3ch to count as first tr, 1tr into same place, 1ch, miss 1tr, *2tr into next tr, 1ch, miss 1tr, rep from * to end, join with ss to 3rd of 3ch. 14grs of 2tr. Break off A and join in B to sp between first 2tr of round.
4th round 4ch, 1tr into same place, 2ch, *(1tr, 1ch, 1tr) between 2tr of gr, 2ch, rep from * to end, join with ss to 3rd of 4ch.
5th round 4ch, 1tr between tr, 3ch, *(1tr, 1ch, 1tr) – called 1 gr – in 1ch sp of gr, 3ch, rep from * to end, join with ss to 3rd of 4ch.
6th round 4ch, 1tr between tr, 4ch, *1gr in 1ch sp, 4ch, rep from * to end, join with ss to 3rd of 4ch.
7th round As 6th but working 5ch between gr instead of 4ch.
8th round As 6th but working 6ch between gr.
9th round As 6th but working 7ch between gr. Break off B and join in C.
10th round 4ch, 1tr between tr, 3ch, *1gr in 7ch loop, 3ch, 1gr in 1ch sp, 3ch, rep from * ending with 1 gr in 7ch loop, 3ch, join with ss to 3rd of 4ch. 28grs.
11th–14th rounds As 6th–9th.
Break off C and join in D.
15th round As 10th. 56grs.
Break off D and join in B.

Divide for armholes
16th row 4ch, 1tr between tr, 4ch, *1gr in 1 ch sp, 4ch, rep from * 34 times more, 1gr in 1ch sp, turn, leaving 19grs unworked for back section.
17th row 4ch, 1tr between tr, 5ch, *1gr in 1ch sp, 5ch, rep from * 34 times more, 1gr in 1ch sp, turn.
18th row As 17th but working 6ch between gr.
19th row As 17th but working 7ch between gr. Break off B and join in A.
20th row 4ch, 1tr between tr, 3ch, *1gr in 7ch loop, 3ch, 1gr in 1ch sp, 3ch, rep from * omitting 3ch at end of last rep, turn. 73grs.
21st row 4ch, 1tr between tr, 3ch, *1gr in 1ch sp, 3ch, rep from * omitting 3ch at end of last rep, turn.
Rep 21st row 9 times more,

working 4 rows A, 1 row C and 4 rows D.

Shoulder straps

Break off D and join in B.
Next row Make 36ch, into 5th ch from hook work 1tr, 3ch, miss 3ch, *1gr into next ch, 3ch, miss 3ch, rep from * 6 times more, work in patt to end of row, using a separate length of B make 32ch and fasten off yarn, return to main yarn and work across these 32ch with **miss 3ch, 3ch, 1gr in next ch, rep from ** to end, turn.
Next row As 21st, working across all sts including straps. Fasten off.

Back section

Return to where 19gr were left, with RS facing miss

first 4grs, rejoin B and patt as given for 21st row across 11grs, turn and leave rem 4grs unworked.
Continue across these 11grs, rep 21st row 4 times more. Fasten off.

To make up

Join ends of straps to each side of top of back section. Using No. 4·50 hook, B and with RS facing, work 1 row dc round all edges, holding in neckline and armholes to make a firm edge.
Press under a damp cloth with a warm iron.

Lacing
Using No. 4·50 hook and 2 strands B, make chain 20in long. Fasten off.
Thread lacing through edges at front waist to tie.

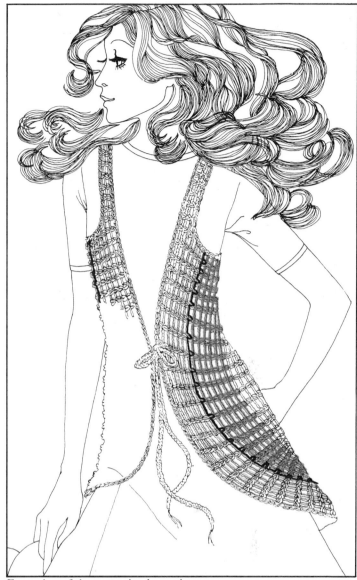

Front view of the pretty circular waistcoat

stunning sunny time stripes

A sizzle of breathtaking stripes shown here in a combination of white, blue, green and orange makes this striking beach set. Halter topped, with a zip fastened skirt, it is simple to make in rows of half treble and is the sun seekers' answer to summer days.

Sizes
Top. To fit 32[34:36]in bust
Skirt. 34[36:38]in hips
Length, 22in
The figures in brackets [] refer to the 34 and 36in sizes respectively

---

Tension for this design
11 sts and 8 rows to 2in over htr worked on No.3·00 hook

Materials shown here
Wendy Invitation Crochet Cotton
6[6:7] balls main shade, A
6[6:6] balls contrast colour, B
3[3:4] balls each of two contrast colours, C and D
One No.3·00 (ISR) crochet hook
Two buttons
22in open-ended zip fastener
Waist length elastic

Skirt back

Using No.3·00 hook and B, make 73[79:85]ch and beg at waist.
1st row Into 3rd ch from hook work 1htr, work 1htr into each ch to end, turn. 71[77:83] sts.
2nd row 2ch to count as first htr, work 1htr into each st to end. Turn.
3rd row Join in A and work as 2nd row.
4th row Join in C and work as 2nd row.
5th row Join in D, 2ch, 1htr into next st, work 2htr into next st, 1 htr into each of next 15[17:19] sts, work 2htr in next st, 1htr into each of next 33[35:37] sts, work 2htr into next st, 1htr into each of next 15[17:19] sts, work 2htr into next st, 1htr into each of next 2 sts. Turn. 75[81:87] sts.
Continue in htr without shaping, working 2 rows A and 1 row B.
9th row Using B, 2ch, 1htr into next st, work 2htr into next st, 1htr into each of next 16[18:20] sts, work 2htr into next st, 1htr into each of next 35[37:39] sts, work 2htr into next st, 1htr into each of next 16[18:20] sts, work 2htr into next st, 1htr into each of next 2 sts. Turn. 79[85:91] sts.
Continue to work in striped patt of 1 row A, 1 row C, 1 row D, 2 rows A and 2 rows B, *at the same time* inc as before on every 4th row 5 times more, then on every following 10th row until work measures 22in from beg, ending with 2 rows B. Fasten off.

Skirt front

Work as given for Back.

Halter top

Using No.3·00 hook and B, make 135[139:143]ch.
Work first 2 rows as given for Skirt back, 133[137:141] sts.
Continue in stripes, reversing order of colours given for Skirt and working 2 rows A, 1 row D, 1 row C, 1 row A and 2 rows B throughout.

Shape top
3rd row 2ch, miss one st, 1htr into each of next 46[47: 48] sts, work 3htr into next st, 1htr into each of next 35[37:39] sts, work 3htr into next st, 1htr into each of next 40[41:42] sts, 1dc in next st, turn.
4th row 2ch, miss one st, 1htr into each of next 40[41:42] sts, work 3htr into next st, 1htr into each of next 37[39:41] sts, work 3htr into next st, work in htr to last 8 sts, 1dc in next st, turn.
5th row 2ch, miss one st, 1htr into each of next 40[41: 42] sts, work 3htr into next st, 1htr into each of next 39[41:43] sts, work 3htr into next st, work in htr to last 8 sts, 1dc into next st, turn.
Continue to inc in this way on next 5 rows, keeping inc sts in line, at the same time work one st less at beg and 7 sts less at end of these rows. 101[105:109] sts.
Next row 2ch, miss one st, patt to last 8 sts, 1dc into next st, turn.
Rep last row 3 times more. 69[73:77] sts.
Next row 2ch, miss one st, patt to last 4[5:6] sts, 1dc into next st, turn.

Rep last row 3 times more. 53 sts.
Next row 2ch, miss one st, patt to last 4 sts, 1dc into next st, turn.
Rep last row 11 times more. Fasten off.

Straps

Using No.3·00 hook and B, make 138[143:148]ch.
Work first row as given for Skirt back.
Continue in htr, working 1 row A, 1 row D and 1 row C. Fasten off.
Make second strap in same way.

To make up

Skirt. Press each piece under a damp cloth with a warm iron. Join right side seam. Sew zip into left side seam with slide at bottom of skirt. Sew elastic at waist with casing st. Press seam.
Top. Press as given for Skirt. Sew on straps, beginning at back and round to point at top, leaving 8 inches of strap free for halter neck. Sew on button to one side of back and second button to end of one strap. Make button loops on other sides to correspond. Press seams.

▼ *Close-up showing the detail of the bust darts and halter neckline*

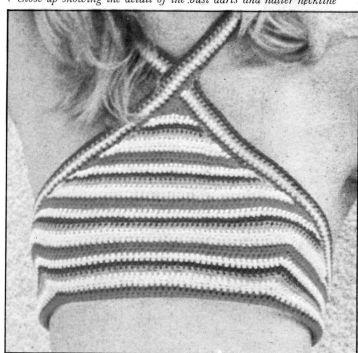

Pretty cover-up

Here is a pretty hostess apron which has been designed to look feminine and attractive and still give maximum coverage in the kitchen. The main section is worked in an interesting new stitch.

Size

To fit waist 24–26in, adjustable
Length from shoulder to hem, 38in

Tension for this design
6ddc and 5 rows to 1in worked on No. 3·00 hook

Materials shown here

Twilley's Crysette 12 balls
One No. 3·00 (ISR) crochet hook
2 buttons

Apron

Using No. 3·00 hook, make 49ch.

1st row Insert hook into 2nd ch from hook, yrh and draw through, yrh and draw through one loop, yrh and draw through 2 loops – called 1ddc (double double crochet) – 1ddc into each ch to end, turn. 48 sts.

2nd row 2ch, miss first ddc, 1ddc into each of next 9ddc, 2ddc into next ddc, 1ddc into each ddc to last 11ddc, 2ddc into next ddc, 1ddc into each ddc to end, 1ddc into 2nd of 2ch, turn.

3rd row 2ch, miss first ddc, *1ddc into next ddc, rep from * to end, 1ddc into 2nd of 2ch, turn.
Rep last row 4 times more.

then 2nd row once.
Continue in this way, inc on every 6th row until there are 80 sts.
Fasten off.

Edging
1st row With RS facing, rejoin yarn to side edge at waist and work 96ddc into row ends down edge of apron, 2ddc at corner, 84ddc along lower edge, 2ddc at corner and 96ddc up other edge, turn.
2nd row 4ch, *miss 1ddc, 1tr into next ddc, 1ch, rep from * to corner, (1tr, 2ch) twice into corner sp, 1tr into same sp, 1ch, rep from * along lower edge, work corner as before, rep from * up second side edge ending with 1tr into last ddc, turn.
3rd row 4ch, (1dtr into first tr, 2ch, ss into top of dtr – called 1 picot –) 4 times, *2ch, miss 2 sps, 1dc into next sp, 2ch, miss 2 sps, (1dtr, 1 picot) 7 times into next sp, rep from * 6 times more, 2ch, miss 2 sps, 1dc into next sp, 2ch, miss 2 sps, (1dtr, 1 picot) 3 times into each of next 4 sps, beg at * work along lower edge and other side edge in the same way, working second corner as before and ending with 2ch, miss 2 sps, 1dc into next sp, 2ch, miss 2 sps, (1dtr, 1 picot) 4 times into 3rd of 4ch, 1dtr into same place, turn.
4th row Ss to first picot, *3ch, 1dc into next picot, rep from * to end of first gr, 1dc into first picot of next gr, rep from * all round counting the 12 picots at each corner as one gr, and ending with 3ch, 1dc into last picot, turn.
5th row 3ch, 1tr into last dc made, (3ch, keeping last loop of each st on hook work 3tr into next 3ch sp, yrh and draw through all loops on hook – called 1cl –) 3 times, *1ch, (1cl into next 3ch sp, 3ch) 5 times, 1cl into next 3ch sp*, rep from * to * 6 times more, **1ch, (1cl into next 3ch sp, 3ch) 10 times round corner, 1cl into next 3ch sp**, rep from * to * 6 times along lower edge,

then from ** to ** round second corner, then from * to * up second side edge, ending with 3ch, 2tr into first ss of 4th row, turn.
6th row (3ch, 1cl into next 3ch sp) 3 times, *1ch, (1cl into next 3ch loop, 3ch) 4 times, 1cl into next 3ch loop*, rep from * to * 6 times more, **1ch, (1cl into next 3ch loop, 3ch) 9 times round corner, 1cl into next 3ch loop**, rep from * to * 6 times then from ** to ** once for second corner, then from * to * up second side edge, ending with 1ch, (1cl into next 3ch loop, 3ch) twice, 1cl into last 3ch loop, 1tr into 3rd of 3ch, turn.
7th row *4ch, 1dc into next 3ch sp, rep from * all round, ending with 1ch, 1tr into 3rd of 3ch, turn.
8th row 3dc into first 4ch loop, *(2dc, 3ch, 1 picot into top of last dc worked, 2dc) into next 4ch loop, rep from * to last loop, 3dc into last loop.
Fasten off.

Waistband

Using No. 3·00 hook, make 59ch, without breaking off yarn and with RS facing, work 12ddc into top of apron edging, 48ddc into top of apron skirt, 12ddc into top of second apron edging, make 60ch, turn.
2nd row 1dc into 2nd ch from hook, 1dc into each ch, 1dc into each ddc, 1dc into each ch, turn. 190dc.
3rd row 1ch, 1dc into each dc to end, turn.
Rep last row 3 times more.
Next row (buttonhole) 1dc into each of next 4dc, 4ch, miss 4dc, 1dc into each of next 32dc, 4ch, miss 4dc, 1dc into each dc to end, turn.
Next row As 3rd but working 4dc into each 4ch loop.
Rep 3rd row 4 times more.
Fasten off.

Straps

Using No. 3·00 hook, make 25ch.
1st row As 1st row of apron.

Back view showing fastening

24ddc.
2nd row As 3rd row of apron.
3rd row 1ch, 1ddc into each of next 9ddc, leaving last loop of each st on hook work 1ddc into each of the next 2ddc, yrh and draw through all loops on hook – called dec 1 – turn.
4th row 1ddc into each st, turn.
5th row 1ddc into each st to within last 2 sts, dec 1, turn.
Rep last 2 rows until 8 sts rem.
Continue in ddc without shaping until strap measures 30in.
Fasten off.
Rejoin yarn to 13ddc on waistband, dec 1, 1ddc into each st to end, turn.
Work to correspond with first strap, reversing shapings.
Fasten off.

Edging
Rejoin yarn to outer edge of strap at waist.
Work 156dc along outer

edge, turn.
Work rows 2 to 8 of apron edging, omitting shaping at corners and reading dc for ddc on 2nd row.
Fasten off.
Work edging on second strap in same way.
Position straps centrally on waistband and stitch in place.

Button loops
Join yarn to end of strap on frill edge, work 10dc along frill edge, 8dc along end of strap, turn.
Next row 1ch, 1dc into each of 2dc, 4ch, miss 4dc, 1dc into next 2dc, turn.
Next row 1ch, 1dc into each of next 2dc, 4dc into 4ch loop, 2dc into last 2dc.
Fasten off.

To make up

Position buttons on waistband to correspond with buttonholes on other end of waistband and straps.
Press under a damp cloth using a warm iron.

Cobwebby shawl in hairpin crochet

This wisp of a shawl in luxurious mohair is made in hairpin crochet. Strips of loops with double crochet down the centre are joined in fan-shaped groupings for a cobweb effect.

Size
52in along neck edge, measured without fringe 35in from centre neck edge to centre point, measured without fringe

Tension for this design
Each strip is worked on a hairpin frame measuring 3in across

Materials shown here
Pingouin Mohair
5 50gr balls
One Quadframe or crochet fork measuring 3in across
One No. 3.50 (ISR) Aero crochet hook

Working the strips
1st strip Work 15 loops on either side of a double crochet centre stitch.
2nd strip As for first strip but working 45 loops.
3rd strip As for first strip but working 75 loops.
4th strip As for first strip but working 105 loops.
5th strip As for first strip but working 135 loops.
6th strip As for first strip but working 165 loops.
7th strip As for first strip but working 195 loops.
8th strip As for first strip but working 225 loops.
9th strip As for first strip but working 255 loops.
Finish off all ends.

Grouping the loops
Work along one side of each strip, using No. 3.50 hook. Group the first 3 loops together and join yarn with ss, *(3ch, group next 3 loops together and work 1dc into the group) 4 times, 5ch, group the next 15 loops together and work 1dc into the group, 5ch, 1dc into next 3 loops rep from * to end of strip. Work along second side of each strip as follows. Group the first 15 loops together and join in yarn with ss, 5ch, group the next 3 loops together and work 1dc into the group, rep from * as given for first side to the end of the strip.

To join the strips together
Using No. 3.50 hook, on second side of the first strip join in yarn with ss to first group of 3 loops, 3ch, 1dc into fourth group of 3 loops on first side of second strip, 3ch, 1dc into second group of 3 loops on first strip, 3ch, 1dc into fifth group of 3 loops on second strip, 3ch, 1dc into third group of 3 loops of first strip, 3ch, 1dc into group of 15 loops on second strip, 3ch 1dc into fourth group of 3 loops on first strip, continue in this manner, keeping the 15 loop groups which form the points of the fan shape alternated with the 3 loop groups which form the open edges of the fan shape.

Working the edging
Using No. 3.50 hook, join yarn with ss to last 3 loop group on last strip and work down one side of shawl towards the point and then back up the other side as follows.
1st row 7ch, *1dc into centre

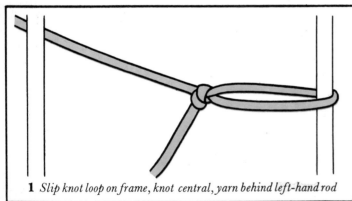

1 *Slip knot loop on frame, knot central, yarn behind left-hand rod*

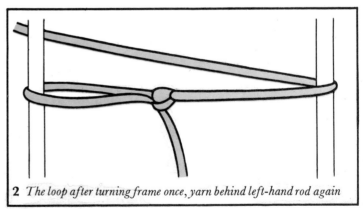

2 *The loop after turning frame once, yarn behind left-hand rod again*

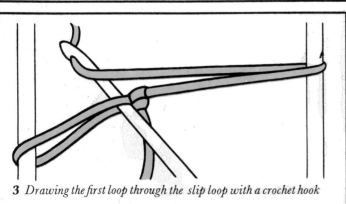

3 *Drawing the first loop through the slip loop with a crochet hook*

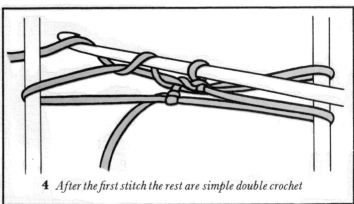

4 *After the first stitch the rest are simple double crochet*

dc of strip, 7ch, 1dc into 15 loop group point, 7ch, 1dc into 3ch loop joining the two strips, 7ch, 1dc into last 3 loop group of next strip, 7ch, 1dc into next 3ch loop joining the two strips, rep from * down edge to point and back up the opposite edge. Turn. **2nd row** 5ch, 1dc into first 7ch loop, *7ch, 1dc into next 7ch loop, rep from *ending with 5ch, 1dc into last dc.

Adding the fringe
Make 46 tassels each of six 24in lengths of yarn, fold each group of six strands in half and knot one into each 7ch loop and one into each of the two 5ch loops.
Make a slip knot in the yarn and place it on the right-hand rod. Draw the loop out so that the knot is exactly central between the bars. Hold the yarn behind the left rod with the index finger and thumb of the left hand and turn the frame towards you from right to left until the right-hand rod has reversed to the left side.
The yarn will now pass round the other rod and should be held again by the left hand behind the left-hand rod. Insert crochet hook through the loop, yarn round hook and draw loop through. Yarn round hook and draw through loop. Turn frame. *Insert the crochet hook through the loop and draw a single thread through so that there are two loops on the crochet hook, yarn round hook and draw through both loops to complete the double crochet. Keeping the loop on the hook, pass the hook through to the back of the frame and turn the frame towards you from right to left as before. Repeat from *, turning the frame after each stitch and always in the same direction.

Deeply fringed, soft and clinging, the perfect shawl for cooler evenings.

Daisy work jacket

A simple crochet jacket becomes something special when covered in tiny coloured daisies. It is ideal as a cover-up over a simple evening dress, or even as an unusual finishing touch to a bridesmaid's outfit.

Sizes

To fit 32[34:36:38]in bust
Length, 14¾[15:15¼:15½]in
Sleeve seam, 6[6:6:6]in
The figures in brackets [] refer to the 34, 36 and 38in bust sizes respectively

---

Tension for this design
6dc and 8 rows to 1in worked on No. 3·50 hook
Each daisy measures 1¾in diameter

Materials shown here

Twilley's Cortina
15[16:17:18] 1oz balls main shade, A, Mulberry
4 1oz balls contrast colour, B, Royal Purple
4 1oz balls contrast colour, C, Lavender
One No. 3·00 (ISR) crochet hook
One No. 3·50 (ISR) crochet hook
Twilley's multi-fleur loom

Back

Using No. 3·50 hook and A, make 97[103:109:115] ch.
1st row 1dc into 2nd ch from hook, *1dc into next ch, rep from * to end, turn. 96[102:108:115] ch.
2nd row 1ch, *1dc into next dc, rep from * to end, turn.
Rep 2nd row 62 times more.

Shape armholes

Next row Ss to 7th dc, 1ch, *1dc into next dc, rep from * to last 6dc, turn.
Dec one st at each end of each of next 7[9:11:13] rows.
70[72:74:76] dc.
Work 42 rows more without shaping.

Shape shoulders

Next row Ss to 7th dc, 1ch, *1dc into next dc, rep from * to last 6dc, turn.
Rep last row twice more. 34[36:38:40] dc.
Fasten off.

Front

Using No. 3·50 hook and A, make 46[49:52:55] ch.
Work as given for Back to armhole shaping. 45[48:51:54] ch.

Shape armhole

Next row Ss to 7th dc, 1ch, *1dc into next dc, rep from * to end, turn.
Dec one st at armhole edge on each of next 7[9:11:13] rows. 32[33:34:35] dc.
Work 21 rows more without shaping.

Shape neck

Next row Ss to 7th dc, 1ch, *1dc into next dc, rep from * to end, turn.
Dec one st at neck edge on each of next 8[9:10:11] rows. 18dc.
Work 12[11:10:9] rows more without shaping.

Shape shoulder

Next row Ss to 7th dc, 1ch, *1dc into next dc, rep from * to end, turn.
Next row 1ch, *1dc into next dc, rep from * to last 6dc, turn.
Fasten off.
Work a second Front in the same way.

Sleeves

Using No. 3·50 hook and A, make 70[73:76:79] ch.
1st row 1dc into 2nd ch from hook, *1dc into next ch, rep from * to end, turn. 69[72:75:78] dc.
2nd row 1ch, *1dc into next dc, rep from * to end, turn.
Work 2nd row 46 times more.

Shape top

Next row Ss to 7th dc, 1ch, *1dc into next dc, rep from * to last 6dc, turn.
Dec one st at each end of next and following 10[11:12:13] alt rows.
Work 1 row.
Dec one st at each end of each of next 12 rows.
11[12:13:14] dc.
Fasten off.

Front and neck edgings

Join shoulder seams.
Using No. 3·50 hook and A, with RS facing, join yarn to lower edge of Right Front at corner with ss.
1st row 1dc into same place as ss, *miss next row end, 1dc into next row end, rep from * to corner, 3dc into corner, 1dc into each of 6dc at neck edge, 1dc into every alt row end up side of neck, 1dc into each dc along back neck, 1dc into every alt row end down side of neck, 1dc into each of 6dc at neck edge, 3dc into corner, 1dc into every alt row end to lower corner of Left Front, turn.
2nd row 1ch, 1dc into each dc all round, working 3dc into centre dc at each corner, turn.
Rep 2nd row 4 times more.
Fasten off.

Collar

Using No. 3·50 hook and A, with RS facing, join yarn to centre dc of 3 corner dc at top of Right Front edge.
1st row 1ch, work in dc to centre dc of 3 corner dc on Left Front, dec 6 sts evenly across the row, turn.
Change to No. 3·00 hook.
2nd row 1ch, *1dc into next dc, rep from * to end, turn.
Rep 2nd row 9 times more.
Fasten off.
Join side seams.
Using No. 3·50 hook and A, with RS facing, rejoin yarn to lower corner of Right Front and work 1 row dc all round, including lower edge and working 2dc into each lower corner st and 3dc into

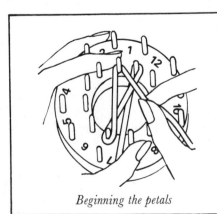

Beginning the petals

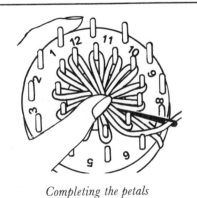

Completing the petals

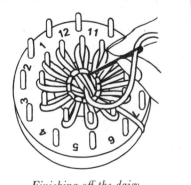

Finishing off the daisy

each corner st on collar.
Fasten off.

Daisies

Winding

Using the multi-fleur loom, secure the end of the yarn at space 7 with a piece of clear adhesive tape. Use the inner circle of pegs only. Take the yarn across to space 1, round the peg to space 12, across to space 6, round the peg to space 7. Wind the yarn round the same pegs twice more. Continuing with the yarn at space 7, take it across to space 2, round the peg to space 1, across to space 7, round the peg to space 8. Wind the yarn round the same pegs twice more. Continue winding the inner pegs in this way until there are 12 petals in all, ending with the yarn at space 6. Cut the yarn, leaving about sixteen inches for fastening off.

Thread the end into a tapestry needle, pass round the inner peg to space 7 and push the needle through to the back at centre, taking care not to split the yarn. Finish off by bringing the needle up through space 12, pull tightly against centre back of flower, push needle through to the back between the strands in space 1.

Continue this backstitch until every petal has a crossbar, keeping the stitch as firm and near the centre as possible. End with the yarn at the back of the loom in space 10. Push the needle through from back to front at centre and then from front to back at the inner edge of any backstitch.

Gently remove the flower from the loom and fasten off the end securely on the wrong side. Trim long ends.

Make 150 flowers in each of the three colours.

To make up

Press lightly under a dry cloth, using a warm iron. Join sleeve seam. Press seams lightly. Stitch daisies to jacket at random.

Introducing Aran crochet

This poncho suit with the Aran look is crocheted, not knitted. It is interesting to work, as well as making a smart addition to any wardrobe.

Sizes

To fit 34[36:38]in bust
36[38:40]in hips
Trousers. Inside leg, 28in, adjustable
Poncho. Length at side, 24in

Tension for this design
9 sts to 2in and 7 rows to 3in over tr worked on No. 4.00 hook

---

Materials shown here

Emu Scotch Double Knitting
Trousers. 21[22:23] 1oz balls
Poncho. 22 1oz balls
One No. 4.00 (ISR) crochet hook
One No. 6.00 (ISR) crochet hook
Waist length elastic

Trousers right leg

Using No. 4.00 hook, make 92[97:102]ch.
1st row 1tr into 3rd ch from hook, *1tr into next ch, rep from * to end. 90[95:100] sts.
2nd row 3ch to count as first tr, *1tr into next tr, rep from * to end.
Rep 2nd row until work measures 22in from beg. Adjust length here if required.
Inc one st at each end of next and every following 3rd row until there are 100[105:110] sts.
Work one row.

Shape crutch

Next row Ss over first 5 sts, 1tr into each tr to last 3 sts, turn.
Next row Ss over first 2 sts, 1tr into each tr to last 3 sts, turn.
Next row Ss over first 2 sts, 1tr into each tr to last 2 sts, turn.
Dec one st at end (front edge) of next and following 3 alt rows, then every 4th row twice, *at the same time* dec one st at beg (back edge) of next and following 4 rows, then every alt row 6 times. 66[71:76] sts.
Continue without shaping until work measures 9½[10:10½]in from beg of crutch shaping, ending at back edge.

Shape back

1st row Patt over 48[52:56] sts, turn.
2nd row Ss over first 12[13:14] sts, patt to end.
3rd row Patt over first 24[26:28] sts, turn.
4th row As 2nd.
Work 3 rows across all sts.
Fasten off.

Trousers left leg

Work as given for Right leg, reversing all shaping.

Poncho

Using No. 4.00 hook, make 94ch, join with ss to form a ring (neck edge).
1st round 3ch to count as first tr, *1tr into next ch, rep from * to end, ss to 3rd of 3ch. 94 sts.
2nd round 3ch to count as first tr, *2tr into next tr, 1tr into each of next 20tr, 2tr into next tr*, 1tr into each of next 2tr, rep from * to *, 1tr into next tr, rep from * to *, 1tr into each of next 2tr, rep from * to *, ss to 3rd of 3ch. 102 sts.
3rd round 3ch to count as first tr, *2tr into next tr, 1tr into each of next 48tr, 2tr into next tr*, 1tr into next tr, rep from * to *, ss to 3rd of 3ch. 106 sts.
4th round 3ch to count as first tr, *2tr into next tr, 1tr into each of next 23tr, 2tr into next tr*, 1tr into each of next 2tr, rep from * to *, 1tr into next tr, rep from * to *, 1tr into each of next 2tr, rep from * to *, ss to 3rd of 3ch. 114 sts.
5th round 3ch to count as first tr, *2tr into next tr, 1tr into each of next 54tr, 2tr into next tr*, 1tr into next tr, rep from * to *, ss to 3rd of 3ch. 118 sts.
Continue in this way, inc (8tr in next round and 4tr in following round) 8 times more. 214 sts.
Continue inc 4tr on every round (i.e. at centre back and centre front only) 35 times.

Poncho surface crochet

Using No. 6.00 hook and 2 strands of yarn throughout, beg at lower edge. Insert hook in sp between centre back st where rounds started and the next st and draw a loop through. Hold yarn at back of work, *insert hook into same sp on next row up, draw loop through the st and the loop on hook, thus working a ss and not drawing yarn too tight, rep from * into each row to neck edge. Fasten off.
Rep along other side of the centre back st, thus forming a double line of ss.
Work in the same way at either side of centre front st. Find the 2 sts at centre of work between centre front and back sts to make the side edge. Work a single line ss in the same way between these 2 sts at each side.
Beg at centre back, count 7 sts, mark the sp between the 7th and 8th sts, count 12 sts and mark next sp, count 9 sts and mark next sp, *count 9 sts and mark next sp, count 12 sts and mark next sp, count 9 sts and mark next sp, rep from * once more thus coming to centre of side edge which has already been worked, rep from * twice more, count 9 sts, mark next sp, count 12 sts and mark next sp, count 7 sts thus coming to centre front. Continue in this way until the centre back is reached.
Beg with first marked sp to the left of one side edge, insert hook into first row and draw through loop. Continue as before but moving one sp to the left on each of next 12 rows, then one sp to the right on each of next 12 rows and continue in this way to the top.
Fasten off.
At next marked sp to the left, insert hook into first row and draw through loop and work as the previous line but beg with one sp to the right on each of next 12 rows and then one sp to the left on each of next 12 rows.
At next marked sp work a straight line to the top.
Continue in this way, working one diamond panel, then one straight line and making sure that where lines meet at centre front and back they do so on the same row.

Neckband

With WS facing, using No. 4.00 hook and single yarn, join yarn to centre back neck, 3ch, 1tr into each of foundation ch, ending with ss into 3rd of 3ch.
Work in tr for 5 rounds more.
Fasten off.

To make up

Trousers. Press pieces under a damp cloth, using a warm iron.
Join back and front seams.
Join leg seams.
Press seams.
Sew elastic to inside waist with casing stitch.
Poncho. Press as given for Trousers.
Turn 3 rows of Neckband over to RS.
Using No. 4.00 hook and yarn double, make a cord of ch 37 inches long and thread through 2nd row of tr at neck edge to tie at centre front. Make a small tassel at each end of the cord.

Deep bands of chevrons in flattering subtle colours make an attractive evening skirt. Easy to make, the skirt is worked all in one piece.

Sizes
To fit 34/36[38/40]in hips
Length, 40in, adjustable
The figures in brackets [ ] refer to the 38/40in hip size

Tension for this design
1 patt (10 sts) to 1¾in and 7 rows to 4in worked on No. 3·00 hook

Materials shown here
Original Art Needlework Industries Shetland 2 ply
6[7] hanks dark green, A
6[7] hanks silver grey, B
4[5] hanks light green, C
One No. 3·00 (ISR) crochet hook
7in zip fastener
Waist length elastic or petersham

Skirt

Using No. 3·00 hook and A, beg at top of skirt, make 165[185]ch.

1st row 2dtr into 5th ch from hook, *1dtr into each of next 2ch, miss 2ch, 1dtr into next ch, miss 2ch, 1dtr into each of next 2ch, 5dtr into next ch. rep from *, ending with 3dtr into last ch instead of 5dtr. 16[18] patts.

2nd row 4ch, work 2dtr into the first (edge) dtr, *1dtr into each of next 2dtr, miss 2dtr, 1dtr into next dtr, miss 2dtr, 1dtr into each of next 2dtr, 5dtr into next dtr, rep from *, ending with 3dtr into 4th of 4ch.
Rep 2nd row 5 times more.

8th row 4ch, work 3dtr into the first (edge) dtr, *1dtr into each of next 2dtr, miss 2dtr, 1dtr into next dtr, miss 2dtr, 1dtr into each of next 2dtr, 7dtr into next dtr, rep from *, ending with 4dtr into 4th of 4ch.

9th row 4ch, work 2dtr into the first (edge) dtr, *1dtr into each of next 3dtr, miss 2dtr, 1dtr into next dtr,

miss 2dtr, 1dtr into each of next 3dtr, 5dtr into next dtr, rep from *, ending with 3dtr into 4th of 4ch.
Rep last row 5 times more.
Break off A and join in B.
Rep 9th row once more.

16th row 4ch, work 3dtr into the first (edge) dtr, *1dtr into each of next 3dtr, miss 2dtr, 1dtr into next dtr, miss 2dtr, 1dtr into each of next 3dtr, 7dtr into next dtr, rep from *, ending with 4dtr into 4th of 4ch.

17th row 4ch, work 2dtr into the first (edge) dtr, *1dtr into each of next 4dtr, miss 2dtr, 1dtr into next dtr, miss 2dtr, 1dtr into each of next 4dtr, 5dtr into next dtr, rep from *, ending with 3dtr into 4th of 4ch.

Continue in this way, inc 2 sts in each patt on every 8th row 6 times more, *at the same time* work 11 rows more in B, 14 rows C, 14 rows B, 14 rows A.
Fasten off.

NB Length of skirt may be adjusted by adding or subtracting an equal number of rows to or from each stripe.

To make up

Press work very lightly under a damp cloth, using a warm iron.
Join centre back seam, leaving 7in open at top for zip. Sew in zip.
Sew elastic or petersham in place at waist.
Press seam lightly.

Elegance for evening

▲ *Left to right : jumper and shorts with car motif, dress with sun motif, bolero and skirt with butterfly motif*

Shape sides
1st row Work 15gr, omit 1ch, patt to last 15gr, omit 1ch, patt to end. Turn.
Work 5 rows patt, noting that 1gr has been dec by omitting 1ch.

7th row Work 2gr, omit 1ch, patt to last 2gr, omit 1ch, patt to end. Turn.
Work 5 rows patt.

13th row Work in patt, omitting 1ch between 14th and 15th gr from each end. Turn. Work 5 rows patt.
19th row As 7th.
Work 5 rows patt.
25th row Work in patt, omitting 1ch between 13th and 14th gr from each end. Turn. 36[40:44] gr.
Continue without shaping

until work measures 12[13: 14]in from beg.**

Shape armhole and divide for back opening
Next row Ss over first 2gr, patt 16[18:20] gr, turn.
Complete this side first.
Dec 1gr at armhole edge on every alt row 2[3:4] times.
Continue without shaping.

until armhole measures 5[5½:6]in from beg, ending at side edge.

Shape shoulder
Next row Ss over first 3gr, patt to end. Turn.
Next row Patt to last 3gr, turn.
Next row Ss over first 2[3:3] gr, patt to end. 6[6:7] gr.

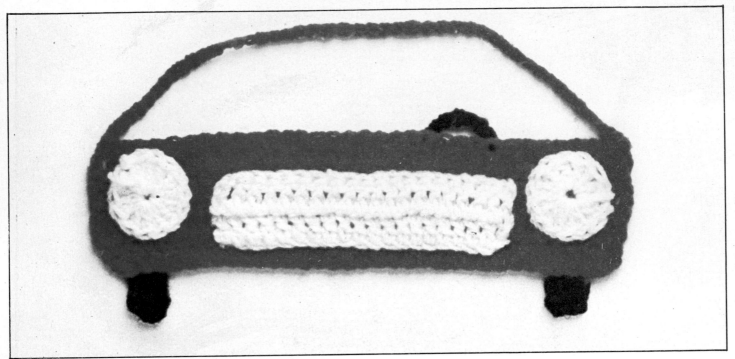

▲ *Close-up detail showing the motor car motif which is appliquéd onto the top of the jumper and shorts outfit*

Fasten off.

Return to where work was left, rejoin yarn and complete to match first side, reversing shaping.

Front

Work as given for Back to **.

Shape armholes

Next row Ss over first 2gr, patt to last 2gr, turn.

Dec 1gr at each end of every alt row 2[3:4] times.

Continue without shaping until armholes measure 3[3½:4]in from beg.

Shape neck

Next row Patt 12[13:14] gr, turn.

Complete this side first.

Dec 1gr at neck edge on next 4[4:5] rows. 8[9:9] gr.

Continue without shaping until armhole measures same as Back to shoulder, ending at side edge.

Shape shoulder

Next row Ss over first 3gr, patt to end. Turn.

Next row Patt to last 3gr, turn.

Fasten off.

Return to where work was left, miss 4gr in centre, rejoin yarn to rem sts and complete to match first side, reversing shaping.

Sleeves

Work as given for jumper Sleeves.

Neckband

Join shoulder seams.

Using No.3·00 hook and A, with RS facing, work a row of dc up side edge of opening, round neck and down other side of opening. Fasten off.

To make up

Press as given for Jumper. Set in sleeves. Join side and sleeve seams. Press seams.

Sew in zip to back neck.

Sun motif. Using No.3·00 hook and B, make 11ch.

1st row *Ss into 2nd ch from hook, 1dc in next ch, 2dc in next ch, 1htr into next ch, 1htr and 1tr in next ch, 1tr in next ch, 1dtr in each of next 4ch, work 11ch, ss to 6th st from end of last petal (ie the 2nd tr), rep from * and continue until 14 petals have been worked.

Fasten off. Join into a circle.

Using No.3·00 hook and B, make 11ch for mouth, ss in 2nd ch and next ch, 1dc in next ch, 1htr in each of next 4ch, 1dc in next ch, ss into each of next 2ch. Fasten off.

Using No.3·00 hook and B, make 2ch for each eye. Work

9dc into first ch, then ss to 2nd ch. Fasten off.

Sew on parts of motif to centre front of dress.

Skirt and bolero

Sizes

To fit 22[24:26]in chest

Bolero. Length to shoulder, 9[10:11]in

Skirt. Length, 9[10:11]in

The figures in brackets [] refer to the 24 and 26in sizes respectively

---

Tension for this design

22 sts and 12 rows to 4in over patt worked on No.3·50 hook

Materials shown here

Patons Cameo Crepe 8[9:10] balls main shade, A
1 ball each of contrast colours, B and C
One No. 3·50 (ISR) crochet hook
4 buttons
Waist length elastic
NB Yarn is used double throughout.

Skirt

Using No. 3·50 hook and A used double throughout, make 130[142:154] ch and

work in one piece from waist edge.

1st row Into 4th ch from hook work 1htr, *1ch, miss 1ch, 1htr in next ch, rep from * to end. Turn. 65[71:77] htr and 64[70:76] ch sp.

2nd row 3ch, 1htr in first ch sp, *1ch, 1htr in next ch sp, rep from * to end. Turn.

3rd row As 2nd.

4th row 3ch, (1htr in ch sp, 1ch) 7 times, (1htr, 1ch) twice in next ch sp—called inc 1 —, *patt 15[16:17] sts, inc 1, rep from * twice more, patt to end. Turn.

Keeping inc in line above each other, continue inc 4 times in this way on following 4th[5th:6th] row 4 times more.

Continue without shaping until work measures 8[9:10]in from beg, or 1in less than required length.

Shape corners

Dec 1htr and 1ch at each end of next 3 rows.

Fasten off.

Bolero

Using No.3·50 hook and A used double throughout, make 114[126:138] ch and work in one piece to underarm.

Work 1st row as given for Skirt. 57[63:69] htr and 56[62:68] ch sp.

▲ *Close-up detail of the sun motif which is appliquéd to the dress*

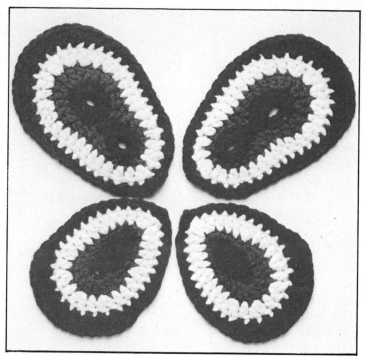

▲ *Close-up detail of the butterfly which is appliquéd to the bolero*

Continue in patt as given for Skirt, inc 1 at each end of next 5 rows. 67[73:79] htr. Continue without shaping until work measures 3[3½:4]in from beg.

Divide for armholes
Next row Patt over first 15[16:18] sp (ie 16[17:19] htr), turn and complete right front on these sts.
Dec 1htr and 1ch at armhole edge on next 3[3:4] rows.
Work 0[1:1] row.
Dec 1htr and 1ch at front edge on next and following 6[7:8] alt rows. 6htr.
Continue without shaping until armhole measures 6[6½:7]in from beg. Fasten off.
Return to where work was left, miss 2[3:3] ch sp, rejoin yarn to next sp, 3ch, patt over next 30[32:34] sp for back, turn. 31[33:35] htr.
Dec 1htr and 1ch at each end of next 3[3:4] rows.
24[27:27] htr.
Continue without shaping until armholes measure 4[4½:5]in from beg.

Shape neck
Next row Patt over first 9[10:10] sp, turn. 10[11:11] htr.
Dec 1htr and 1ch at neck edge on next 4[5:5] rows.
Continue without shaping until armhole measures same as front. Fasten off.

Return to where work was left, miss 6 sp in centre, rejoin yarn to rem sts and complete other side of neck to match first side, reversing shaping.
Return to where work was left at underarm, miss first 2[3:3] sp, rejoin yarn to next sp and patt to end.
Complete to match right front, reversing shaping.

Small butterfly wings

Using No.3·50 hook and B used double, make 10 ch.
1st round Into 4th ch from hook work 1tr, 1dtr into each of next 3ch, 1tr in next ch, 1htr in next ch, ss in last ch. Break off B.
2nd round Using A double, join to ss, 1ch, work along commencing ch working 1dc into each of first 4ch, 1htr into each of next 2ch, 2tr into each of next 4ch and 2tr into first tr, continue round work making 1htr into each of next 2 sts, 1dc into each of next 4 sts, ss to first ch. Break off A.
3rd round Using C double, join to ss, 3ch, 1tr in ss, 1 tr into each of first 3dc, 2 tr into next dc, 1tr into each of next 3 sts, 2tr in next st, (1tr in next st, 2tr in next st) 3 times, (1tr into each of next 3 sts, 2tr in next st) twice, ss to

3ch. Break off C.
4th round Using B double join to ss, 1ch, 1dc in ss, then continue round working 6dc, 5htr, 2tr in each of next 9 sts, 5htr, 6dc, ss to first ch. Fasten off.
Make second wing in same way.

Large butterfly wings

Using No.3·50 hook and B double, make 6ch. Join with ss to first ch to form circle.
1st round 2ch, work 11htr into circle. Join with ss to 2nd of first 2ch. Break off and leave.
Using No.3·50 hook and B double, make 6ch. Join with ss to first ch to form circle.
1st round 2ch, work 15htr into circle. Join with ss to 2nd of first 2ch, join one st of this piece to one st of first piece with ss. Break off B.
Using No.3·50 hook and A used double, join to 6th st of first circle from join of 2 circles counting to the right, 1ch, 1dc into each of next 3 sts, 1htr in next st, 1tr in next st, 1tr in first st of 2nd piece, continue round this circle working 2htr, 3tr, 2tr into each of next 3 sts, work 3tr, 2htr, 1tr, then continue round first piece working 1tr, 1htr, 3dc, 1dc in same place

as join, ss to first ch. Break off A.
Next round Using C double, join to ss, 3ch, continue round working 11tr, 2tr in next st, 1tr, 2tr in next 4 sts, 1tr, 2tr in next st, 11tr, 1tr in ss, ss to 3ch. Break off C.
Next round Using B double, join to ss, 1ch, (1dc in next st, 2dc in next st) twice, continue round working 4dc, 6htr, 1tr, 2tr in each of next 8 sts, 1tr, 6htr, 4dc, (2dc in next st, 1dc in next st) twice, ss to 1ch. Fasten off.
Make second wing in same way.

To make up

Skirt. Press under a damp cloth with a warm iron. Using No.3·00 hook and B, work 1 row dc round all edges. Fasten off.
Join centre front edge from top of shaped corners to waist.
Join elastic into a circle and sew inside waist edge using casing st.
Bolero. Press as given for Skirt. Join shoulder seams. Using No.3·50 hook and B double, work 1 row of dc round all edges, making 4 button loops on straight part of right front. Fasten off.
Sew one large and one small butterfly wing to each front.
Sew buttons to left front.

Pull-on hat

A quick little pull-on hat to crochet. Make it in navy, white or red to wear with the reversible coat and pin on a bright brooch somewhere just for fun.

Size
To fit average adult head

Tension for this design
About 1 loop to 1in over patt worked on No. 4·50 hook and using yarn double

---

Materials shown here
Wendy Double Knitting Nylonised
3 1oz balls
One No. 4·50 (ISR) Aero crochet hook

Hat

Using No. 4·50 hook and yarn double throughout, make 4ch. Join with ss into first ch to form a circle.
1st round *4ch, 1dc into circle, rep from * 3 times more.
2nd round *4ch, 1dc into loop, 4ch, 1dc into next dc, rep from * 3 times more.
3rd round Ss to centre of first loop of last round, *4ch, 1dc into next loop, rep from * 6 times more, 4ch, 1dc into ss.
4th round *4ch, 1dc into loop, 4ch, 1dc into next dc, rep from * 7 times more.
5th round Ss to centre of first loop of last round, *4ch, 1dc into next loop, rep from * 14 times more, 4ch, 1dc into ss.
Rep 5th round 3 times more.
9th round Ss to centre of first loop of last round, *4ch, 1dc into same loop, (4ch, 1dc into next loop) 4 times, rep from * 3 times more, 1dc into ss. 20 loops.
10th round Ss to centre of first loop of last round, *4ch,

1dc into next loop, rep from * 18 times more, 4ch, 1dc into ss.
Rep 10th round 10 times more.
21st round *2dc into next loop, 1dc into next dc, rep from * to end of round ending with ss into first dc.
22nd round 1ch, *1dc into back of next dc, rep from * to end of round, ending with ss into first ch.
Rep 22nd round 5 times more. Fasten off.

To make up

Darn in all ends neatly. Press lightly under a damp cloth using a warm iron.

▼ *Enlarged detail of the simple stitch used for the pull-on*

HOME SEWING

To make this elegant
patchwork table setting
see page 118

Crash Course Home sewing

Know How

Plain seam
With right sides together, machine or back-stitch to the distance of the seam allowance from edge of fabric.

Neatening seams
Either use the zig-zag on your machine or turn under the raw edge of seam allowance and machine close to edge, or oversew closely by hand.

Flat fell seam
Join as for a plain seam and trim one side of seam allowance to within ¼ inch of stitching line. Turn over raw edge to the other side and fold over trimmed edge. Tack and machine near the edge.

French seam
With wrong sides facing, pin and stitch seam ¼ inch from seam line inside seam allowance. Trim close to stitching and lightly press stitched seam towards front. Turn article inside out. Working on wrong side, pin, tack and stitch along original seam line, encasing raw edges in seam.

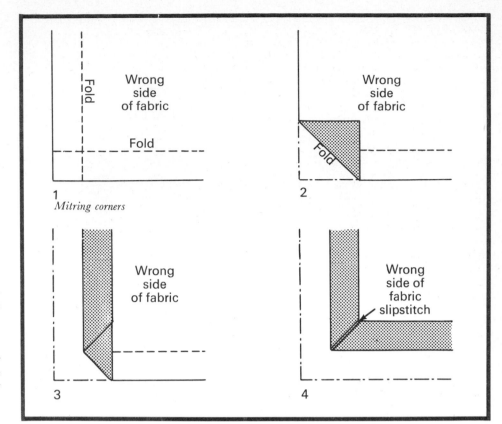

Mitring corners

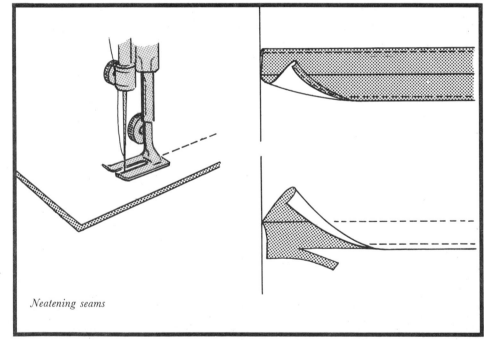

Neatening seams

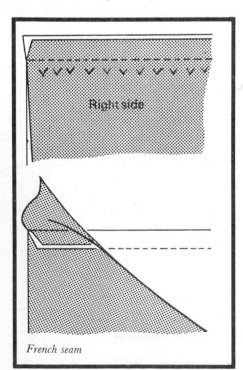

French seam

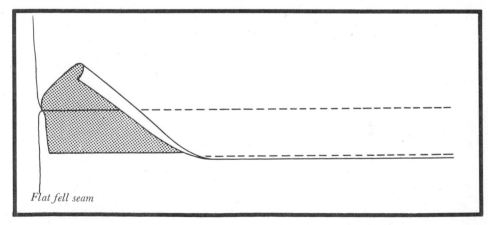

Flat fell seam

Piping

Piping cord can be bought in six thicknesses, depending on the purpose for which it is intended. Numbers 1 and 2 are fine cords used mainly for eiderdowns and cushions made of finer fabrics such as silk. Bias strips to cover these should be 1¼ inches wide; numbers 3 and 4 are for loose covers and cushions, bias strips for these should be 1½ inches wide; numbers 5 and 6 are used for thicker materials where a bolder edge is required, bias strips for these should be 1¾ inches wide. Measure length of piping required, then cut bias strips of the appropriate width to the length required, joining as shown in figure 1. As piping cord can shrink it is advisable to boil cord before using. Cover piping cord with bias strip (figure 2) using a piping or zipper foot on your sewing machine or just tack if you prefer. ¼ yard of 48 inch wide fabric will make about 7 yards of 1½ inch wide bias strip. Here is a very quick method of joining lengths of bias strips and will give about 5¼ yards of 1½ inch bias strips from ¼ yard 36 inch wide fabric (figure 3). To apply piping, tack the covered cord to right side of fabric, with stitching or tacking lines of piping matching stitching lines of fabric section. Clip outside edges of bias strip at corners and curves (figure 4). With right sides together stitch other section which is being joined using a piping or zipper foot on your machine.

1. Joining piping cord

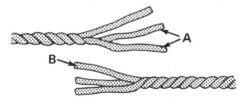

Cut cord to overlap 1 inch and unravel and cut away two strands A. Cut away one strand B.

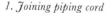

Twist remaining ends and stitch together.

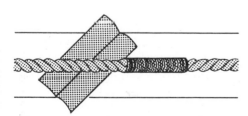

Final join in crossway strip and cord

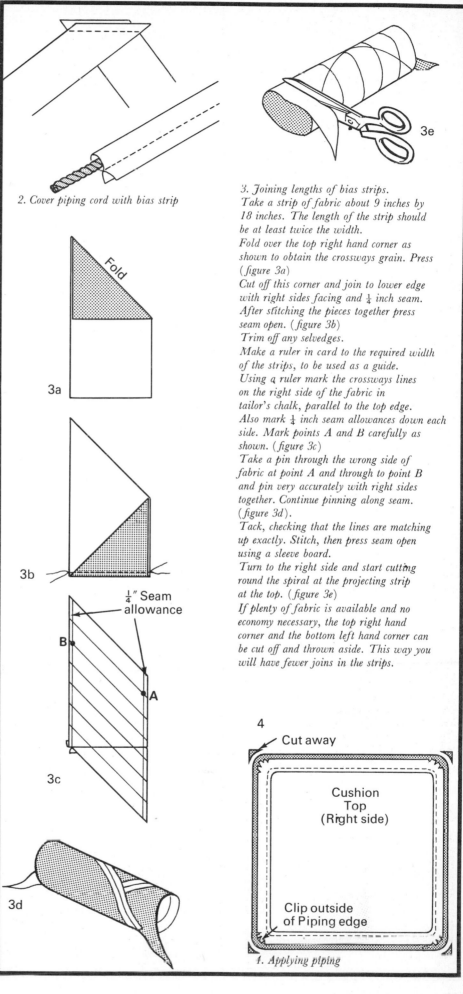

2. Cover piping cord with bias strip

Fold

3a

3b

¼" Seam allowance

B

A

3c

3d

3e

3. Joining lengths of bias strips.
Take a strip of fabric about 9 inches by 18 inches. The length of the strip should be at least twice the width.
Fold over the top right hand corner as shown to obtain the crossways grain. Press (figure 3a)
Cut off this corner and join to lower edge with right sides facing and ¼ inch seam. After stitching the pieces together press seam open. (figure 3b)
Trim off any selvedges.
Make a ruler in card to the required width of the strips, to be used as a guide.
Using a ruler mark the crossways lines on the right side of the fabric in tailor's chalk, parallel to the top edge. Also mark ¼ inch seam allowances down each side. Mark points A and B carefully as shown. (figure 3c)
Take a pin through the wrong side of fabric at point A and through to point B and pin very accurately with right sides together. Continue pinning along seam. (figure 3d).
Tack, checking that the lines are matching up exactly. Stitch, then press seam open using a sleeve board.
Turn to the right side and start cutting round the spiral at the projecting strip at the top. (figure 3e)
If plenty of fabric is available and no economy necessary, the top right hand corner and the bottom left hand corner can be cut off and thrown aside. This way you will have fewer joins in the strips.

4

Cut away

Cushion
Top
(Right side)

Clip outside
of Piping edge

4. Applying piping

Basic patchwork

You will need

Templates: made from metal, perspex or very stiff card, the exact size of the finished patch.

Stiff paper: for the paper shapes which are tacked into the pieces of fabric to hold the patches firm. These shapes must be very accurately cut.

Sharp pencil; scissors, sharp for fabric, old for paper; fine needle and steel pins; fine sewing cotton for cotton fabrics, silk for silk; mercerised cotton for tacking.

The fabrics to use Don't mix fabrics of different weights in the same piece of work and if the finished article is to be washed avoid mixing fabrics with different washing methods. Check that fabrics are colour-fast by taking a small piece, wetting it thoroughly and pressing it with a warm iron on to a piece of white material to see if the colour runs. Never use fabric that is at all worn as repairs are tedious. If using parts of used fabrics mixed with new, wash the new fabric to prevent risk of shrinking afterwards. If you are working with lightweight fabrics and find that the design needs a material

which is so transparent that turnings show through, use a bonded fibre fabric instead of a paper shape and leave it in the finished work. Avoid fabrics that fray and synthetics as they are difficult to fold.

Making the patches Using the template draw round with sharp pencil and carefully cut out the paper shapes. Press fabric if creased, then using the template as a guide cut out the patches, allowing $\frac{3}{8}$ inch extra for turnings. Try to keep two edges of the template parallel to the grain of the fabric as this strengthens the patch.

Pin the paper shape on the wrong side of the fabric and fold over the turnings. Starting with a knot or back stitch, tack round the patch, using one tacking stitch to hold down each corner. Finish off by making a small extra stitch to hold down each corner and take out pin.

Joining the patches Put the right sides of two patches together and oversew with tiny stitches along one edge. Start by laying end of thread along top of edge and sew over it from right to left. Push the needle through fabric at right angles to edge so that stitches

will be neat and patches will not stretch. To fasten off, work backwards for four stitches. Make sure corners are firm by sewing extra stitches over them. Sew together small units first and join up these groups later when you can plan the finished effect to your satisfaction.

To finish off When all the patches are sewn together, press the patchwork on the wrong side with a warm iron. (If you feel that the front of the work needs pressing too, take out the tacking, leave the paper shapes in to prevent the turnings from making a pressing mark and press gently on the right side). Take out all the paper shapes and tack round the edge of the work from the right side to hold the turnings of the edge patches secure. Press again on the wrong side to remove any marks left by the tacking.

To mount patchwork in place on main article, slip stitch with tiny stitches, all round. Remove edge tacking and press lightly just round edge. If the area of patchwork is quite large, catch it to the ground material at various points.

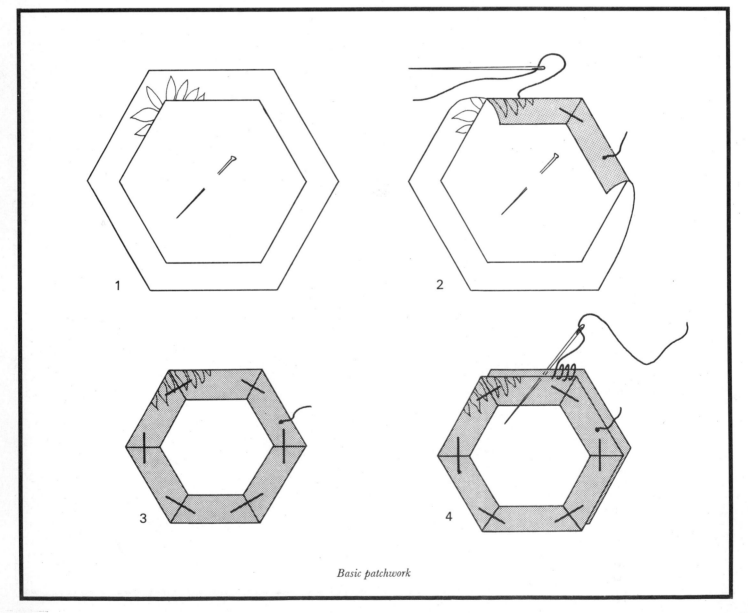

Basic patchwork

Other ways with patchwork

Try a padded velvet patchwork bedspread for a really opulent look. It's expensive, because you'll need new velvet, but at least it combines the virtues of a bedspread and a quilt. The patchwork is quilted onto a Terylene wadding backing and then lined. Prepare Terylene quilting underlay the same size as the bedcover lining and tack stitch any edges together with large cross stitches. Join your patches, and then pin and tack the patchwork section to the wadding. Quilt all round the join lines with straight or zig zag machine stitching through both the layers. When quilting is completed, place lining on bedspread, right sides together and stitch around outer edges, leaving gap for turning. Turn and slipstitch opening.

Another adaptation of normal patchwork is to make a bedcover in suede. Since leather does not fray, you do not need hems or paper backing. Simply butt the edges of the patches together and zigzag stitch on the right side. You may possibly have to use a special leather needle, depending on your machine and the weight of the leather scraps. For a comfortable finish, line the suede patchwork with a firm, non-slip fabric. With any scraps left over, you can make suede patchwork cushions to match.

Fabric-covered wall panels

Not strictly sewing, but a good way of giving your bedroom a co-ordinated look. You can cover slightly padded plywood panels with the same fabric as you've used for your bedspread, and thus do without a separate bedhead altogether. The panels must be cut to the length and depth of the bed by the desired height, preferably down to the skirting board. Narrow fillets of wood must be added around the outer edges of the plywood. These are to take the pins securing the fabric covers. Pad the panels lightly with unbleached wadding or foam plastic sheeting, and cover with fabric tacked to underside. If you machine neaten the fabric edges and use drawing pins to tack it to the panel, it will be easy to remove for washing. Make one or two tiny stitches to hold corners, then screw panels to walls.

Cushions can be decorative as well as useful. You can easily make an eye-catcher from a simple basic shape with clever use of fabric or trimmings.

Cushion fillings depend on the purpose for which the cushion is intended. Feathers and down are luxuriously soft while Terylene wadding is practical and washable. Kapok is useful for garden cushions. Ready cut foam pads can be used as floor cushions and you can adapt these to any shape you wish by cutting with a bread knife! Expanded polystyrene beads are used for filling floor cushions. If you plan to make your own cushion pads, use downproof cambric for feathers and down, sateen for other fillings.

Plain Indian cushions

Cushion cover is perfectly plain, without piping. Cut pattern to required size, then place on fabric to make the most of an exotic border print and give each cushion a slightly different look.

Decorated cushions

Trim plain cushion covers, without piping, with ribbon and braid applique. Cut out cushion covers to required size. Arrange trimming on right side of top before making up and stitch in place by hand, using very small prick stitch. Make your own patterns with various textures and shades of trimming or latticed velvet ribbons. Take trimming right over into seam allowances so that raw ends can be caught into seams when cushion is made up.

Piped cushions

Cut out cushion cover pieces to required size, cut bias strips for piping. For piping details, see page 99. Prepare and tack on piping to right side of cushion top. Tack on half of zip, wrong side uppermost, to centre of one side of cushion top. Stitch all round cushion top as close to piping as possible using a piping or zipper foot on the machine (figure 1).

Tack other half of zip, wrong side uppermost, to back of cushion and stitch (figure 2). With right sides facing tack the two halves of cushion together and stitch on previous stitch line for piping. Neaten ends of zip. Press cushion cover and turn to right side.

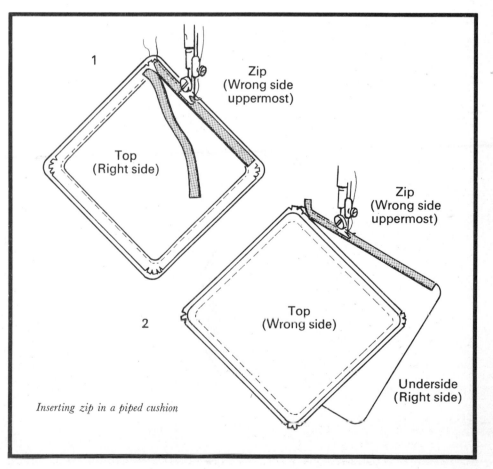

1

Zip
(Wrong side uppermost)

Top
(Right side)

2

Zip
(Wrong side uppermost)

Top
(Wrong side)

Underside
(Right side)

Inserting zip in a piped cushion

Piped bolster cushions

When choosing fabric for a bolster cover, avoid large patterns which might prove difficult to match at seams. Cut out body section and two round ends to required size, plus bias strips for piping. With right sides together, stitch long sides of rectangle at each end, leaving space in centre for zip. Tack this opening together and press seam. Tack zip in position, turn fabric tube right side out and back stitch zip firmly in place. Turn cover to wrong side again. Prepare piping and stitch to right side of bolster ends. Snip seam allowances of tube and piping end at intervals and stitch circles to tube, right sides together. Turn to right side through zip opening. If making your own pad, use down-proof cambric for feather and down fillings, otherwise calico or sateen. Make as bolster cover, omitting piping and zip. Fill through opening in side, then slipstitch opening to close.

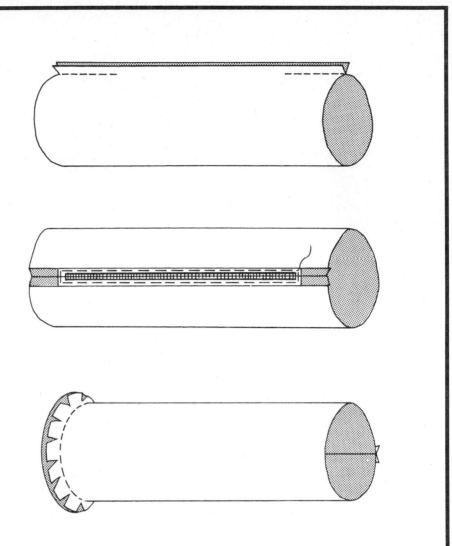

Making a bolster cushion
Cutting plan for 25 inch square piped box cushion cover, 4 inches deep. This would need 2 yards 48 inch wide fabric, 6 yards pre-shrunk piping cord and an 18 inch zip (left)

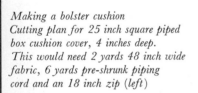

Boxed cushions

Cut out top and bottom cover sections, gusset and bias strips if required for piping. Cut back gusset strip 1 inch deeper if inserting zip. Pin all pieces together round cushion to check fit. Prepare piping (see Crash Course for details)
Cut back gusset in half along the length if using zip. Stitch seams at each end, leaving space for zip in centre. Insert zip. Otherwise, cushion can be fastened with press studs or cover can simply be slipped on cushion through a gap left in gusset seam which is then slipstitched together (see diagram). Stitch piping to top and bottom cushion sections snipping piping seam allowance at corners. Stitch gusset seams then stitch gusset section to the piped top section with right sides together. Snip gusset turning at corners. Attach bottom of cushion cover similarly. Turn right side out and press.

Covering foam cushion shapes

These can be bought ready made in various shapes and sizes. Before making top cover, make an inner cover from strong cambric or sheeting, use same method.

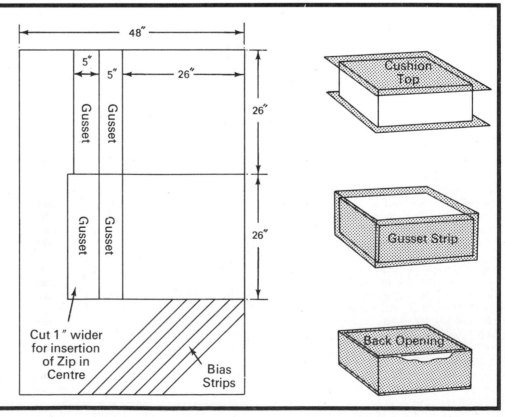

Curtains

Unlined curtains

Fabrics to choose

Some curtains look best with light filtering through them and good fabrics for this are coarsely woven linen and Dralon semi-sheers. It may be necessary to have a second, lightweight curtain close to the window if privacy at night is necessary. Furnishing fabrics usually measure between 48 and 50 inches wide, while sheers and nets come in widths from 36 to 120 inches wide.

Cutting and seaming

Widths of fabric seamed together must have perfectly matched patterns. The design must run continuously across the window and flowers should grow upwards. Remember all the windows in the room must match. Try and finish curtains with a whole pattern if possible.

Place fabric on a large flat surface for cutting. Straighten one end by drawing a thread and cutting along the line. Measure and mark with pins for first width. Fold fabric along line marked with pins and cut along fold. Match pattern if necessary, then cut off second width in same way. Continue until all widths have been cut.

If it is necessary to cut half a width, fold fabric lengthwise and cut along fold. Trim away selvedges and join widths and half widths if necessary with flat fell seams. Use a loose tension and a long machine stitch for seams. A good hem is required at sides to prevent curtains from curling back. Make ½ inch double hems at sides, tack and machine stitch or for a really good looking result stitch by hand. Turn up and hand stitch 1 inch double hem at bottom. Turn top edge of curtain over for 2½ inches and make a tacking line 1½ inches down from folded edge. Cut heading tape the length required plus 2 inch turning allowances. Pin and tack tape to curtain along the line of tacking. Turn ends of tape under, pulling out cord from turned in ends and tack along bottom edge of tape.

Machine both edges of tape to curtain. Stitch in the same direction to prevent any drag in the stitching which would show on the finished curtain.

Secure cords at ends of tape by knotting them together or stitching firmly. Draw cords up from middle of tape and ease fabric so that it is evenly gathered and the correct width for window. Knot cords in the middle and catch them to tape with one or two small stitches to prevent knot from hanging down. Gathers are easily released by cutting these stitches and undoing the knot when curtains need cleaning or laundering.

Wrong side of the finished curtain showing hems and applied gathering tape

Making up sheers and nets

As these fabrics are available in very wide widths, there is no need for widths to be seamed. Some nets are made with decorative, ready-finished hems when even less sewing is necessary. Use Terylene thread for man-made fabrics, a fine needle and tension of 10-12 stitches per inch if using a sewing machine. All sewing should be finished with a double back stitch to prevent stitches from unravelling. If fabric has a very open weave, place tissue paper underneath when machining and tear away the paper afterwards. If you pin Terylene fabric to paper when cutting out it will make it less slippery.

Hems should be double to prevent the ragged edges of net showing when curtains are hung against the light. If using muslin or cotton net remember that shrinkage is possible. Lower hem may be tacked and stitched temporarily until after curtains are washed. When they have shrunk curtains can then be let down.

Make ½ inch double side hems, snipping selvedges to prevent dragging. Neat selvedges may be left as they are.

Use a special lightweight heading tape for gathering up. Apply tape as previously described. If curtains are to be hung on wires, turn over top heading and make a casing as in diagram.

For lined curtains see p. 106.

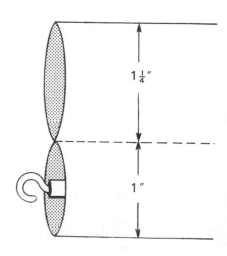

Bedcovers

Bedcovers

A bedroom can be glamorous and cosy or made to do double duty by day with neatly tailored bed covers that transform your bedroom into an elegant lounging area. Fabrics for bed covers should be firmly woven and reasonably crease resistant. Linens are good for pleated frills and leather gives a brand new slant to traditional patchwork quilts (see page 101).

Throw-over bedcover

Fabric will have to be joined to make up the necessary width, so begin by cutting fabric into two lengths, making sure that any design matches at seams.

Cut one length in half lengthwise, to make two half widths. Cut off selvedges so seams do not pull.

With right sides together, tack the two half widths on either side of centre panel so that seams lie on the top of either single or double bed and side panels are the same width. To allow the seams to sit on the top of the bed, centre panel may have to be trimmed.

Join pieces together with flat fell seams. If you wish to make rounded corners, place cover on bed and pin a line where fabric touches the floor at corners of front of bed. Use a large dinner plate or similar rounded object as a guide for shaping curves at corners. Cut away excess fabric, leaving 1¼ inch hem allowance. Turn in ¼ inch then make 1 inch hem all round bedspread. Ease in any fullness at corners with a line of running stitches which are pulled out when hem is turned up. Mitre corners at top of cover.

For bed with foot-board, make bedspread as before, but join half widths along length of bed only as shown in diagram. Mitre all outside corners.

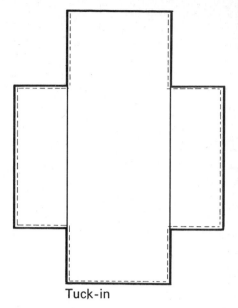

Bedcover showing tuck-in round pillow

Tailored bed-cover

This depends for its good looks on an absolutely perfect fit. It could also be used with a plain tailored valance on a conventional divan. Measure mattress and cut cover in exactly the same way as a boxed cushion. On a double bed, fabric will have to be joined to get the necessary width. Keep main width to centre of bed. Leave bed head corners open. Tack side and foot of bed gussets to top and bottom of cover and slip on to bed to check fit.

Prepare and attach piping in the usual way, snipping corner seam allowances. Pipe round sides and foot of cover only.

Join top of cover to head section of gusset with plain seam. Leave lower head edge open for entire length to allow mattress to be inserted. Neaten side edges of gussets. Stitch one inch wide facing to lower edges of back gusset and bottom of cover and sew on strong press studs, closely spaced, to fasten.

For matching bolster covers, see bolster cushions on page 102.

Duvet cover

Simplify bedmaking by using a continental quilt or duvet instead of conventional top sheets and blankets. A duvet is warm and snug, yet has only a fraction of the weight of ordinary bedding. The cover, made like a giant pillowcase, is detachable for laundering. Patterned covers can be teamed with toning pillows and lower sheets.

To make the cover, cut out the back and front, joining if necessary, also cut a 12 inch deep turn-in strip for pillowcase type closing (or you can face open end of cover with 1 inch wide tape and stitch on press studs to close).

On back and turn-in piece, machine stitch hems from A to B and from C to D on wrong side of fabric (figure 1). With right sides together, tack and machine stitch the turn-in to the front from EG to FH (figure 2). Press both seam allowances down together and make a flat fell seam. Fold down turn-in and tack from G to I and H to J (figure 3). With right sides of front and back together, make flat fell seams from BEG to LM, AFH to KN and LM to KN (figure 4). Turn to right side and press lightly.

Matching cords stitched round very tightly, give 'sausage' effect on bolsters.

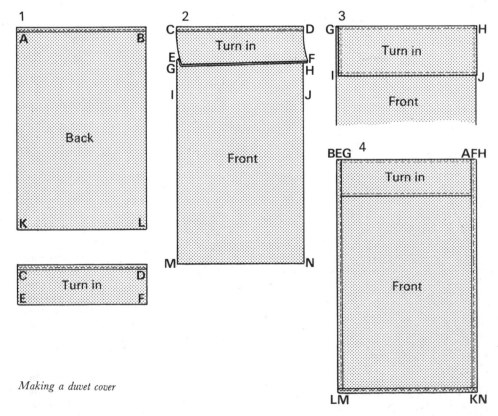

Making a duvet cover

Tablecloths

Fabrics to choose

Washable dress or furnishing fabrics such as cotton, linen, lawn, man-made fibre mixtures and cotton lace can all be used for tablecloths. PVC, although it does not hang as well as fabric, could be used for a nursery or kitchen table. Patterned or coloured sheeting is practical and needs no joining because of its extra width. If the surface of your table needs protecting from hot plates, you can buy heat-proof foam material to put underneath the cloth. This is easily cut to the exact size of the table top.

Making a round tablecloth

First cut a pattern. For this you will need a large square of brown paper with each side a little longer than the radius (or half the diameter) of the tablecloth to be made, a piece of thin string six inches longer than radius of cloth, some chalk and a drawing pin.

Find a large flat surface such as a wooden kitchen table or floor. Tie one end of the string round the chalk and measure radius of cloth plus seam allowance form the chalk along the length of string. Mark this measurement by pushing drawing pin through string. Lay the square of brown paper on to the flat surface and push drawing pin into top left hand corner of paper. Holding the drawing pin firmly, draw an arc with chalk from A at top right hand corner of paper to B at bottom left hand corner (figure 1). Cut along chalk line, this gives pattern for one quarter of the cloth, plus ½ inch seam allowance. Now prepare the fabric, joining widths with flat fell seams if necessary to make a central panel and two narrower side panels. The resulting square of fabric should have each side equal to the diameter of the tablecloth plus seam allowances.

Fold fabric into quarters and pin pattern to folds (figure 2). Cut curved edge. Unpin pattern and unfold fabric.

To make hem of cloth, snip little 'V' notches into edge at 1 inch intervals ⅜ inch deep (figure 3). Turn over the edge for ½ inch, pin and tack. The notches will close up to allow hem to curve (figure 4). Pin and tack bias binding over turned hem to cover raw edge. Stitch binding (figure 5) neatening ends by turning under ¼ inch and overlapping. Machine stitch any trimming required around edge of cloth on right side. If you are using lace or net, see details on page 103 for finishing off hems.

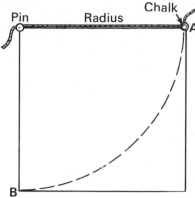

1. Making the paper pattern

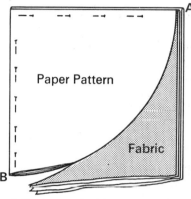

2. Cutting out the fabric

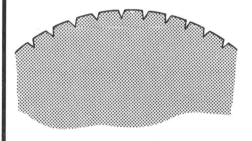

3. Snipping the hem edge

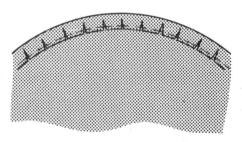

4. Turning over the ½ inch hem

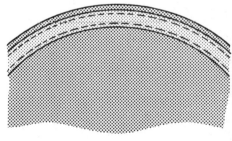

5. Stitching on bias binding

Making a rectangular tablecloth

Cut fabric to required size. If joins have to be made, use either a plain seam or a flat fell seam (preferable for fairly fine fabrics).

For a plain edge, turn in edge for ½ inch, then turn in again to make a 1½ inch hem. Mitre corners and hand-sew or machine stitch the hem.

For a trimmed edge, turn over fabric ½ inch on the right side and pin and tack trimming to cover the raw edge. Sew along both edges of trimming to secure it. If you have to join fabric, make the seams a feature. Sew plain seams, with wrong sides together, trim seam allowance to ¼ inch, then cover raw edges with braid or ribbon.

Patchwork tablecloth

Large-scale patchwork in a limited number of harmonizing colours and designs is quick to make up because of its size. First join triangles to make squares, then join squares to make strips and finally join strips into finished tablecloth. Use plain seams throughout and press seams open. To line the tablecloth, cut a piece of plain toning fabric to the size of the tablecloth. Place cloth and lining together, with wrong sides facing and tack. Bind the edges with contrasting binding with bows tied at the corners. You could obtain a similar effect by using dress fabric, ready-printed with a patchwork design.

Curtain linings and interlinings

Professionally made lined and inter-lined curtains are expensive to buy, so it is a useful accomplishment to be able to make them at home Making good curtains is not difficult, and with a little care really good results can be achieved.

Choosing the fabric

Choose the best quality fabric you can afford for your curtains, bearing in mind the aspect of the room and the existing colour scheme. Next to the carpet, curtains give the largest amount of colour and texture to a room so it is essential that the right fabric is chosen. Remember when choosing curtain material that some fabrics drape better than others. Always ask to see the fabric draped before you buy it—it can look very different lying flat on a counter. Check, too, whether the fabric is washable or needs dry-cleaning, whether it is shrink resistant and whether it will fade if exposed to strong sunlight.

Large abstract and geometric patterns are usually too overpowering for the average living room and if a patterned fabric is used it should be of a small design and in keeping with the size of the room. More fabric will be needed if it is patterned. A large pattern repeat can be expensive too; extra material must be allowed for matching the pattern and there is often some wastage.

Make quite sure that the pattern is printed correctly on the grain of the fabric as otherwise this can present problems when making the curtains.

Linings and interlinings

Linings

Linings are used in curtains for several reasons:

▲ *Properly lined, curtains will drape softly and evenly*

a. A lining helps a curtain to drape better.

b. A lining protects the curtain fabric from sun and light, and also from dust and dirt which damage the curtain fabric and make it wear out more quickly.

c. A lining can act as an insulator if a metal insulated lining called Milium is used. Milium will also make a curtain draught proof and is therefore particularly useful when used to curtain a door. Cotton sateen is normally used for lining curtains. This fabric is usually 48 inches wide and the colours most often used are fawn and white. Although cotton sateen does come in various colours, it is desirable to line all the curtains in the house with the same colour, if possible, to give a uniform effect from the outside of the house. An exception must be made for curtains with a white background where a matching white lining is more suitable.

Interlinings

It greatly improves the appearance of most curtains if they are interlined. This makes them drape better and shows off the texture or pattern of the fabric to best advantage. Interlining gives a curtain a padded luxurious look and is certainly well worth the extra trouble involved.

Bump and domette are the usual fabrics used for interlining curtains although a flannelette sheet would be quite suitable. Bump is rather like a very thick flannelette sheet and is fawn or white in colour and fluffy. Domette is similar to bump but not quite so fluffy. Both materials are good insulators.

Interlined curtains are very expensive if made professionally. All the work is done by hand and this adds considerably to the cost.

Detachable linings

It is now possible to make curtains with detachable linings if a Rufflette curtain lining tape is used. This makes it possible to wash or dry-clean the linings separately, which is quite useful as they often seem to need cleaning before the curtains do.

When a detachable lining is used the curtains and linings are made separately but are attached to the same hooks.

Although detachable linings are very useful in some rooms they do not have quite the professional finish of hand made lined curtains. These have the linings stitched to the curtain round the two sides and bottom. An attached lining prevents dirt and dust from getting in between the curtain and lining fabric, giving more protection to the fabric and making it last longer.

Measuring and cutting curtain fabric

Measure the window and track carefully with a wooden yardstick. A yardstick is invaluable when making curtains because an accurate measurement cannot be obtained with a tape measure.

Curtains should either hang to the sill, 2 to 4 inches below the sill or to the floor. Never use in-between measurements as they will look out of proportion. Floor length curtains should hang to within $\frac{1}{2}$ inch of the floor.

Allow $1\frac{1}{2}$ to 2 times the width of the track for a standard heading, but allow 2 to $2\frac{1}{2}$ times the width of the track if using a fancy heading such as a Regis or Deep Pleat heading.

For top and bottom hems, allow 6 to 8 inch turnings altogether. More fabric must be allowed if a pattern has to be matched, and it is advisable to allow one pattern repeat on each curtain for this purpose.

To get a straight line for cutting draw a thread if possible. If a pattern happens to be badly printed and is not printed on the grain of the fabric, cut to the pattern and not to the thread. Plain material should always be cut to the grain.

Place the fabric on a large table, preferably rectangular, with the selvedge running down the longer edge of the table. The edges of the table can then be used to square up the curtains if a thread cannot be drawn.

Cut out each curtain, being careful to match patterns where necessary.

Cut off all selvedges as this prevents the curtains from puckering.

If it is necessary to join widths of fabric together, the join should come at the sides of the window. Use a plain seam and press it open.

Making a lined curtain

Cutting the lining

Do not try to draw a thread on lining sateen, but square it up on a table or use a set square.

Cut off all selvedges.

Cut the lining the same size as the curtain fabric, joining if necessary. Make a plain seam, with right sides facing, and press open.

Preparing the curtains

1. Turn in $1\frac{1}{2}$ inches at sides and bottom of the curtain fabric.

2. Mitre the two bottom corners.

3. Using matching thread, serge round sides and bottom of curtain.

Locking in the lining

A lining is locked to the curtain fabric to prevent the lining falling away from the top fabric when the curtain is hanging.

First place the curtain on a table with the wrong side uppermost. Lay the lining on top of the curtain, wrong sides together. The raw edges of the lining should be flush with the curtain all round, so trim the sides and the lower edge by the required amount.

4. Fold back the lining at the centre of the curtain and lock lining to curtain as shown. Make long loose stitches to avoid puckering. The locking should start and end 6 to 8 inches from both top and bottom.

To help you work the stitches in a straight line you may find it helpful to make a crease mark on the lining with your thumb.

Locking is usually worked at 12 inch intervals across a curtain. So in a curtain 48 inches wide there would be three rows of locking, one down the middle of the curtain and one to each side 12 inches in from the edge.

5. When the locking is completed, fold in lining at sides and bottom of curtain for 1 inch, mitring corners. Tack.

Make a line of tacking stitches across the curtain 6 inches from the top. This is to keep the lining firmly in place until the heading tape is attached.

Slip stitch lining to curtain round the two sides and bottom of curtain using matching thread and leaving about 6 inches unattached at the top.

Making interlined curtains

Cutting the interlining

The interlining, or bump, is cut to the size of the finished curtain. It is taken to the edge of the curtain and extends up to the top under the heading tape. This means that the interlining should be cut 3 inches narrower than the curtain fabric to allow the edges of the curtain to be turned over $1\frac{1}{2}$ inches.

6. If a join needs to be made in the bump, a lap seam should be used. As bump tends to stretch it is advisable to stitch with two rows of zigzag machine stitching. Alternatively the lapped seam can be sewn by hand.

Position the bump on the curtain $1\frac{1}{2}$ inches up from the lower edge and $1\frac{1}{2}$ inches in from both sides. Lock the bump to curtain fabric in the same way as the lining was locked to the curtain (see figure **4**).

7. Turn in the sides and lower edge $1\frac{1}{2}$ inches, herringbone curtain to bump. Attach the lining as before but this time lock the lining to the bump.

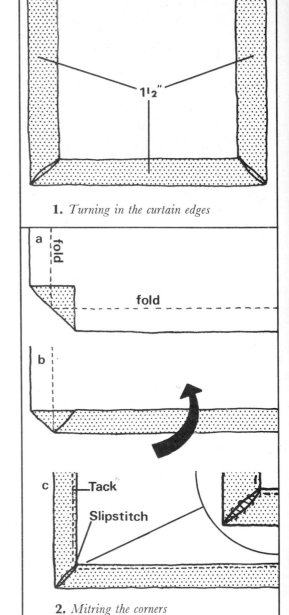

1. *Turning in the curtain edges*

2. *Mitring the corners*

Curtain headings

Choice of heading

There are so many different types of curtain track and heading tape available that it is advisable to give your curtain headings some thought and to decide on the effect required. Decorative curtain poles are very much in fashion again and can look most attractive used with pleated or deeply gathered heading tapes.

Many different effects can be achieved by using the new tracks and headings and it is advisable to find a soft furnishing or hardware shop which displays some of them.

If a lined or interlined curtain is being used, make sure when choosing a track that it is strong enough to take the weight. Interlining adds considerably to the weight of a curtain.

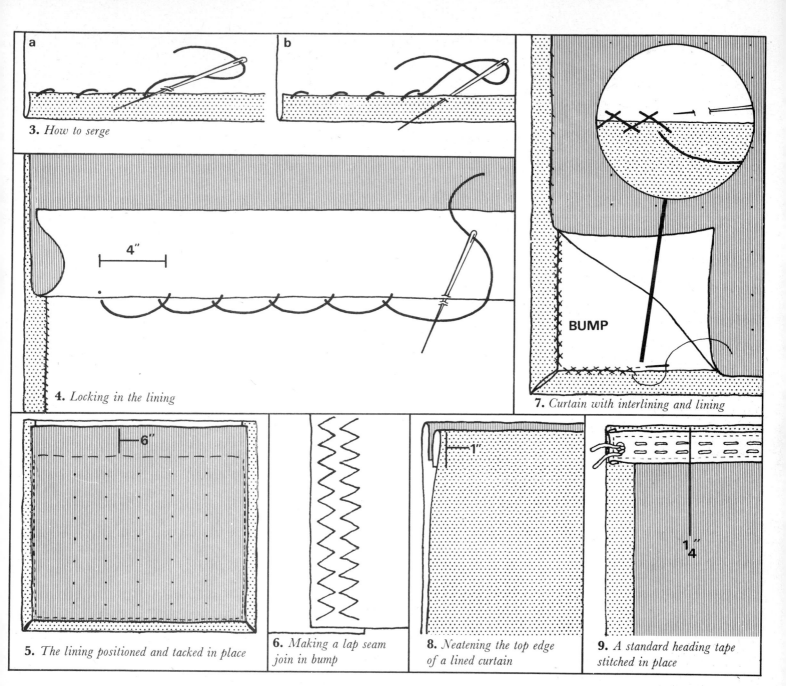

a

b

3. *How to serge*

4″

4. *Locking in the lining*

BUMP

7. *Curtain with interlining and lining*

6″

5. *The lining positioned and tacked in place*

6. *Making a lap seam join in bump*

1″

8. *Neatening the top edge of a lined curtain*

1¼″

9. *A standard heading tape stitched in place*

Tapes and hooks

Here are some of the most widely used heading tapes:

□ Standard heading tape: this is a 1 inch wide tape for even gathering on all types of fabrics where a simple gathered heading is required. The tape comes in a variety of colours and has two cords for drawing up the fullness.

□ Kirsch Easypleat and Rufflette Deep Pleat tape: these are for making pinch pleats easily. No cord is used for drawing up the tapes, but special deep pleat hooks are required and the pleated effect is achieved by inserting the prongs of the hooks in the pockets on the tape. Single, double or triple pleats can be made.

When using the tapes it is necessary to work out carefully the quantity of fabric required and the number of sets of pleats in each curtain. Rufflette produce a tape and fabric calculator for this purpose.

□ Rufflette Regis tape: for making pencil pleats. No special hook is required for this tape, the standard plastic hook is used. The tape is made of nylon and is hard wearing and strong, standing up well to washing and drycleaning. Two cords are used to draw up the tape and so form the pencil pleats.

□ Rufflette Hi-Style tape: this is another way of making pencil pleats. Three cords are used for drawing up the pleats and special Hi-Style hooks are used.

Various detailed leaflets are available on these and other heading styles and can be obtained from most soft furnishing counters.

Applying standard heading tape

Size up curtains to obtain the correct length of tape required. Don't forget to use a wooden yardstick for this.

Trim the top edge of the curtain, leaving about 1 to 2 inches for turnings.

8. Turn in top of curtain and lining 1 to 2 inches as shown. Cut the heading tape to curtain width plus 1 inch.

9. Position and tack heading tape to top of curtain, turning ½ inch under at each end.

Pull out the cords from turned in ends. Machine along top and bottom of tape and along the two sides, taking care not to catch in the cords.

Tie the cords at one end and draw up the cord at other end to the required width. Do not cut off the cord but wind it on to a cord tidy for a neat finish. The cords can then be released easily for dry cleaning or washing.

Press curtains, insert hooks and the curtains are ready for hanging.

Roller blinds

Roller blinds are a pretty window dressing and very practical, but it's important that they work well. Here's how to make perfect roller blinds that work, from home kits.

Measuring for roller and fabric

If the blind is to hang outside a window recess, allow an extra six inches on the width of the roller. Measure the recess accurately if the roller is to hang inside it.

When calculating fabric, the finished width should be 1 inch less than the roller, so that the material clears the brackets on either side.

Natural selvedges can be used for the edges of a blind, but hemmed edges do help the blind to hang better. Allow 1½ inches on each side for hems.

Calculate the length of the blind by putting the roller in the brackets and then measuring from the point where the blind is attached to the roller to the extent of the required drop. Add 8 inches to this measurement to allow for the roller and for the lath casing. If the fabric is to be seamed, allow for matching the pattern in calculations.

Choosing the right fabric

Fabrics should be smooth and firm; holland is ideal and can be purchased in various widths, in patterned designs and in plain colours. If other kinds of fabrics are considered to match a room scheme, choose carefully and avoid materials which are loosely woven or of thick or very thin texture. Closely woven cotton fabrics work quite well. It is usually advisable to have ordinary fabric professionally stiffened for making roller blinds – it helps the movement of the roller, but small blinds can be stiffened at home by using iron-on Vilene. This has to be done very carefully however, because constant wear may cause the bond to break and 'bubbles' will appear.

PVC coated fabrics available in a wide range of widths are ideal for kitchens and bathrooms and for a small blind (not more than 21 inches wide). Vinyl coated wallpaper can be used. Treat the back of it with spray-on waterproofing to make it last longer.

The most professional-looking blinds are those made from a single width of material. Seaming doubles the bulk of fabric on the roller and could cause it to pucker when the blind is rolled up. This doesn't mean that seaming won't work, but care must be taken when choosing the type of fabric.

If a window is particularly wide and fabric isn't available in a width sufficient for the roller, choose either a plain fabric or an all-over pattern which can be used sideways, seaming selvedges together.

Cutting the fabric

This is probably one of the most important stages in making a roller blind. If the material isn't cut accurately and true to the grain, it will roll unevenly and become caught in the bracket.

To make sure the fabric is square, draw a weft thread or cut along it. If this isn't possible, place the material on a table top, matching the selvedge or long edge with the edge of the table. Stick the material on the table top with adhesive tape. The straight of the short edge can be found by folding it over the end of the table. Crease the material and cut it. Straighten both ends in the same way.

Making up the blind fabric

For a smooth running blind, it is important that the side hems are as flat as possible. One simple turn should be used wherever possible, but if the fabric shows a tendency to fray it might have to be turned under twice. Try to choose fabrics which don't fray – it's better in the long run.

Press hems really well before machining and remember that plasticised fabrics cannot be pressed. These will have to be creased manually. Pins shouldn't be used on these fabrics either, they make holes which show. Use adhesive tape instead.

Stitch the side hems with machine stitching using a large zigzag stitch – the actual raw edge should lie in the middle of the zigzag. If your machine won't work zigzag, machine two rows close to the edge.

To make the lath casing, turn over ½ inch to the wrong side. Turn a 1½ inch hem and press carefully. Machine stitch ⅛ inch from the edge to form the casing. Trim the lath so that it is ½ inch shorter and insert it.

When working with PVC or plasticised fabrics remember that tacking will mark the fabric. Use adhesive tape to prepare

Striped blind to match divan cover top and cushions hung cafe curtain style from a rod

Appliqué a design on a roller blind, such as this border, to match painted window surround

the hem for machine stitching. To avoid uneven machine stitches on these fabrics, stick a strip of tissue paper on both sides of the material and stitch through them. Tear the paper away afterwards. A dusting of talcum powder on the surface helps too. Hems can be turned without stitching, using a latex adhesive, but unless great care is taken puckers will show on the right side of the fabric.

A tip about working with stiffened fabrics: they'll crack unless they are kept as flat as possible, so work on a large table.

Finishing the roller blind

Follow the manufacturer's instructions for putting up the brackets and fittings and for cutting the roller and lath to size.

Lay the prepared blind fabric flat on a table, right side up. Turn under ¼ inch

An elegant window effect, using the same fabric for both roller blind and curtains

A roller blind designed for maximum daylight colour keyed to the surrounding wallpaper

Pelmet, wallpaper and roller blind in the same pattern and colourway for room impact

Important: Study the diagrams for hanging the blind very carefully ▼

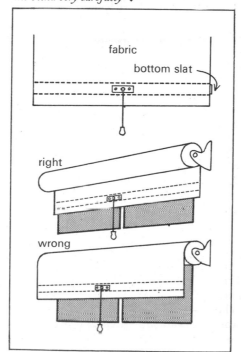

on the raw (upper) edge if the fabric is reasonably thin. Leave it raw if the fabric is too bulky. It is very important that the blind is put onto the roller the right way round. Study the diagram carefully before starting to fix the blind to the roller. The fabric must hang closest to the window. If it is fixed on the wrong side of the roller, as soon as the blind is pulled for the first time, the spring will break and the roller blind will be ruined.

Work from the centre of the roller out towards the ends, and tack the blind to the roller.

If, for any reason, such as an ugly reverse to the fabric, it is desired that the roller be hung in reverse (this is one way, incidentally, of making the actual roller invisible from the room) this can be done by reversing the roller fittings so that the spring end is to the right of the window. A special fitment called a

strap bracket is then required for the other end.

Tensioning the roller

When the blind is properly fixed to the roller, roll it up and place the blind in the brackets, and pull it down to see if it hangs properly.

If it doesn't run back up smoothly, the spring may need tensioning. Take the blind down again and hand roll it. Keep doing this until the tension is right. Be sure not to over-tension, because if the blind is released in such a way that it snaps up the spring can be damaged.

Trimming roller blinds

The bottom edge of a blind can be decorated with various trimmings, rick-rack braid, cotton lace, bobble braid or appliqué. Machine stitch trims into place or, if the fabric is suitable, stick on with latex adhesive.

café curtains

Café curtains originated in France in the old coffee houses and are still to be seen in restaurant windows in many parts of Europe. They usually cover only the lower part of the window, and are used when privacy is required without blocking out daylight. Café curtains are hung in various ways, sometimes they are simply hung on a rod; or they can be gathered on tape for different effects, or can be made with cut-out headings and suspended from hooks or rings. So café curtains are not only functional, they can be decorative too, and make a striking change from the traditional half window nets. Trimmed with braid or matched to roller blinds or pelmets, they are particularly effective in rooms where the windows are extra large and where traditional curtains would be very expensive.

It is worth remembering that café curtains will allow the maximum amount of light into a room; light coming from nearer the ceiling is more valuable than light coming in at a lower level.

Measuring for café curtains

To measure for café curtains first decide on the 'drop' required. This is the finished length of the curtain. It will probably be determined by the amount of privacy needed, but café curtains usually cover half the window. Sometimes two curtains are used, one for the top half of the window and one for the bottom half. These are called 'tiered cafés' and are both made in exactly the same way.

Café curtains usually hang either to the sill or 2 to 4 inches below the sill. Sometimes they hang to the floor, perhaps to cover a radiator, but they should never fall in between unless a window seat or other piece of furniture has to be cleared or they will look out of proportion to the window.

Measure the track with a yardstick or

steel ruler, not a tape measure as these tend to stretch and an accurate measurement cannot be obtained. Allow $1\frac{1}{2}$ times the length of the track if a lined curtain with a scalloped heading is being used. $1\frac{1}{2}$ to $2\frac{1}{2}$ times the length of the track will be necessary if the curtain is unlined or a fancy heading tape is being used. The width needed depends on the weight and texture of the fabric—lighter more delicate fabrics look better with extra fullness.

Allow 6 inches for turnings (i.e. for top and bottom hems), if using a standard or deep heading tape. For scalloped headings more allowance is necessary for the scallop. Allow extra material if using a patterned fabric and work out the repeats to see if the curtain lengths will cut economically. Remember when choosing the fabric to ask the size of the pattern repeat as large repeats can be expensive.

Linings

It is not usually necessary to line café curtains. If they are unlined the maximum of light will filter through. However, some fabrics may look more effective used with a light cotton lining and less fullness, particularly where a pattern can be shown to advantage.

Tracks and headings

Decorative brass poles or wooden or plastic rods can be used for hanging café curtains in exactly the same way as traditional curtains. Brass or plastic or wooden rings can be sewn to the top of the curtain or clip-on rings can be used.

Scalloped café curtains

These instructions are for unlined café curtains.

Fabric requirements.

To calculate the length decide on the drop of the curtain. Also decide on the depth of the scallop required and add this measurement plus 5 inches for turnings to the curtain length.

Allow $1\frac{1}{2}$ times the measurement of the track for the width of the curtain depending on the fabric used. In the case of a scalloped heading less fullness may be necessary to show up the shaped top to advantage. Sheer material is not usually suitable for scalloped headings for this reason.

Sides and hem

First cut off the selvedges to avoid pulling, and fold and tack $\frac{1}{2}$ inch double hems at both sides of the curtain. Turn up the bottom hem 2 inches and make a 1 inch double hem.

Hand or machine stitch side and bottom hems. Hand stitched hems look better

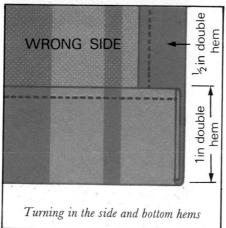

Turning in the side and bottom hems

and hang well, and really are worth the extra trouble.

Working out scallops

To make a paper pattern for the scallops, cut a piece of paper as wide as the curtain fabric and about 12 inches deep. A piece of wallpaper or lining paper is ideal for this.

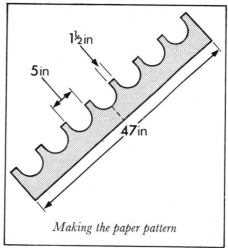

Making the paper pattern

Draw a line across the paper about 3 inches down from the upper edge. Decide at this point how deep you want the scallops to be. Draw another line the depth of the scallop below the first line. Now mark the paper vertically down the middle because it is easier to plan scallops on a narrower width. Plan one half of the width first and then trace off another half for accurate placing.

Use a pair of compasses and a pencil for drawing scallops and remember that the shape of the scallop will depend on where you place the compass point. Experiment by moving the point until you have a segment that fits your plan. Start drawing the scallops and leave $1\frac{1}{2}$ inches between each scallop and approximately $1\frac{1}{2}$ inches at each end of the curtain. When all the scallops have been drawn in, cut the scallops out for a pattern.

Making up the curtain

With right side of fabric up, fold over top of the curtain to the depth of the scallops plus 3 inches. Tack.

Place and pin the prepared paper pattern to the fold and mark round the scallops with tailor's chalk. Remove the pattern and machine stitch on the marked line. Cut out scallops $\frac{1}{4}$ inch outside the stitching line. Clip into curves and trim corners diagonally.

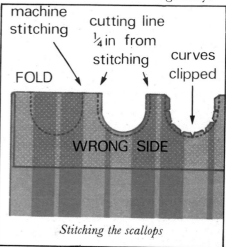

Stitching the scallops

Turn facing to wrong side and press well. Finish the lower edge of the facing with a $\frac{1}{2}$ inch hem and slip stitch hem at the sides of the curtain.

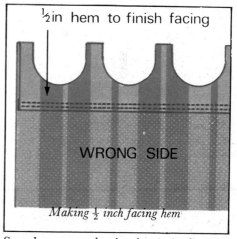

Making $\frac{1}{2}$ inch facing hem

Sew brass or plastic rings to the top of the scallops using buttonhole twist thread.

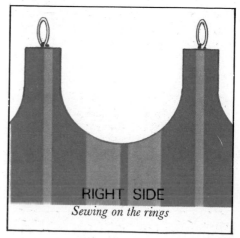

Sewing on the rings

Making pretty pillowcases

Pillowcases are cheap and easy to make, whether plain or with a decorative edging. Choose a fabric to match, tone or contrast with sheets and bedroom décor to make an interesting and unusual focal point.

Plain pillowcases with a 'housewife' flap are very straightforward and easy to make. The flap is cut in one with one side of the pillowcase.

To make a pair of plain pillowcases, finished size $18\frac{1}{2}$ inches by $28\frac{1}{2}$ inches, you will need: $1\frac{1}{4}$ yards of 70 inch wide cotton sheeting.

Cut the piece of cotton sheeting into two so that each piece measures 70 inches by $22\frac{1}{2}$ inches. Each piece makes one pillowcase.

Making a plain pillowcase

Cut each piece of cotton sheeting as follows:

One piece measuring 35 inches wide by $19\frac{1}{2}$ inches deep (piece A)
One piece measuring $31\frac{1}{2}$ inches wide by $19\frac{1}{2}$ inches deep (piece B)

1. Make a narrow hem on one short side of piece A.
2. Make a one inch hem on one short side of piece B.
3. Place piece A on piece B, right sides facing and matching corners x and y (diagram 1).
4. Fold the flap of piece A over B (diagram 2).
Stitch all round three sides of the pillowcase through all thicknesses, leaving the top edge unstitched (diagram 3). Trim corners, turn to right side and press.

Plain edged pillowcases

These are a little more complicated to make and require more fabric. To make a pair of pillowcases, finished size including edge $31\frac{1}{2}$ inches wide by $22\frac{1}{2}$ inches deep, you will need $2\frac{5}{8}$ yards of 45 inch wide fabric.

Cut the fabric as shown in diagram 4.
1. Turn a narrow hem on one short side of piece B. Fold this side six inches to the wrong side and press (diagram 5).

2. Place piece B, wrong sides of fabric facing, on top of piece A, centring it exactly (diagram 6).
3. Fold sides and bottom of piece A along fold lines, turn a narrow hem and tack to piece B, mitring corners (diagram 7a and b). Machine stitch.
Fold down top edge, turning under a narrow hem so that the hem just meets the fold of the flap piece. Mitre the corners, tack and machine stitch, making sure that the stitches do not catch the flap of B.
Trim corners, turn to right side and press.
Finish off the edge of the pillowcase by working two rows of zigzag machine stitching with the machine set to satin stitch, placing the rows $\frac{1}{2}$ inch apart (diagram 8).

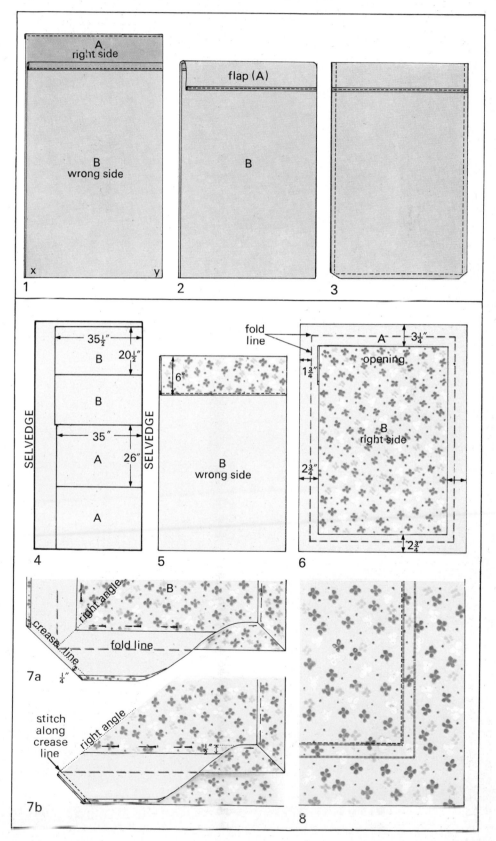

Make this ingenious tidy-all to hang behind a door or on a wall. It is the perfect way to keep safe easily mislaid household items – from brushes to screwdrivers.

You will need:

- [ ] 1¼ yards 36 inch wide navy cotton sailcloth
- [ ] 3 yards white bias binding
- [ ] 1 20 inch length of ¼ inch diameter bamboo or dowel
- [ ] matching thread

Cutting out the pieces

From the navy sailcloth cut one piece 22 inches by 29 inches for the back of the tidy, and for the pockets two pieces each 15 inches by 9 inches, one piece 14 inches by 6½ inches, one piece 11½ inches by 6¼ inches and one piece 6 inches by 4½ inches.

To make the tidy

Turn under and stitch a 1 inch hem on the two long sides of the big piece of sailcloth, then turn under one short side and hem in the same way, using matching thread. Turn under the remaining short side for 1 inch and stitch a ¼ inch hem, leaving a ¾ inch channel to take the bamboo or dowel.

The lower pockets Bind one long side of each of the two 15 inch by 9 inch pieces of sailcloth with bias binding. Turn under and stitch a ½ inch hem on the two short sides of each of these two pieces. With the bound edge uppermost, position the pieces in the lower corners of the backing fabric, so that each piece is ½ inch from the bottom and ½ inch in from the edge.

Stitch the outer side seams, keeping the pockets lined up with the edge and bottom of the main fabric piece. Position and pin the pocket inner edges 2 inches apart. Tack and stitch.

The pocket pleats Make one equal pleat in either side of the two pockets, lining up the top fold with the pocket side seam and keeping the fabric smooth

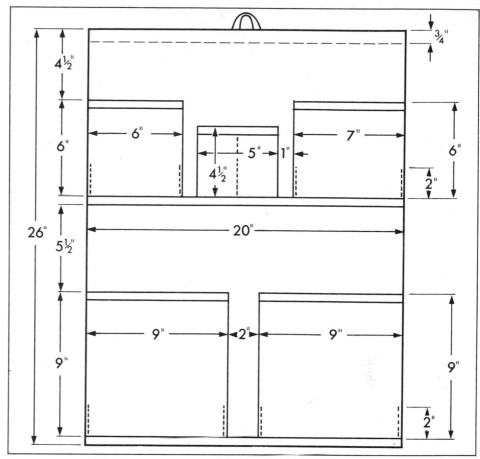

Finished measurements of the tidy, not including side pleats

across the centre of the pocket (Fig. 1). The pocket fronts should measure 9 inches across when pleated on either side. Pin, tack and sew each pleat for 2 inches up the side seam, working from the bottom edge of the pocket.

Place a 21 inch length of bias binding across the bottom of the tidy, to cover the bottom edges of the two pockets. Tack and sew along the upper and lower edges of the binding, stitching through all thicknesses of fabric. Neaten the ends of the bias binding by turning them to the back of the tidy and stitching securely.

The top pockets Bind one long edge of the 14 inch by 6½ inch piece of fabric with bias binding. Turn under and stitch a ½ inch hem on the short sides. Place this pocket ½ inch from the right hand edge of the backing piece, with the lower, unbound edge 6 inches above the lower right hand pocket. Pin, tack and stitch the outer side seam. Pleat the pocket as described for the bottom pockets, so that it measures 7 inches across when completed. Tack and stitch the inner side seam. Stitch up each pleat for 2 inches, working from the bottom of the pocket.

Bind one long edge of the 11½ inch by 6¼ inch piece of fabric with bias binding. Turn under and stitch a ½ inch hem on both short sides. Position this pocket ½ inch from the left hand edge of the

backing piece, with the lower, unbound edge 6 inches above the bottom left hand pocket. Pin, tack and stitch the outer side seam. Pleat the pocket as previously described so that when completed it measures 6 inches across. Tack and stitch the inner side seam. Stitch up each pleat for 2 inches, working from the bottom of the pocket.

Bind one long edge of the 6 inch by 4½ inch piece of fabric with bias binding. Turn under and stitch a ½ inch hem on both short sides. Position this piece centrally between the two top pockets. Stitch the pocket down flat around the three unbound edges. Run another seam vertically up the centre of the pocket, to form a subdivision.

Cut another 21 inch length of bias binding and place it across the bottom of the three top pockets. Stitch down as described for the lower strip of binding, turning the ends of the bias binding to the back to neaten.

Finishing off the tidy

Cut a 3 inch length of white bias binding and fold it in half. Place it at the top centre back of the tidy and stitch it down very firmly with navy thread, making sure that you do not stitch through the fold. Press the tidy, then slip the bamboo or dowel into the fold at the top.

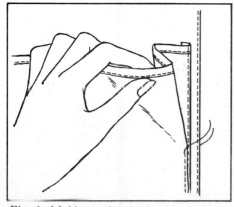

Fig 1 Making a pleat in the side of a pocket

New setting for patchwork

Here is a new way with patchwork to make a delightful table setting. The patchwork place mats are sewn onto the tablecloth and are interlined with heat-resistant Milium and bonded fibre fabric to protect a polished table. Matching patchwork-trimmed napkins complete the setting. The materials given here are for making the tablecloth illustrated, but alternative colour schemes can be worked out from the quantities given.

To make a tablecloth with a finished diameter of 72 inches and two 12 inch square napkins you will need:

- ☐ 2 yards 72 inch wide unbleached calico
- ☐ 9 yards 1 inch wide bias binding in dark brown

For the patchwork place mats and napkin trims you will need:

- ☐ $\frac{1}{4}$ yard 36 inch wide plain dark brown fine poplin
- ☐ $\frac{1}{4}$ yard 36 inch wide plain gold cotton batiste
- ☐ $\frac{1}{4}$ yard 36 inch wide patterned lawn, predominantly dark brown
- ☐ $\frac{1}{4}$ yard 36 inch wide patterned lawn, predominantly light brown
- ☐ $\frac{1}{2}$ yard 36 inch wide Milium lining
- ☐ $\frac{1}{2}$ yard 36 inch wide heavy bonded fibre fabric interlining
- ☐ Tracing paper, stiff card, several sheets of writing paper
- ☐ Scalpel or craft knife, metal straight edge
- ☐ Paper glue

Preparing the fabrics

Wash all the fabrics in hot water. Iron while still damp with a medium hot iron. This will prevent any uneven shrinkage after the cloth is made up. Press any creases out of the Milium and bonded fibre fabric interlining and press any creases out of the bias binding. Fold the bias binding in half along its length and press carefully, making a very sharp crease where it is folded. The edges of the bias binding are left folded.

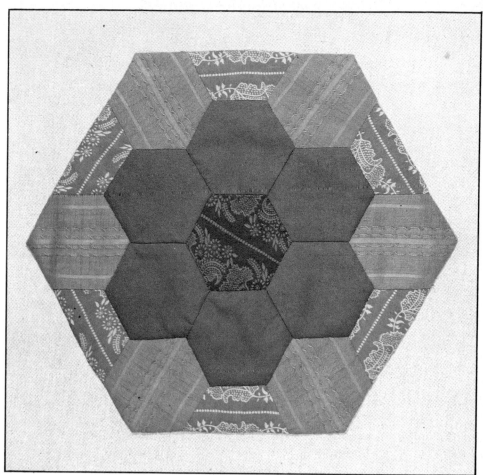

▲ Arrangement of the patchwork shapes for the place mat
▼ The patchwork trim in place on the napkin

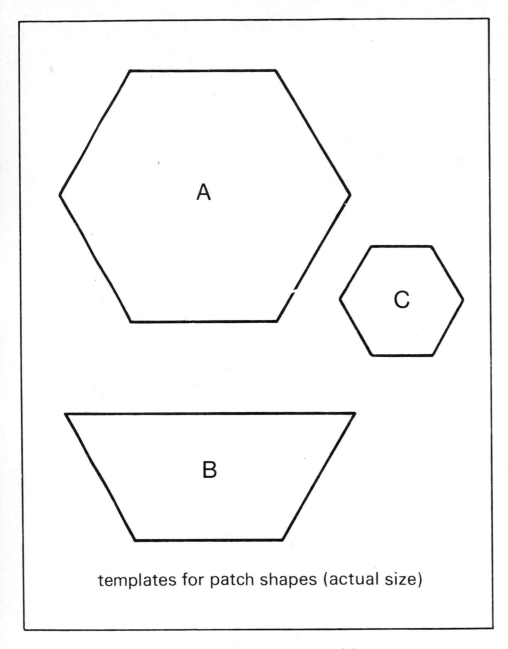

templates for patch shapes (actual size)

1. Cutting out the circular cloth from a folded square of fabric

4a. The patchwork fabric tacked to the paper

Making the tablecloth and napkins

Fold the fabric in half across its width and then in half again to form a square 36 inches by 36 inches.

1. Cut out a circle as shown in the diagram.

2. The napkins are cut from the fabric corners left over. If preferred, the remaining two corners of fabric can be used to make two spare napkins. There will be enough patchwork fabric to trim all four napkins, but an extra 3 yards of bias binding will be required.

Press the squares of calico carefully, pulling them into shape at the corners if they are at all distorted.

Binding the tablecloth and napkins

3. Tack and machine stitch the folded bias binding over the raw edge of the tablecloth as shown. Press.

The napkins are bound in the same way as the cloth, but the corners are mitred by folding the bias binding. Press the

napkins carefully.

Templates and papers for patchwork

All tracing and cutting for patchwork shapes must be as exact as possible. Trace the templates for patch shapes A, B and C. Glue the tracings to the stiff card and cut along the traced lines with a scalpel or craft knife against a metal straight edge, cutting through both tracing paper and card.

Use the card templates to cut out the papers. Place the templates onto the writing paper and draw round them with a sharp pencil held at a right angle to the paper. Cut out the papers.

Cut 26 papers in shape A, 12 papers in shape B and 14 papers in shape C.

Preparing and making the patchwork

Pin the papers to the fabric with at least $\frac{1}{2}$ inch turning allowance showing round

each patch for shapes A and B and $\frac{1}{4}$ inch turning allowance showing round each patch for shape C.

Cut out round each paper leaving the correct turning allowances.

Tablecloth

Using shape A, cut 12 brown poplin patches, 12 gold batiste patches and 2 dark brown patterned patches.

Using shape B, cut 12 pale brown patterned patches.

Napkins

Using shape C, cut 6 dark brown patterned patches, 6 gold batiste patches and 2 pale brown patterned patches. (If four napkins are being made, double the amounts of both papers and patches).

4. Pin and tack the turnings on all the patches. Remove the pins.

Join the patches by placing two together, right sides facing, and oversewing one edge with tiny stitches. Join further

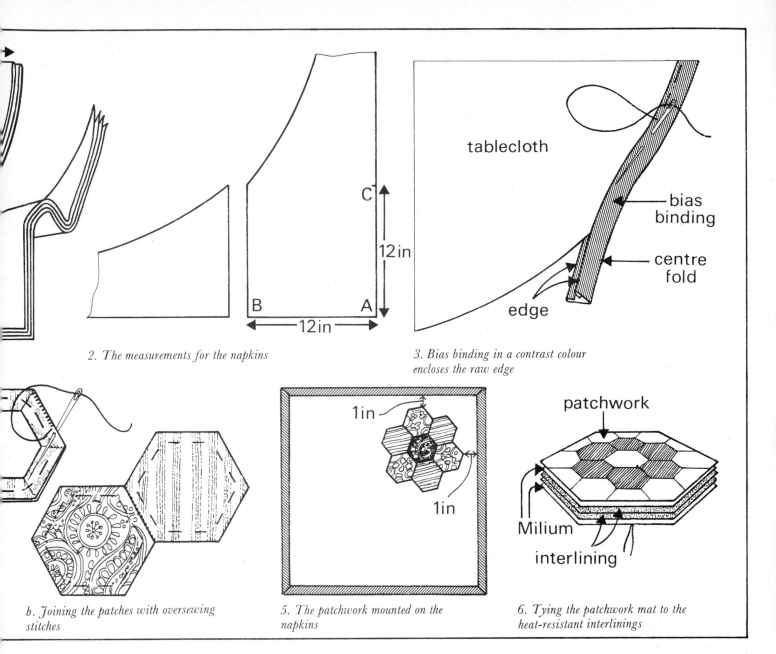

2. The measurements for the napkins

3. Bias binding in a contrast colour
encloses the raw edge

b. Joining the patches with oversewing
stitches

5. The patchwork mounted on the
napkins

6. Tying the patchwork mat to the
heat-resistant interlinings

patches in the same way. Follow the detail pictures of the tablecloth and napkin patchwork arrangement.

Press the joined patchwork carefully on both sides.

Remove the tacking stitches and pull out the papers. Retack the edges, making sure that the turnings are folded under neatly.

Mounting the patchwork
5. The napkins. Place the finished napkin patchwork on one corner of the napkin one inch from each edge, and pin through the central patch. Pin and tack the outer edges of the patchwork, placing the pinheads at the edge and points towards the centre to avoid puckering, and keeping the napkin smooth and flat.

Press the patchwork again and slip stitch it to the napkin round the outer edges. Remove the tacking stitches.

For each tablecloth place mat, place the finished patchwork face downwards on the Milium lining. Draw round the patchwork, remove the patchwork and re-draw the outline $\frac{1}{2}$ inch smaller all round. Cut this shape out.

Using the Milium shape as a pattern, cut two interlining shapes from the heavy bonded fibre fabric.

6. Place the patchwork right side down on a flat surface. Place a Milium shape, silver side down, on top of it. Place two bonded fibre fabric interlining shapes on top and then the other Milium shape, silver side down. Make sure that all the pieces are exactly centred on the patchwork and that there is a $\frac{1}{2}$ inch turning allowance of patchwork showing round the edges.

Tack all the layers together. Turn the layers over so that the patchwork is on top.

Using matching thread, 'tie' all the layers together by inserting the needle from the back, through all the layers and out at the top through one of the points of the centre patch. Leave at least 4 inches of thread free underneath and return the needle through, close to the first hole, back through all the layers and out again at the back. Tie the loose ends together in a firm knot.

Tie down the corners of all the patches in the same way.

The tablecloth. Place the tablecloth over the table so that the overhang is equal all round. Mark the position of the edge of the table on the tablecloth with tacking stitches.

Place two patchwork mats opposite each other, 2 inches from the tacked line which marks the edge of the table. Pin the tied patchwork onto the tablecloth, keeping the cloth and patchwork absolutely flat. Tack and then slip stitch the patchwork into place.

Remove all the tacking and re-press on the wrong side.

A fine edge

You will need:

To make a tablecloth 69 inches square and two napkins 14½ inches square

- [ ] 4 yards 36 inch wide patterned cotton fabric (if the fabric has a very dominant pattern, buy enough extra fabric to match it up on the join)
- [ ] 5 yards 36 inch wide plain cotton fabric in a toning colour
- [ ] matching sewing thread
- [ ] pair of compasses, yard rule, tape measure, pencil

All measurements must be absolutely accurate, so check everything twice. Trim along one edge of each piece of fabric by pulling a thread and cutting along this line. Take all subsequent measurements from this straight edge.

To make the tablecloth

Working on the patterned fabric, draw a thread to get a straight edge and cut off exactly 71 inches of fabric. Measure off a second 71 inch piece and trim the edge straight by drawing another thread. If the fabric is patterned and needs to be matched, do this before cutting the second piece.

Working on the plain fabric, measure off and cut another two 71 inch lengths in the same way. Cut the remaining plain fabric into four 15½ inch squares, for the napkins.

Place the patterned fabric pieces right sides together and stitch, taking a ½ inch seam allowance. The joined piece should measure exactly 71 inches square. Press the seam open. Join the patterned fabric in exactly the same way. Place the patterned fabric right side up on a large flat surface, with the seam running horizontally. Place the plain fabric on top, right side down, with the seam running vertically. Match the edges exactly. Pin and tack the two layers together, running lines of tacking stitches from A to B, A to C, A to D, A to E, A to F, A to G, A to H, and A to I (Fig. 1). Remove the pins. Working on the plain side, measure 1 inch in from the edge EC and draw a line, using a pencil and the yard rule, parallel to and one inch from the edge. Repeat with the other three sides. Measure 3 inches in from the edge EC and draw a line, using a pencil and the yard rule, parallel to and 3 inches from the edge. Repeat with the other three sides (Fig. 2).

The scalloped edging

The scallops each measure 4 inches across and 2 inches in depth. They are set 1 inch apart with 14 scallops on each side of the cloth. Set the compasses so that the lead point is exactly 2 inches from the metal point. The scallops are

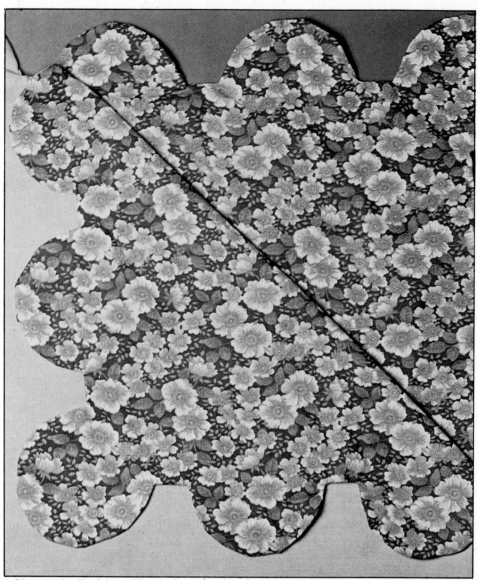

▲ *Close-up detail of the scalloped edge, showing the plain reverse side*

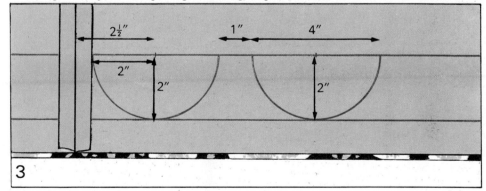

drawn from the inner line with their lowest point touching the outer line. Working on the plain side, mark a point on the inner line 2½ inches from the central seam. Place the compass point on the mark and draw a semi-circle to form the first scallop. The edge of this scallop falls ½ inch from the central seam. From the right-hand edge of the first scallop measure a point 3 inches further along the inner line. Mark this point and draw the next scallop from this (Fig. 3). Continue drawing scallops in this way

until the corner is reached. The final scallop on each side curves right round the corner (Fig. 4). Continue until scallops are drawn right round the cloth. Tack all round the scalloped lines. Using a short machine stitch, stitch round all the scallops on the pencilled line. Remove tacking, trim and clip (Fig. 5).

Press back the seams along three scallops on one side and unpick the stitching on these scallops. Turn the cloth right side out, then retack and hem the opening. Press the tablecloth carefully. It is

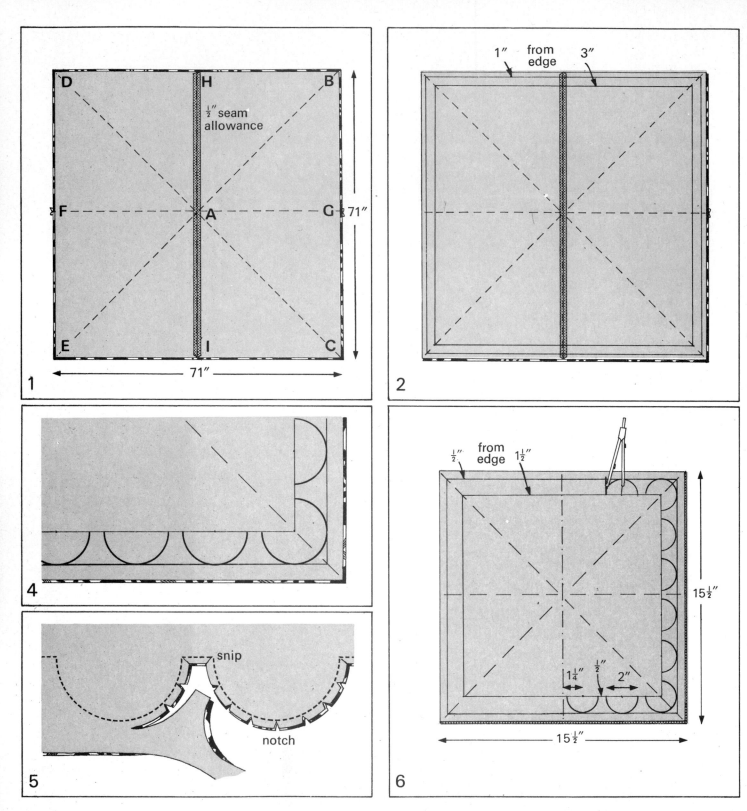

important to do this unpicking and re-sewing to keep the shape of the scallops even.

If desired, two rows of top-stitching can be worked around the scallops $\frac{1}{4}$ inch and $\frac{1}{2}$ inch in from the edge. This helps to keep the scallops in position, and makes pressing easier.

The napkins

To make the napkins, tack two 15½ inch squares right sides together as shown in Fig. 1. The scallops are 1 inch deep and 2 inches across, and are set $\frac{1}{2}$ inch apart. Draw a line parallel to each edge and $\frac{1}{2}$ inch in from the edge. Draw a second line parallel to each edge and 1½ inches in from the edge. Fold the napkin exactly in half, and mark the centre line. Measure 1¼ inches from the centre line along the inner line and mark this point. Set the compasses so that the lead point is exactly 1 inch from the metal point. Place the metal point of the compasses at the marked point and draw a scallop.

From the right-hand edge of the first scallop mark a point 1½ inches along the inner line and draw the second scallop from this. Continue drawing scallops in this way right round the square. Tack and stitch the scallops exactly as described for the tablecloth. Turn the napkin to the right side and hem the opening. If desired, a double row of top-stitching, in a toning or contrasting colour, can be worked around the scallops $\frac{1}{4}$ inch and $\frac{1}{2}$ inch from the edge of the napkin.

124

Cushion comfort

Giant, squashy cushions make a cheap and attractive alternative to conventional furniture. Make this huge, segmented cushion in a riot of contrasting colours for a brilliant effect, or in subtle, toning shades for a restful room.

125

You will need:

- [ ] 1 yard 60 inch wide jersey in navy
- [ ] 1 yard 60 inch wide jersey in beige
- [ ] 1 yard 60 inch wide jersey patterned in beige/brown

or

- [ ] 1¼ yards of the same colours in 36 inch wide fabric
- [ ] 1 8 pint can of Polybeads and 1 4 pint can of Polybeads

Making the cushion

Draw up a paper pattern from the graph, in which one square equals one inch. Cut one bottom section and one top section from the navy jersey. Cut two navy side segments, two beige side segments and two patterned side segments. With right sides together, pin one long side of a navy segment to one long side of a beige segment. Tack and machine stitch, taking ½ inch seam allowance. Stitch a second seam ⅛ inch in from the first, for strength. Pin the long side of a patterned segment to the beige segment, and stitch in the same way. Continue alternating the segments until a circular shape is formed.

With right sides together, pin and tack the top section in position. Stitch the seam twice, as for the sides. Pin in the bottom section and stitch in the same way around 5 sides. Trim seams and press flat. Turn the cushion through to the right side.

Preparing the filling

To prepare the Polybeads, take a large saucepan with a close-fitting lid. Check how many pints it holds. Leave 2 inches of water in the bottom of the pan, and bring it to the boil. When the water is boiling, pour in one heaped teaspoonful of Polybeads for every pint of the saucepan's capacity. Stir the beads after one minute and again after three minutes, replacing the lid securely each time. After four minutes 'cooking' the beads are ready. Ladle the beads into the drying bag supplied, and repeat the process.

Close the neck of the drying bag and leave the beads to dry for four days in a well-ventilated place.

Filling the cushion

Use a rubber band to attach one end of the cardboard tube supplied with the Polybeads to the drying bag. Push the other end of the tube through the unstitched cushion seam and pour in the Polybeads. Fill the cushion two-thirds full. Pin the final seam and oversew it. It is worth keeping the cardboard tube and drying bag for removing the Polybeads when the cover needs to be cleaned.

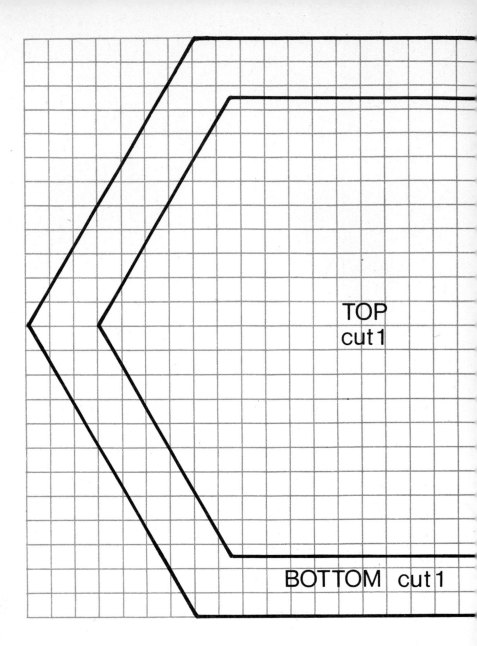

TOP
cut 1

BOTTOM cut 1

graph pattern for floor cu
one square=one inch

seam allowance includ

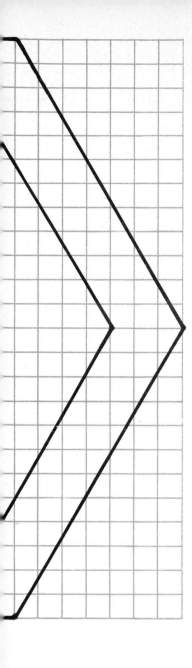

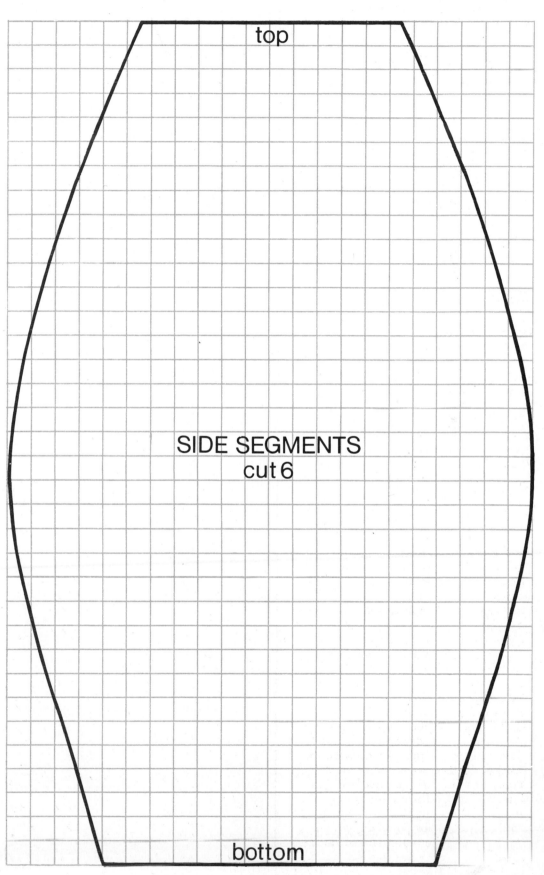

top

SIDE SEGMENTS
cut 6

bottom

Crazy patchwork cushion

One side of this beautiful cushion has been covered in crazy patchwork. This form of patchwork is completely random, not only in the choice and arrangement of the different fabrics but also in the way that the irregular shapes of the patchwork pieces themselves are built up. Here, scraps of silk, velvet and satin fabrics have been used.

In many ways the technique is closer to appliqué than patchwork, as the pieces are stitched to a ground material and not to each other. The raw edges are turned under and each piece is pinned onto the base, slightly overlapping its neighbours. No papers or templates are used in the process.

The patchwork pieces look most attractive sewn onto the backing fabric with different embroidery stitches. As long as the pieces are anchored securely, the embroidery can be as simple or elaborate as you wish. In this piece, simple lines of cross stitch, chain stitch, stem stitch and blanket stitch have been worked in embroidery threads chosen to contrast with the fabrics. Little sequins or pearls sewn into the centre of a patch, or a cluster of beads on a rather plain material, also add interest and variety to the work.

If you decide to work a large piece of patchwork in this manner, it is probably best to complete sections in squares or rectangles and then join these together, rather than try to handle one enormous piece all at once.

The advantage of crazy patchwork is that any scraps of material that are too small to be used up in a geometric design can be incorporated with larger pieces, and the random effect can be used to create a truly vivid splash of colour.

To make this beautiful quilt
see page 152

EMBROIDERY

Crash Course Embroidery

Enlarging a design

With a ruler and pencil, enclose the outline drawing in a square or rectangle. Draw centre lines horizontally and vertically, divide these again, and draw a separate rectangle to the size required and divide in the same manner. Copy the outlines from the smaller to the larger squares. Letters and figures help to identify the squares.

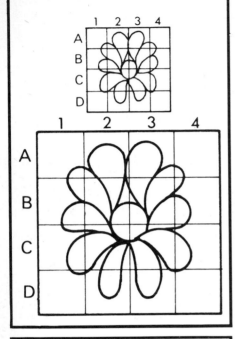

To prepare the fabric

Oversew the edges of the fabric to prevent fraying during working.

To work from a chart

With running stitch, mark the centres of the linen or canvas. Each square on the chart represents a stitch. Follow the pattern on the chart and work each stitch on to the canvas. When working in cross stitch, begin at one end and work the design and background in rows. To begin, work a few stitches, leaving a length of thread on the surface. Thread into the back of the worked stitches, and fasten off in the same way. Or, where possible, bring the thread to the front of the canvas and leave. The next stitches will cover the loose thread left at the back, and the thread at the front is cut off.

To trace the drawn outline

Tack horizontal and vertical centre lines on to the fabric. Trace the given outline on to tissue paper, mark the centres, and pin the tracing into position on the fabric. Use the tacked lines as a guide. With running stitch and one strand of cotton, outline the design. Use the colour of the finished embroidery. A smaller stitch on the surface than underneath allows for the easy removal of the tissue paper. Remove the pins and tear the paper away carefully. Round-ended tweezers are useful for pulling off any fragments of tissue paper caught in the stitches. The guide lines and colours are laid out clearly on the fabric and they become part of the embroidery and need not be removed when the work is finished. For organdie: draw the traced line on to the tissue paper with a pen. Pin to the BACK of the organdie. The design can be seen through the fabric and outlined with running stitch. There is no need to pierce the paper.

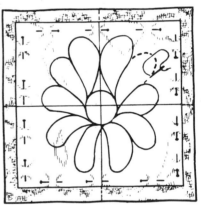

Embroidery frames

A frame is helpful for the even working of some techniques. There are two basic types, the ring and the slate frame.

The ring frame. It consists of an inner and an outer ring, the outer has an adjustable screw, and the fabric is gripped taut between the two rings. Easily positioned and removed it is useful for working on a large area and is also useful when an embroidery has a variety of stitches, some of which may be worked more easily in and some out of the frame.
Rings with a screw clamp for fixing to the table, or with a stand, are the most useful as they leave both hands free for working.
To mount the fabric: separate the inner and outer rings, and place the fabric over the inner ring. A square of tissue paper will prevent the rings marking fabric. Push the outer ring into position, and tear away the centre of the tissue paper and tighten the ring screw. To avoid stretching the fabric, ensure that the weave lies vertical and horizontal.

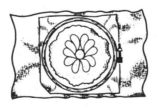

The slate frame. This holds the whole area of the fabric firmly and is obtainable in several sizes from 18″ wide.
When the fabric is mounted, support the frame between two tables or a table and chair. Both hands should be free to work, one above and one below the fabric. The diagram shows how to mount the fabric. Mark the centres of the webbing at each end of the frame, make a single turning at each end of the fabric to be mounted and mark the centre. Place the centres right sides together and oversew fabric to frame. Begin at the centre and work outward, and repeat at the opposite end. Insert the side slats and fix in position

with split pins. The fabric should be taut, but not strained. Tack a hem along the sides, laying in a piece of string to strengthen it. Begin at the centre and, with a packing needle and fine string, lace the side of the fabric to the side supports. Tighten evenly at each side and knot the string firmly.

Pressing and stretching

To press embroidery – pad a large, flat surface with a blanket and ironing cloth. Lay the embroidery face downward and press with a damp cloth.

To stretch canvas work – pad a board with clean, damp blotting paper. Place the canvas work face upward on the blotting paper, and starting at the centre fix one end of the canvas with drawing pins. Align the horizontal threads with the edge of the board. Repeat at the opposite end and at the sides. Leave to dry for at least twenty four hours.

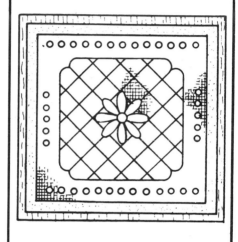

To prepare embroidery for a picture frame

Cut a piece of cardboard or hardboard to fit the frame, mark centres and match with the embroidery. Turn the edges of the fabric over the card and stitch firmly in place with strong thread. Start from the centre and work outward. Tighten the thread so that there is an even pull on the fabric and fasten off securely, and repeat for the two remaining sides. When choosing a frame allow sufficient depth to prevent the embroidery pressing on the glass. Embroidery shows to best advantage unglazed.

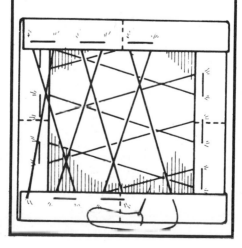

Making up with an interlining

(Belt, spectacle case, shopping bag and handbag etc.) The basic method is the same for each.

Cut interlining, eg Vilene, to fit within the hem lines. Lay the decorated fabric face downward and pin the interlining in

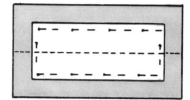

position. Snip at the corner as shown so that the fabric lies flat. With open herringbone, stitch the seam allowance to the interlining, cut a lining the same

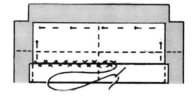

size as the decorated fabric, turn in slightly more than the seam allowance and slip stitch into position.

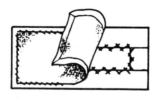

Mounting a spectacle case into a metal frame

Follow the interlining and lining instructions. Measure the side opening of the metal frame and mark the measurement onto the embroidery. Oversew the side seam as far as the opening. Fit the embroidery to the inside of the frame and with a strong thread oversew through the punched holes.

Marking circular cloths and mats

Measure and mark the centre of the fabric. Cut a length of string, measuring from the centre to the required extent of the circumference. Fasten a pencil at one end and a drawing pin at the other, fix the drawing pin at the centre mark and draw the circle, keeping the string taut.

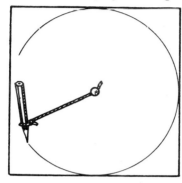

For a small circle, cut a strip of card, at one end make a hole for the pencil point and at the other fix a drawing pin. It may be used in the same way as the string and will accurately repeat a series of mats of the same size.

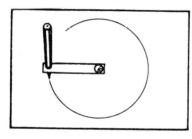

Joining the fabric for a large cloth. If the fabric has to be joined, stitch the seam and press open before marking the circle. Two side seams are less conspicuous and the circle may be cut from slightly less fabric if two side seams are stitched. Cut the length required, and divide the remaining piece down the centre. Match centres of each piece and join the two half pieces, one each side of the whole. Press seam open, mark the circle as shown, and cut the circle and stitch the hem when the embroidery is complete.

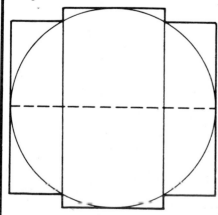

Stitch library

The stitches shown are easily worked. Allow the threads to lie easily on the surface of the fabric. It should not be pulled out of shape by the stitch. To prevent threads from knotting: With a woollen thread stitch in the direction of the natural lie of the wool. Run a hand along the thread. In one direction the hairs lie flatter than in the other. For 6-strand floss: cut the length of thread, not more than 18 inches for a trouble-free needleful. Divide at the centre for the number of strands required. They will separate easily without knotting.

Stem stitch

Use for straight and curved lines. Notice the position of the thread for left- and right-hand curves. Begin on the traced line and work inward when used to fill a shape.

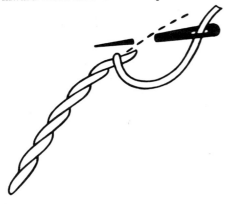

French knot

To make a well-shaped knot, as the needle returns into the fabric, keep the thread taut.

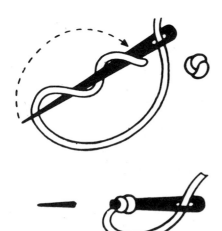

Cross-stitch

For an even appearance, work one row below another. The stitches should cross in the same direction throughout the work.

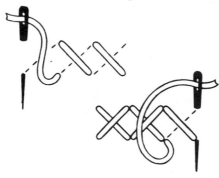

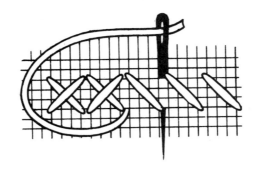

Herringbone stitch (closed)

The movements of the needle are the same as for open herringbone stitch, but the needle comes out close to the previous stitch.

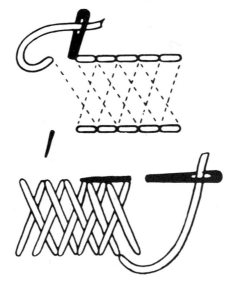

Herringbone stitch (open)

Work vertically upward, or from left · to right.

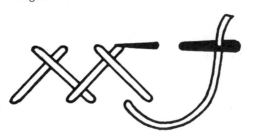

Feather stitch (half)

The needle goes in to one side of the previous stitch. The position of the needle and thread is the same as in chain stitch.

Long and short stitch

Work it as in the diagram for a broken surface. For a smooth surface, work the first row as shown. On the second row, bring the needle UP through the previous stitch. Best worked in a frame.

Rumanian stitch

Take a long stitch across the shape to be worked and tie it down with a slanting stitch.

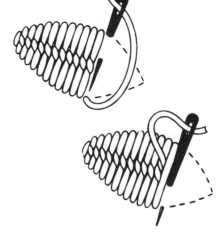

Running stitch

Use the stitch as an outline, or in rows as filling stitch.

Satin stitch

Most easily worked in a frame. The movements of the needle are simple. Hold the thread in position before inserting the needle. The stitches will lie smoothly side by side. For a raised effect, first pad with running stitches.

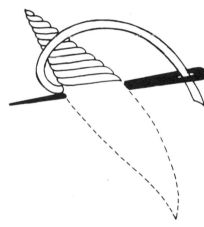

Surface satin stitch

Economical in thread. In relation to satin stitch, it has a slightly broken surface.

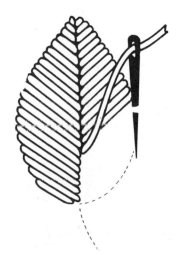

Slip stitch

Holds the hem in position with very little stitching showing on the right side.

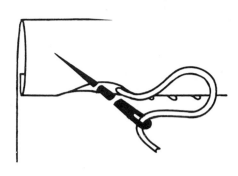

Blanket stitch

The thread loops underneath the needle which lies vertically in the fabric.

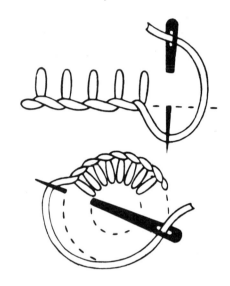

Chain stitch

The needle returns to the place where it came out. The thread loops under it. Chain stitch may be worked in straight or curved lines. Use it in circles or rows to fill a shape. When used as a filling, begin at the outer edge and work inward.

Detached chain

Each stitch is held down separately with the working thread. Finish a row of chain stitch in this manner. The method for making a point in a line of chain stitch is also shown.

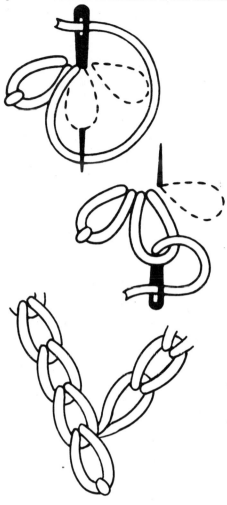

Couching

More easily worked with the fabric in a frame. With a large needle, take a thick thread to the back of the fabric. On the surface, tie it down with small stitches in a color-matched, thin thread. If the embroidery is to be laundered, stitch at frequent intervals to prevent the line pulling out of shape. Work it as a single line or in rows.

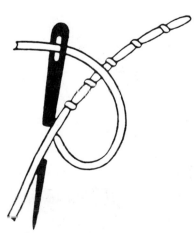

How to 'read' patterns

Colours

Some embroidery patterns are given with precise colour references – as for example, with the shading of leaves and flowers where the relationship between tones is important. With other designs, however, colour is entirely a matter of personal preference. But do remember to be generous with the amount of yarn you use. Embroidery should always be rich and colourful.

Stitches

The fully illustrated Stitch Library on pages 132 and 133 should be extremely useful for new embroiderers, both to practise from and as a constant source of reference. You'll soon notice that embroidery stitches can be made to work for you creatively, just as paint does for an artist.

There are three types of embroidery patterns for you to work from: tracing patterns, graphs and charts. Explanatory notes and diagrams are given with each, and for precise details on different stitches, refer to the Stitch Library on the previous pages.

Materials

Material requirements may read something like this: D.M.C. six-strand floss. 1.666 scarlet (4). This is what it means; the first number (in this case 1) always refers to the area on the pattern where this thread is to be used. This is followed by the manufacturer's colour number (666) and the colour description (scarlet). The last figure in parentheses refers to the probable number of skeins or balls of thread you will need.

Monogram alphabet

This is an alphabet of letters with many uses. Embroider it in one of the three styles – gay, formal or pretty – and use one letter, or a combination on towels, clothing, handkerchiefs or scarves. Transfer the letter outline to the fabric by using dressmaker's carbon paper, and begin by working the outlines. For the chain stitch letters, work as many rows of chain as will fit comfortably within the outline.

Floral motif in pastel shades

Add a personal touch to guest towels with sprigs of hand embroidered flowers. Work the embroidery in pastel shades on a fine linen towel, and position it centrally just above a hemstitched border.

Materials required:
- [ ] linen guest towel
- [ ] Anchor Stranded Cotton in the following colours: 0158 pale kingfisher blue, 0159 kingfisher blue, 0213 pale forest green, 0214 medium forest green, 0216 forest green, 0386 ecru, 0387 cream, 0379 snuff brown, 048 pale rose pink, 050 rose pink

To work the embroidery

Trace the designs onto the guest towels using dressmakers' carbon paper. Centre the flowers and extend the small circles of satin stitch across the width of the towels.

Use the working chart as a guide to the colours and stitches used for each area of the design. Give special attention to keeping the wrong side of the work as neat as possible.

Extend the satin stitch 'spots' across the width of the guest towel

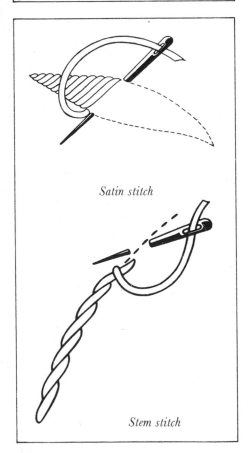

Satin stitch

Stem stitch

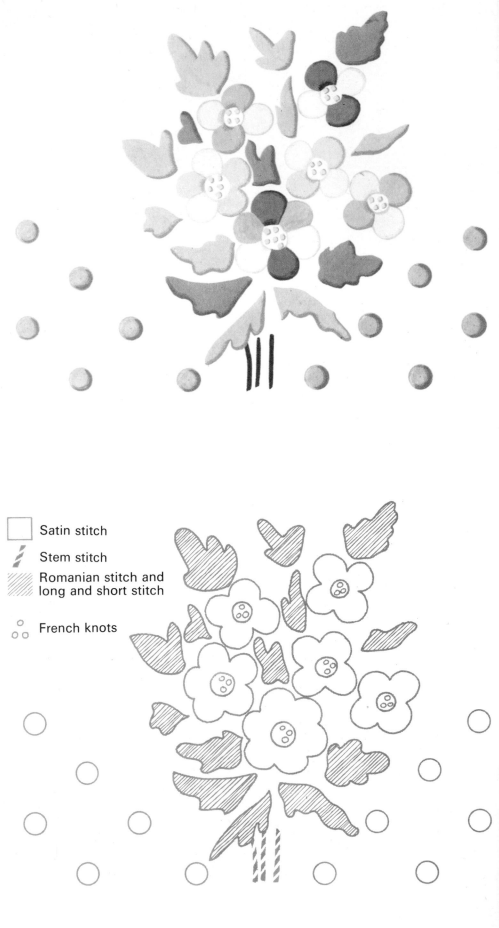

☐ Satin stitch

⟋ Stem stitch

▨ Romanian stitch and long and short stitch

⚬ ⚬⚬ French knots

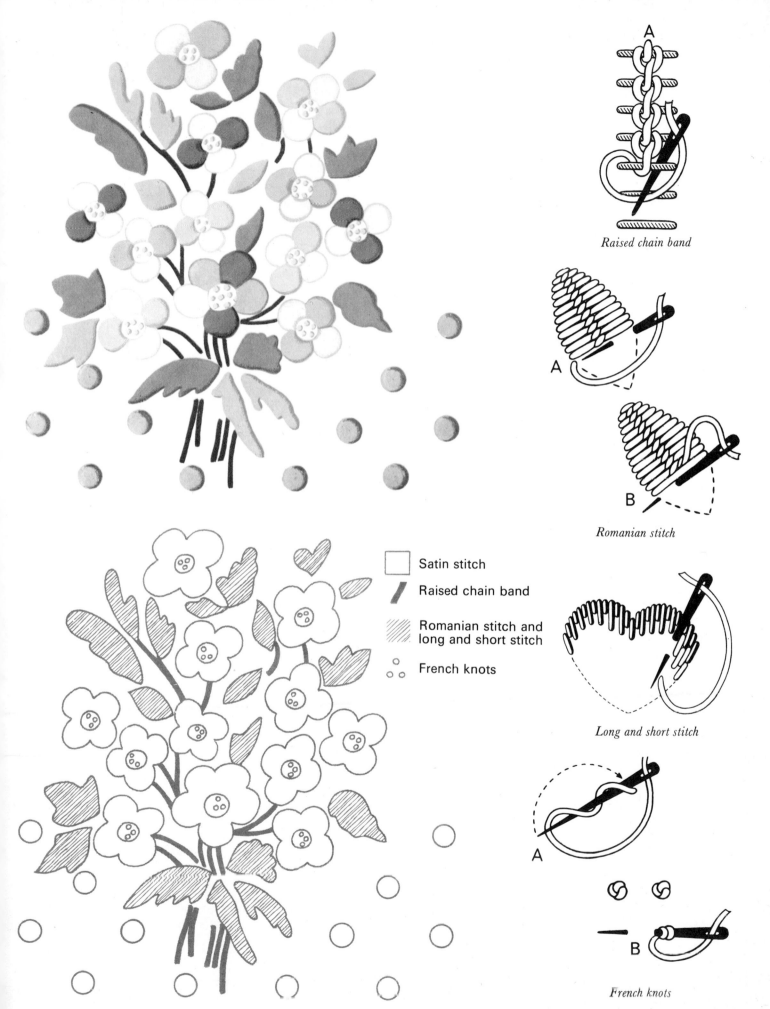

Satin stitch

Raised chain band

Romanian stitch and long and short stitch

French knots

Raised chain band

Romanian stitch

Long and short stitch

French knots

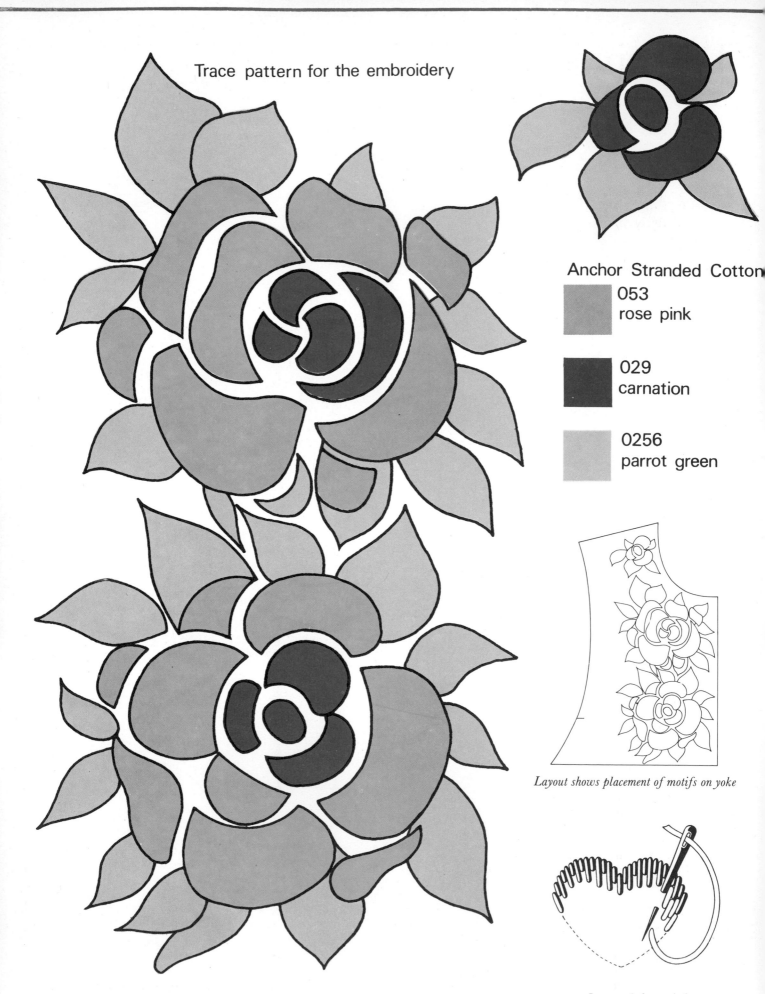

Trace pattern for the embroidery

Anchor Stranded Cotton

053
rose pink

029
carnation

0256
parrot green

Layout shows placement of motifs on yoke

Long and short stitch

The romance
of roses

These vivid roses are bold, pretty embroidery motifs which may be worked entirely in long and short stitch.

To work the embroidery

Materials required
☐ Anchor Stranded Cotton in the following colours and quantities:
   3 skeins 053 rose pink
   2 skeins 029 carnation
   3 skeins 0256 parrot green
☐ No. 5 embroidery needle

Placing the motifs
For the embroidery on the yoke, use the motifs once as shown in the trace pattern and once reversed as a mirror image for the second yoke piece. Use an alternating mirror image of the small rose motifs, working three on each cuff.

Method of working
After tracing the motifs onto the two yoke pieces and cuffs, work the embroidery in long and short stitch, using three strands of stranded cotton in the needle. This should be done before making up the dress.

Adapting the motifs

As a pleasing alternative, group four of the large motifs in the centre of a small linen tablecloth. Place one small motif in the corner of each of a set of matching napkins. Gold and orange on a background of beige linen would be a warm combination, perhaps with olive-green leaves.

Or work a row of the smaller roses on a strip of fabric to be used as curtain tiebacks, using the same fabric as the curtains. The result is particularly gay if the fabric is spotted or striped.

Another idea is to work the roses in appliqué on a bedspread, using scraps of cotton fabric (try combining solid colours and prints, as in patchwork). Individual petals and leaves can be stitched to the background fabric either by hand or machine.

Large and small roses are versatile embroidery motifs, used either singly or in groups

Rows
and rows
of rosebuds

The repetition of a simple floral pattern on the shoulders and sleeves of this sheer blouse creates an especially appealing effect. The adaptability of this very feminine motif makes it equally suitable for a border and for larger areas.

The arrangement of the rosebud chains can be varied according to the style of the garment or shape of the article on which it is worked. For instance, several rows of embroidery might be worked at the edge of the sleeves and the work at the shoulders omitted altogether. Or the rosebuds could be positioned either horizontally or vertically along the yoke of a nightdress.

Silk or gros grain cushions with a floral border might be attractively piled on a bed or chaise. Or, for a charming and imaginative gift, make a small sachet of silk filled with lavender. Work the rosebud chains across one side and trim the sachet with cord or braid. Another idea is to trim the patch pockets on a long wool skirt with several rosebud chains.

To work the embroidery
Green and orange stranded cotton are required for the blouse shown. Extend the trace pattern given for the embroidery to include nine flowers in a row. Trace the flowers onto the sleeves in consecutive rows, making certain to align them carefully. Ideally, the embroidery should be worked before the garment is made up, but this is not essential.

Using four strands of cotton in the needle, work the stem, sprigs and leaves in green and the rosebuds in orange. The stem is worked in stem stitch and the sprigs are in large chain stitch held with a cross stitch. The calyx of each flower, its leaves and the rosebud itself are all worked in satin stitch in the appropriate colours.

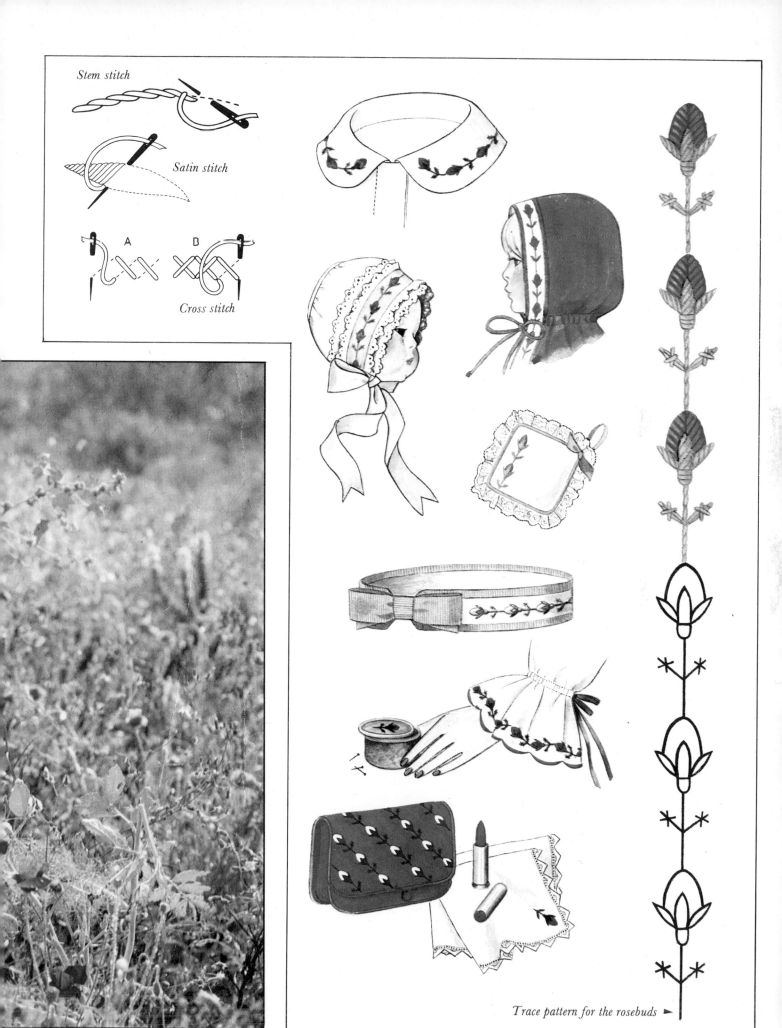

Stem stitch

Satin stitch

A B

Cross stitch

Trace pattern for the rosebuds ▶

Flowers strewn across a smock

These little sprays of Alpine flowers add charm and colour to a muslin smock and can be scattered at random or arranged more formally, depending upon the style of the yoke. A few possibilities are suggested, but the fun of embroidering these motifs lies mainly in the individual's own choice of colour and placement.

To work the embroidery

To work the flowers shown on this smock only four stitches are used, and they are worked throughout with two strands of thread in the needle. The entire motif is first outlined with a double running stitch in black. The gentians, edelweiss and leaves are then worked in twisted chain stitch, and detached chain stitch is used for the Alpine roses and forget-me-nots. A few French knots complete the centres of the flowers. A stitch detail of the double running stitch (sometimes known as Holbein stitch) is given to illustrate how the outline of the motif is worked. A line of running stitches is worked, all stitches being made equal in length and the spaces between them the same length as the individual stitches. On the return journey the stitches are worked over the empty spaces left in the first series of stitches, so that an unbroken line is thus completed.

For the smock illustrated here, one skein each of Anchor stranded cottons 0403, 064, 025, 0157, 0160, 0260, 0204, 0386 and 0212 is required.

Other ideas

These, or similar flowers, would be every bit as appealing on the bodice or yoke of a nightdress. Or a summery linen handbag or canvas needlework bag might well profit from a touch of floral embroidery.

Trace pattern of Alpine flowers for yoke

Double running stitch (or Holbein stitch)

Twisted chain stitch

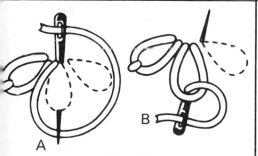

Detached chain stitch

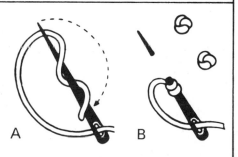

French knot

Ideas for embroidery on a smock

Smart ways with smocking

No other form of embroidery is quite so simple yet effective – hence the enduring popularity of smocking. Through the combined devices of gathering into pleats and subsequent decorative stitching, the appearance of the fabric's surface and of the whole garment is altered in the most attractive way.

Originally used to control fullness in (and even to help waterproof) farm workers' and shepherds' heavy garments, smocking has evolved as a decorative means of transforming a full range of babies', children's and adult garments. Any garment with fullness to be gathered in may be worked in this way, using either a few rows or wide bands of smocking. Some of the possibilities for blouses and smocks are illustrated here, showing some areas which lend themselves particularly well to this form of decorative embroidery.

Fabrics for smocking
The best background for smocking is a smooth, even-textured fabric: cotton, silk, cotton and wool mixtures or fine woollens are all suitable. The work is

▲ *Smocking on bodice combines trellis stitch and feather stitch*

▲ *A long panel on a bodice*

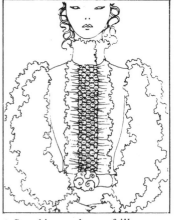

▲ *Traditional-look smocking*

▲ *Smocking gathers a frill*

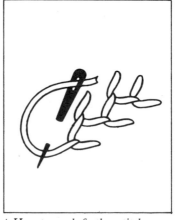

▲ *How to work feather stitch*

done on the material before the garment is made up. Allow about three times the required finished length, as it is particularly important not to skimp on material; this factor is crucial to the effectiveness of a piece of work.

Colour possibilities

As the decorative value of smocking does not depend on the colour – too much colour actually detracts from the effect of the stitching – plan ahead to make quite certain that the colour scheme is kept simple. There are three possibilities to consider when smocking: one may use threads in the same colour as the background fabric, threads in a contrasting colour, or threads of various colours. The effectiveness of both matching and contrasting threads is exemplified by the two blouses illustrated. On the pink blouse, a little colour has been introduced with some floral embroidery on the bodice, whereas the smocking itself is merely a part of the textured backdrop. Conversely, on the green bodice, coloured threads draw particular attention to the smocked areas.

Stitches and threads

Many different stitches are used in smocking, including variations on stem stitch, chevron and feather stitch. Coton à broder and Pearl cotton are particularly suitable threads for this type of stitchery, as they are strong and will not twist (as is sometimes the case with stranded cotton).

Smocking transfers

Before smocking, the area to be worked on must be marked out with rows of dots. As this marking must be very accurate, the use of a transfer for smocking dots will prove invaluable. Transfers are available in various gauges: the spacing of the dots required depends on the weight of the material used and the smocking design itself.

▲ *Surface honeycomb stitch reduces fullness at waist and upper sleeve*

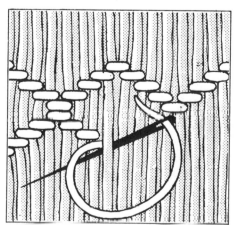

▲ *Trellis stitch*

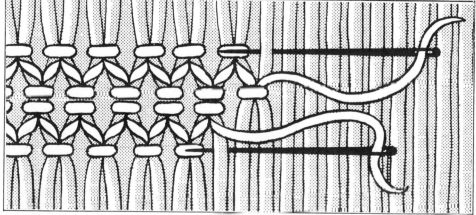

▲ *Surface honeycomb stitch. The thread remains on the right side of the work*

Cross stitch in fashion

A motif worked in a single stitch gives this peasant-style blouse its colourful appeal—and it's quite astonishing just how adaptable this kind of motif can be. It could be used for a linen tablecloth and matching napkins, a bedspread, bed linen, tea cloths, a curtain edging or even a hatband. The secret lies in deciding just how much of the motif can be used effectively.

To work cross stitch
For this type of embroidery on counted threads, it is important to maintain an even, regular appearance; for this reason, the upper half of all the stitches must lie in one direction. Cross stitch may be worked from left to right or right to left, however, keeping this in mind.

For filling large areas of solid cross stitch it is possible to work the first stitch of each cross in one direction and then return along the same row, completing each stitch. Although quicker than working one complete cross at a time, the results are less satisfactory. After working one row of cross stitch, begin the next using the points at which the needle has moved in and out of the material for the first row. In this way, each row of stitches is immediately adjacent to the next.

Embroidery on the blouse
The fabric for cross stitch embroidery should be of even weave and depending upon the density of the material used, embroider with either four or six strands of stranded cotton in the needle. Cross stitch can be worked on cotton, lawn, organdie, linen, or even-weave man-made fibre fabrics.

The following colours in Anchor Stranded Cotton have been used for the blouse illustrated
0187 medium jade green
0189 dark jade green
076 medium old rose
078 dark old rose
0403 black

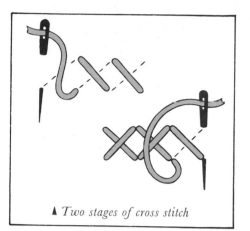

▲ *Two stages of cross stitch*

Ways with cross stitch motifs

Work the entire motif in the centre of a bright-coloured linen tablecloth and repeat the border area round the edge of the cloth. Napkins might be in a contrasting colour perhaps gold napkins with a grey-green cloth, and with the embroidery worked in the same shades as on the tablecloth. Keep the embroidery on the napkins relatively simple; the stylized floral motif alone echoes the feeling of the larger piece. The motif could be repeated all over a bedspread or worked just across the top, with the border edging the entire piece. Try the motif in thick embroidery cotton on coarsely woven linen. For a smaller piece of embroidery work the border pattern alone on a strip of vibrant-coloured silk as a hatband . . . perfect trim for a large, floppy hat in felt or straw. Work the whole motif as a repeat around the edge of a full skirt or as a panel down the front of a dress. The single central flower motif could be embroidered on a knitted or crocheted sweater—or try the motif as a pattern for canvas work enlarged for a brilliant cushion or on fine mark canvas for a beautiful accessory.

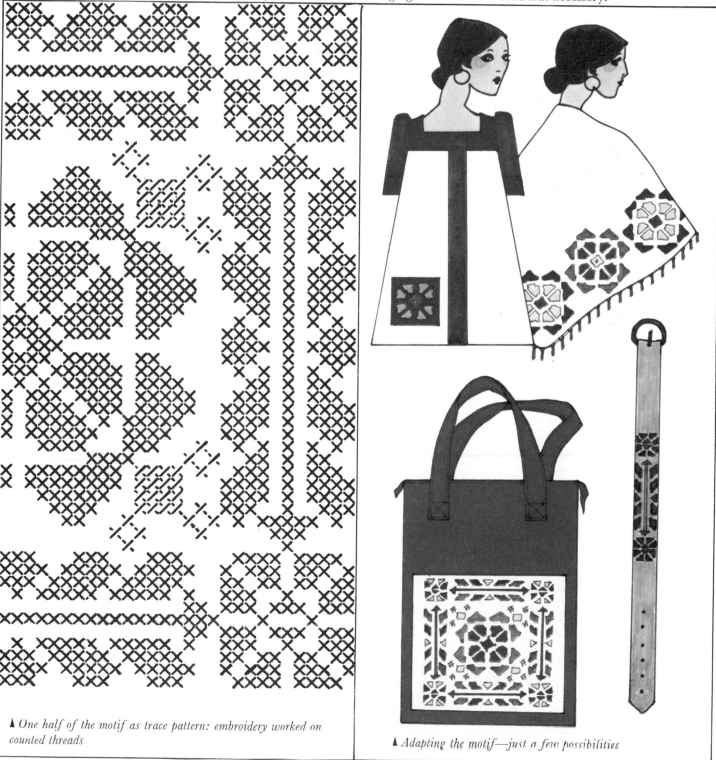

▲ *One half of the motif as trace pattern: embroidery worked on counted threads*

▲ *Adapting the motif—just a few possibilities*

Bold and beautiful

It's astonishing how a simple, colourful floral motif can transform a plain garment into something quite special, with a distinct peasant touch about it. The stitches used for this motif couldn't be simpler—satin stitch, chain stitch and stem stitch. The embroidery shown here has been worked on felt, but for a dressier garment substitute velvet—and team up the waistcoat with crepe trousers or a long, sashed skirt. There's no need to limit yourself to embroidery silks, either; a range of crewel wools would be just as appropriate for working a bold design such as this. A variety of thicknesses and textures is possible through the use of several strands of wool or a combination of embroidery silks or crochet cotton and crewel wool or even metallic threads.

The trace pattern for the floral motif is given life-size so that you can work the embroidery just as it appears on the waistcoat, repeating the motifs as required. Alternatively, use a portion of the design on a pocket or cuffs. Work the motif on a canvas tote bag to make yours just a bit different from all the others—centre the embroidery on a sash and then sew the sash to the front of a tunic, leaving the ends free to be tied at the back. A long cotton skirt with a flounce at the bottom takes on a casual, countrified air with half of the motif worked diagonally on both sides at pocket level. A more ambitious project would be to decorate a long skirt with two panels of the embroidery from waist to hem. These are just a few of the many ways you can use this brilliant design. To work the embroidery as shown the following colours are suggested, using two thicknesses of Anchor Stranded Cotton:·

0301	gorse yellow
0264	pale moss green
0268	dark moss green
0334	flame red

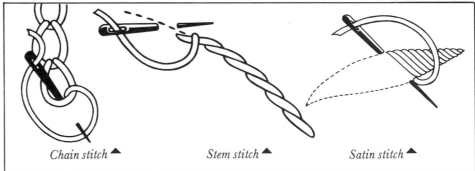

Chain stitch ▲   *Stem stitch* ▲   *Satin stitch* ▲

Uses for the entire motif or one section of it : on a cuff, a sash and a long skirt

Embroidery shown full size for the trace pattern

▼ *A portion of the motif in alternative colours*

Decorative beading

From the very earliest times, man has used natural objects, such as seeds, stones, pieces of polished bone and even teeth as ornaments. Variations in form, texture and materials have resulted in the wide range of beads and bead-like ornaments available today. After several revivals, bead-work has reached a peak of versatility: anything is possible and acceptable. And so great is the diversity from tiny, sparkling bugle beads and rocailles to big, crusty hand-made beads from Persia, Holland and India – that the choice and combinations of beads are entirely a matter of personal preference.

The term 'bead embroidery' generally refers to the application of beads alone to embellish an article, although another effective device is to incorporate stitchery into the design.

For either method, balance in colour and shape is of fundamental importance, whether using geometric or natural shapes, a symmetrical or asymmetrical design.

Here are a few pointers on working with beads. Any material is suitable as a background fabric, although most materials should be backed to support the weight of the beads. The work should be done in a frame, ideally before the garment is made up. A fine needle or tambour needle and silk sewing thread are the only other materials required.

Try to forget the idea that bead embroidery is suitable only for neat collar and cuff borders. Put beads anywhere, as few or as many as you like. Use them to make pictures on a garment, like simplistic paintings or strip cartoons. Combine beading with quilting and padding to make designs in relief. Make beaded cuffs that spill over the edge of the fabric to become beaded bracelets.

Fasten a dress or blouse with beads instead of buttons and, if you like, string together a necklace or choker to match the beading on the garment.

Use your imagination to discover new ways to convert, personalize and dress up a wide range of items with beads.

Cosy quilt

- ☐ ½ yard each of six cotton fabrics (for this quilt: red, pink, blue check, orange check, red flowered spot and red spot)
- ☐ Red and blue machine twist
- ☐ Tailor's chalk
- ☐ Yardstick
- ☐ Glass-headed pins
- ☐ Tracing paper

Here's a bright, appealing quilt for a child which is certain to make even naptime seem like a good idea. It's quite a temptation to make, too, as any sewing machine can do the appliqué and quilting required. What lucky child wouldn't consider this the 'prize' among his birthday or Christmas gifts?

To make the quilt

Materials required for quilt 50 inches by 60 inches

- ☐ 3½ yards blue cotton for backing, 36 inches wide
- ☐ 3 yards Terylene wadding, 36 inches wide

Cutting out the quilt

Cut the blue backing material into two lengths each 1¾ yards long. Placing right sides together, stitch along one long side and press the seam open. Trim backing to 59 inches by 69 inches. Cut the wadding into two 1½ yard lengths and trim each to 50 inches by 30 inches. Lay the 30 inch sides together, making the wadding the same size as the finished quilt, 50 inches by 60inches. There is no need to tack the two pieces of wadding together as a gentle press with a warm iron will join the fibres. Lay the wadding on the centre of the backing, facing the wrong side of this fabric. Tack together (figure 1).

Cutting out the squares and motifs

Using the various cotton fabrics that you have chosen – bright prints are

▼ One of the motifs used to decorate the quilt

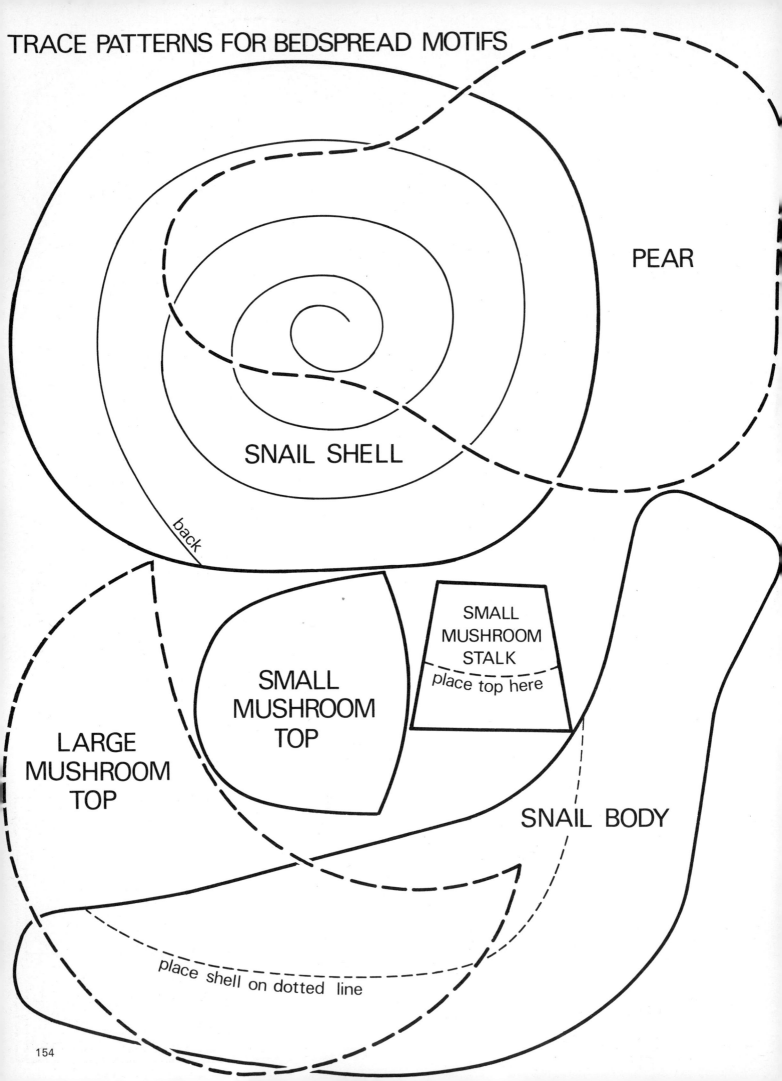

TRACE PATTERNS FOR BEDSPREAD MOTIFS

PEAR

SNAIL SHELL

back

SMALL
MUSHROOM
STALK
place top here

SMALL
MUSHROOM
TOP

LARGE
MUSHROOM
TOP

SNAIL BODY

place shell on dotted line

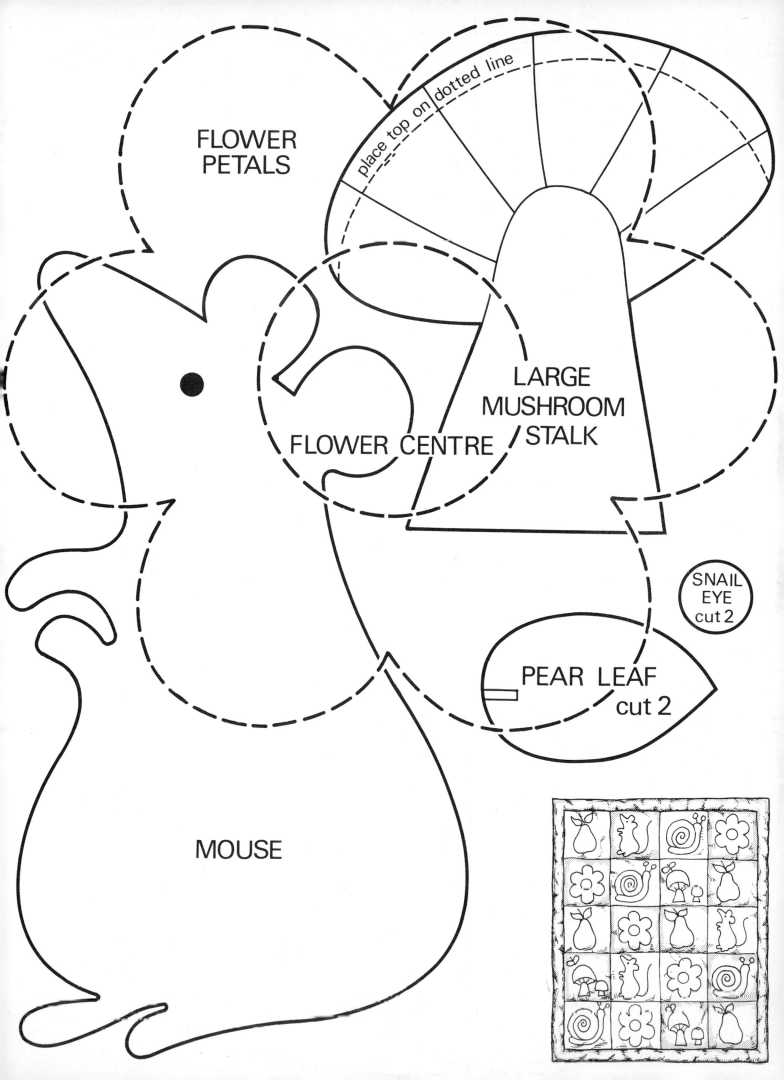

FLOWER
PETALS

place top on dotted line

LARGE
MUSHROOM
STALK

FLOWER CENTRE

SNAIL
EYE
cut 2

PEAR LEAF
cut 2

MOUSE

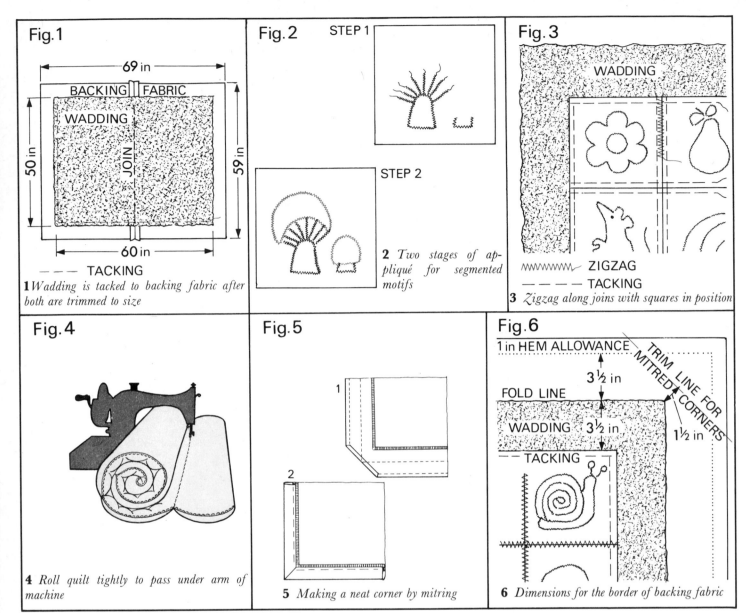

Fig. 1

69 in

BACKING FABRIC

WADDING

JOIN

50 in

59 in

60 in

- - - - TACKING

1 *Wadding is tacked to backing fabric after both are trimmed to size*

Fig. 2

STEP 1

STEP 2

2 *Two stages of appliqué for segmented motifs*

Fig. 3

WADDING

〜〜〜〜〜 ZIGZAG

- - - - - TACKING

3 *Zigzag along joins with squares in position*

Fig. 4

4 *Roll quilt tightly to pass under arm of machine*

Fig. 5

1

2

5 *Making a neat corner by mitring*

Fig. 6

1 in HEM ALLOWANCE

TRIM LINE FOR MITRED CORNERS

3½ in

FOLD LINE

WADDING 3½ in

1½ in

- - TACKING

6 *Dimensions for the border of backing fabric*

cheerful – plan an arrangement of these which will harmonise and balance well. Cut into twenty 12 inch squares; this dimension will include a ¾ inch seam allowance.

Using the trace pattern for the motifs, trace each separately onto tracing paper and cut out. Cut out twenty motifs from the various fabrics, remembering that no seam allowance is required for these as the pieces are sewn along the rough edge with zigzag stitch.

Sewing on the motifs

Tack one motif in the centre of each square and, placing a sheet of thin paper under the square to keep the material from puckering, machine stitch along the edge of the motifs using zigzag stitch. (Do not use this supplementary layer of paper when quilting; this applies only to appliqué.) When using one section of the motif over another (e.g. the mushroom), first tack and stitch the lower part onto the square, then tack and stitch the upper part on

(figure 2).

Tear away the paper from the under side of the stitching and press each square with a damp cloth.

Stitching the quilt together

Machine stitch the squares together, using a ¾ inch seam allowance. When this has been completed, the joined squares will number four on one side and five on the other. Press the seams open. Lay the joined squares onto the wadding, right side up. Pin these layers together and tack round the edges, then tack around the sides of each machined square. This will hold the squares in position when the machine quilting of each section is done.

Stitch along the joins between the squares, using the fancy stitch of your choice. A fairly open stitch will probably create the best effect and contrasts nicely with the zigzag used for appliqué (figure 3).

To avoid difficulty in passing the bulk of the quilt under the arm of the ma-

chine while stitching, roll it up tightly and have someone help you hold it as you stitch (figure 4).

Finishing the edges

Trim the corner of the backing fabric as indicated, then mitre and tack (figure 5). Turn the excess backing material which extends beyond the rim of wadding over to the front of the quilt to form a border (figure 6). Allow 1 inch turning and tack. Machine stitch along the joining of border edge and appliqué squares, and stitch again round the outside edge of the border, ¼ inch from the folded edge.

Tidy up the back of the quilt by trimming machine threads and remove tacking stitches.

Note: When making quilts, use glass-headed pins. Count out the number you need before starting to work and again after removing them, to make quite certain that none is left in the work. Use only one needle, and take great care not to lose it.

Design with simple circles

These cushions are three colourful variations on the theme of circles. A vibrant range of colours—and just a few stitches—combine to make all three. A striking effect could be achieved by matching one embroidered cushion with others in plain fabrics chosen to pick up the embroidery thread colours.

Materials you will need

To make each cushion 14 inches square:

- ☐ 2 17 inch squares of furnishing cotton
- ☐ 1 16 inch square cushion pad
- ☐ Crewel needles, No.6 and No.7
- ☐ Contrast bias binding
- ☐ Coats Anchor Stranded Cotton in the following colours and quantities: **Cushion A** 1 skein each **1.** 074 pale old rose, **2.** 09 geranium, **3.** 0315 tangerine, **4.** 052 rose pink; 2 skeins each **5.** 076 old rose, **6.** 087 cyclamen; 4 skeins **7.** 0333 flame. **Cushion B** 1 skein each **1.** 0125 indigo, **2.** 0186 jade, **3.** 0849 grey blue, **4.** 0109 parma violet; 2 skeins each **5.** 0142 electric blue, **6.** 0122 delphinium. **Cushion C** 1 skein each **1.** 0125 indigo, **2.** 061 magenta, **3.** 097 violet, **4.** 0889 bark, **5.** 0122 delphinium, **6.** 0853 tawny beige, **7.** 0893 muted pink, **8.** 0117 periwinkle, **9.** 0164 kingfisher.

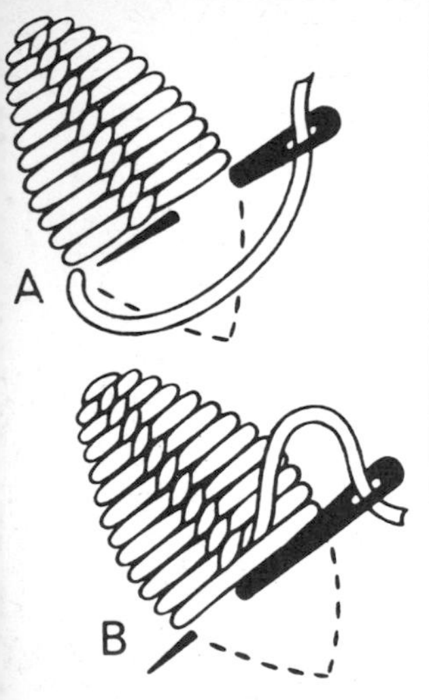

Cushion A

To work the embroidery

Oversew the edges of the fabric. With running stitches, mark the vertical and horizontal centres and transfer the design to the fabric. A portion of each design is given full size on the following pages; the remaining portions can be drawn to scale accordingly, using a pair of compasses.

Work the Roumanian stitch circles with two strands of cotton in the needle. Angle them toward the centre point; they will be closely packed on the inner line and fan out slightly on the outer. With three strands in the needle, fill the centres with stem stitch circles and buttonhole wheels as shown in the diagram. The large buttonhole wheels are worked with three strands of cotton in the needle and the scattered stem stitch circles and French knots require six strands.

Cushion B

To work the embroidery

Use three strands of cotton for the buttonhole wheels and six for the French knots. Angle the large buttonhole wheels toward the centre point. The inner wheels form an eyelet at the centre. Take the needle from the same central point as you work round.

Cushion C

To work the embroidery

Work the chain stitch flowers with three strands of cotton. Stitch in a spiral from the outer edge to the centre. The violet flowers are worked in a long detached chain stitch angled toward the centre point. Work a smaller, second stitch within each petal. The florets in the delphinium are made with closely stitched buttonhole wheels. Use four strands in the needle.

To make up the cushions

Press the embroidery face down over a thick pad. Decorate the edges of the cushions with a bias binding piping. Match it to one of the colours in the embroidery. Pin the two cushion pieces, right sides together, with the folded bias binding sandwiched between the two layers. The fold of the binding faces into the centre. Stitch three sides together through all layers. On the fourth side, the binding is stitched to the seam line of the embroidered square. Turn to the right side and press. Insert the cushion pad and close with oversewing, with a zip, or with press studs.

Roumanian stitch

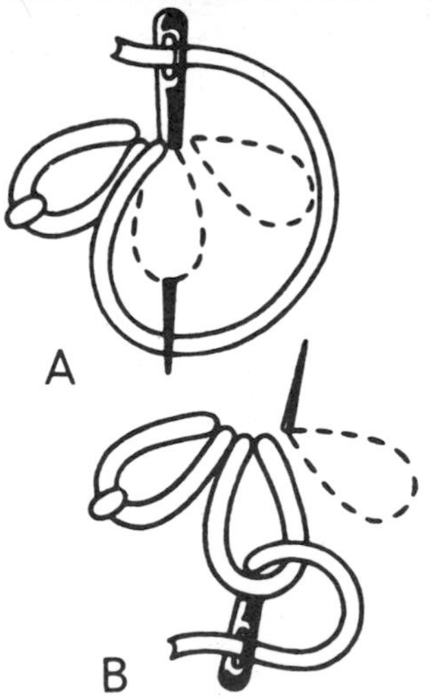

Detached chain stitch

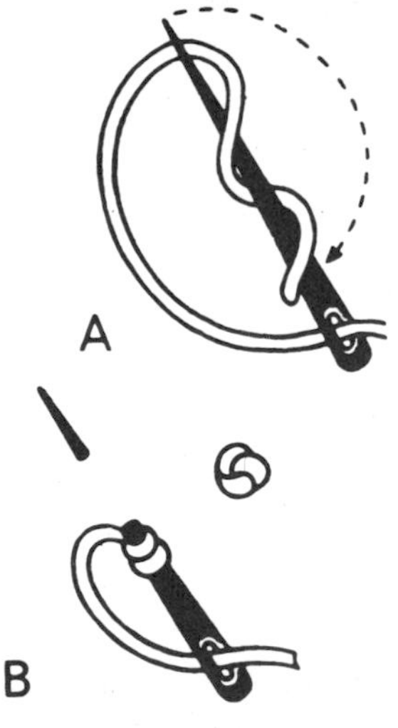

French knot

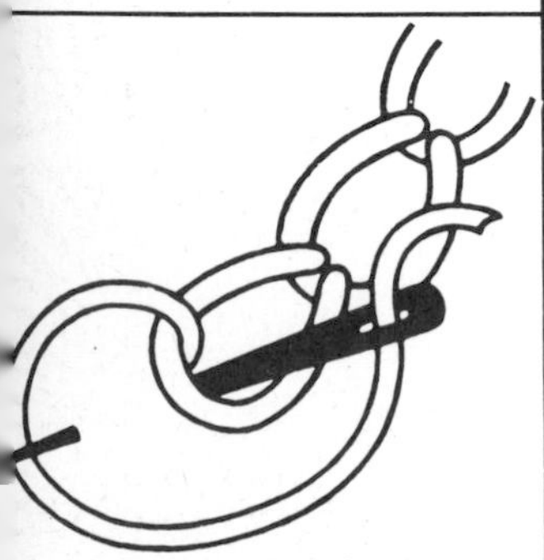

Chain stitch

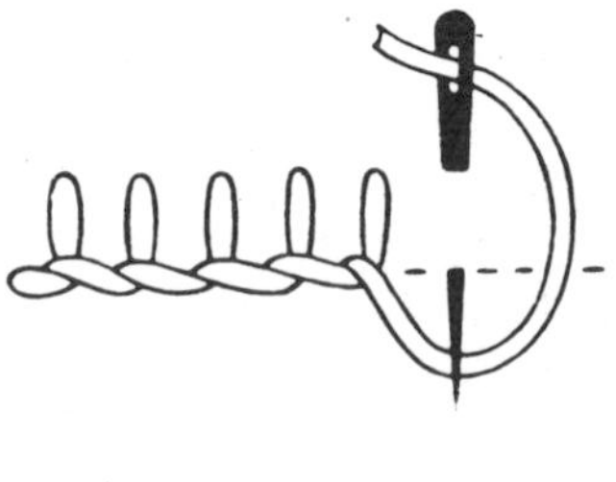

Buttonhole stitch

Stem stitch

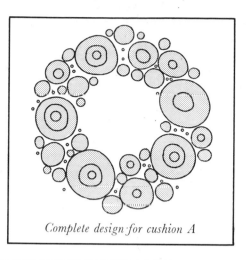

Complete design for cushion A

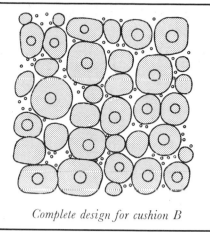

Complete design for cushion B

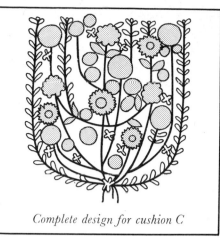

Complete design for cushion C

Trace pattern for cushion A

Colour Key		
1.	074	pale old rose
2.	09	geranium
3.	0315	tangerine
4.	052	rose pink
5.	076	old rose
6.	087	cyclamen
7.	0333	flame

Trace pattern for cushion B

Colour Key		
1.	0125	indigo
2.	0186	jade
3.	0849	grey blue
4.	0109	parma violet
5.	0142	electric blue
6.	0122	delphinium

Trace pattern for cushion C

Colour Key
1. 0125 indigo
2. 061 magenta
3. 097 violet
4. 0889 bark
5. 0122 delphinium
6. 0853 tawny beige
7. 0893 muted pink
8. 0117 periwinkle
9. 0164 kingfisher

Continue outer leaf pattern
to match opposite side

MACRAME

To make this beaded
jacket see page 182

Crash Course Macramé

Setting on threads

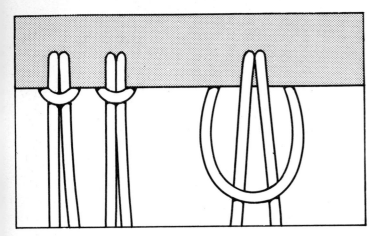

To work onto fabric

Threads must be about eight times the length of the finished work and then folded in half to form doubled threads. Pull the doubled threads. Pull the doubled thread through the material with a crochet hook and knot the ends through the loop. Pull the knot firmly up to the edge of the fabric but not so tightly that the fabric puckers.

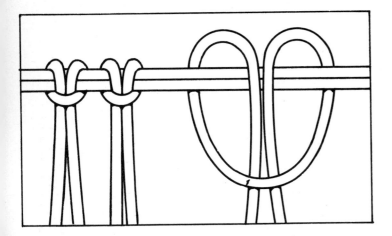

To work separately

Cut a length of yarn about six inches longer than the finished width of the work. Pin to the top of knotting board with overhand knots so that it is taut and running under the setting on knots.

Cut working threads eight times the length of the finished work. Fold each thread in half and tie onto the foundation thread by holding the doubled strand in front of the foundation thread, fold it over the back and pull the ends through the loop, tightening the knot round the foundation thread. Having the doubled threads four times the length of the finished work is only a guide. The thicker the thread is, the more length will be used up by each knot.

The set on threads are pushed close together and it helps to prevent tangling if each thread is wound into a small ball secured with an elastic band. The thread can then be fed out as it is required.

Horizontal cording

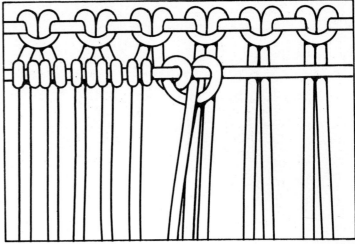

The set on threads are usually secured with one row of horizontal cording which is worked using the basic knot of all macramé.

Each knot is worked over a central core and this can either be a second foundation thread introduced from the side of the work or by using the outer edge thread. A separate thread should be six inches longer than the finished width of the work, the same as the first foundation thread. The central core is called the knot bearer or leader and this is held taut by the right hand, running horizontally under the set on knots. Working from left to right, bring up each single knotting thread in turn and wrap it round the knot bearer to form a knot. Repeat the same movement a second time to form a double knot.

Pull the knot tight and repeat with the next thread along.

As well as making a firm base for beginning or finishing a piece of macramé, horizontal cording can be used within the design but always using one of the knotting threads as leader and not a separate foundation thread.

Double horizontal cording

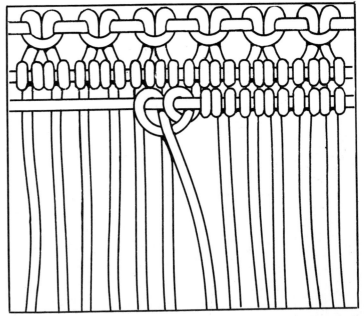

Introduce a third foundation thread or use the outer edge thread and work another line of cording from right to left. The knots will be worked in the same way as explained above but the thread will be knotted round clockwise as opposed to anti-clockwise.

Diagonal cording (stage 1)

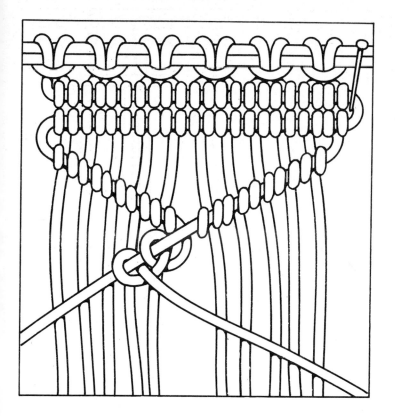

Double diagonal cording (stage 1)

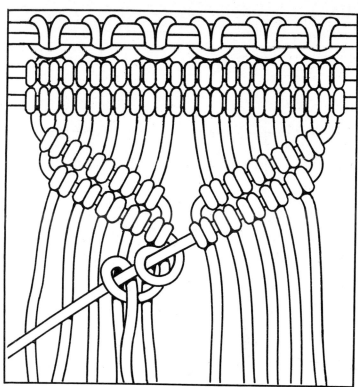

This is worked in the same way as horizontal cording, using one of the knotting threads as a leader, which is held diagonally downwards to either right or left, depending on which way the work is intended to slope.

The thread next to the leader is knotted round it in the same double knot as for horizontal cording. Continue along the row until a diagonal bar is formed.

Cross leaders in the middle as shown in diagram stage 2.

Work one row of diagonal cording on the right and left using the first and last thread as a leader. Take the outside threads and work another row of diagonal cording parallel to the rows already done.

Cord the leader on the right

across to the left. Cord the next thread in the section on the left, across to the left. Complete the cross by cording the leader on the left across to the right. Cord the next thread in the section on the right, across to the right.

Diagonal cording (stage 2)

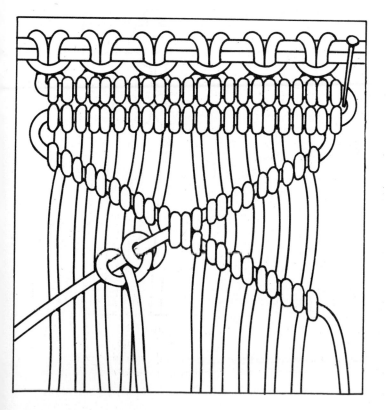

Double diagonal cording (stage 2)

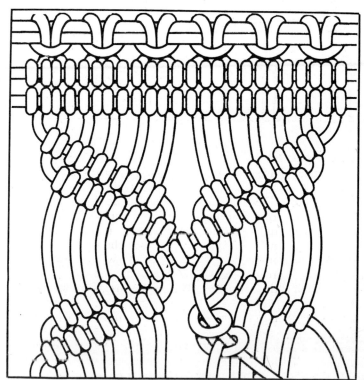

Flat knots

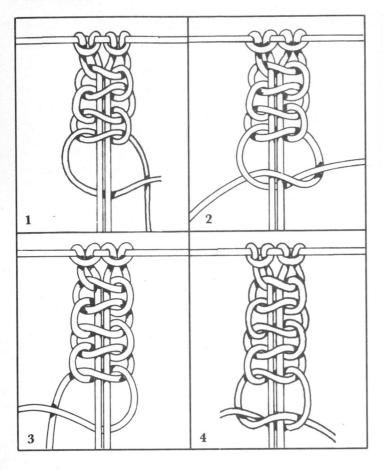

Alternating flat knots

To work flat knots, four threads, or multiples of four, are required. The two centre threads act as a core and the two outer threads are knotted round them. Hold the centre threads taut by winding them round the third finger of the left hand or by securing them to the bottom of the board with a bulldog clip.

Form the right-hand thread into a loop with the end passing under the centre core and over the left-hand thread. Bring the left-hand thread over the core and thread it through the loop from the front of the work.

Pull both ends up until the knot closes tightly round the centre core. This completes the first part of the knot.

Repeat the process in reverse by forming the left-hand thread into a loop and passing the right-hand thread through the loop. Draw up tight. If only one half of the flat knot is repeated continuously the resulting braid will spiral and it depends on whether the first stage or the second stage is used which

way the work will spiral.

Finishing off

Turn back the threads and sew them down at the back of the fabric for about a quarter of an inch, then trim the ends closely. Do the same with the foundation thread. This method is more practical for macramé than darning in the ends as for knitting or crochet because the tightness of the knots makes too firm a fabric to work into. If there is any likelihood of the yarn fraying allow a slightly longer end.

Adding more threads

If the thread is used up before the work is completed, add an extra length by oversewing one end to the end already incorporated in the work. The threads could also be knotted together providing the knot falls to the back of the work.

Set knots in multiples of four. Work a flat knot on each group.

In the next row leave two threads and with the next four threads work a flat knot. Work another flat knot with the next four and so on until

the end of the row when two threads will remain on either side. These will then be incorporated into the work on the next row.

Continue working the rows in this way so that each knot is formed alternately.

164

Corded diamond and a flat knot

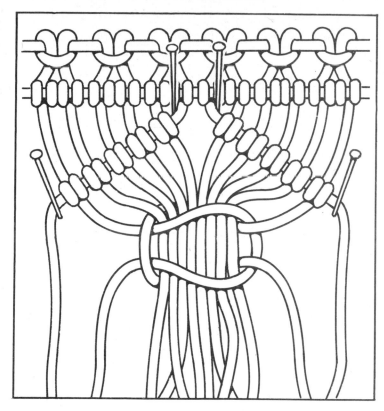

Cord the centre threads out to the left and right diagonally (see diagonal cording page 107).

Omitting both leaders on either side, work a flat knot with the central threads. In the diagram eight threads have been used as a core and two threads used for knotting round them.

Insert a pin just inside each outside leader thread, and cord them back into the centre.

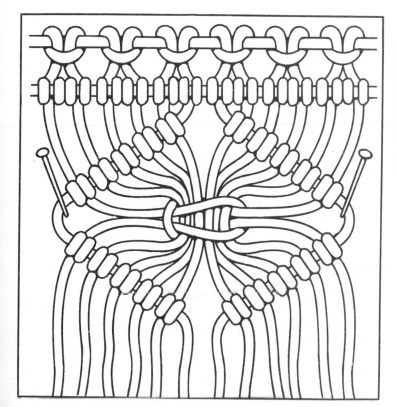

Flat knots with picots

Set on two doubled threads and work one flat knot. Work a second flat knot leaving a space between it and the first one. Push the knot up into place under the first one. The length of thread left between the two knots dictates the size of the picot.

Flat knots with side knots

Set on doubled threads and work a flat knot. Tie an overhand knot (see page 110) on each of the right and left threads using a pin to slide the knots up against the preceding flat knot before finally tightening it. Work a second flat knot.

Flat knots with beads

Set on two doubled threads and work one flat knot. Thread a bead onto each of the left and right-hand threads and work a second flat knot.

N.B. Choose beads which have large holes so that they are easily threaded.

Children's china or wooden threading beads, and small rings available for various purposes from notions departments, all add an attractive three-dimensional look to macramé.

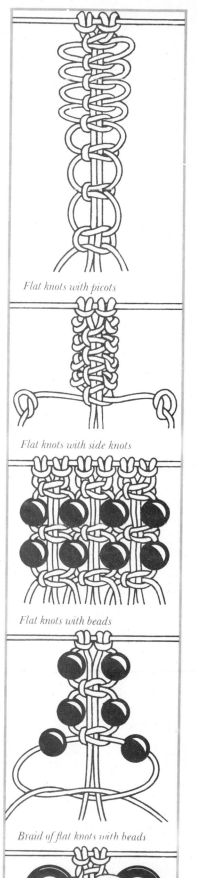

Flat knots with picots

Flat knots with side knots

Flat knots with beads

Braid of flat knots with beads

Overhand knot

An overhand knot can be worked with any number of threads. All thicknesses are held together and used as one to form a loop into which the working end is inserted, top to bottom and front to back. The ends are then pulled to tighten the knot.

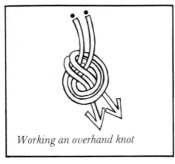

Working an overhand knot

Blackberry-shaped balls

This decorative bobble is usually worked over four threads. Work six flat knots, then using a blunt ended needle, thread the two central threads from front to back

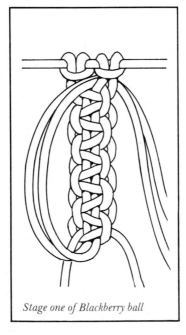

Stage one of Blackberry ball

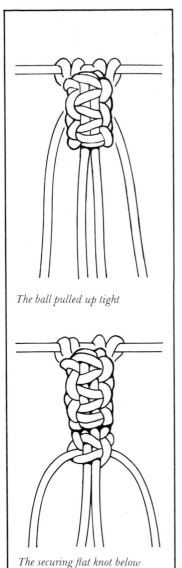

The ball pulled up tight

The securing flat knot below

through the work above the centre of the first knot. Pull up until a little blackberry-shaped roll is formed. The next flat knot which is worked underneath this will then hold the blackberry ball in place.

Picots and scallops

Setting threads onto a foundation cord can be done in more decorative ways than simple knotting by using picots or scallops.

Simple picots. Pin doubled threads behind the foundation cord. Attach to the cord with cording.

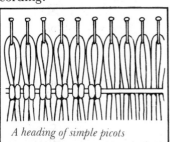

A heading of simple picots

Scallops. Pin doubled threads as for simple picots but using three threads, one inside the other. Keep the spacing even by pinning. Cord to the foundation.

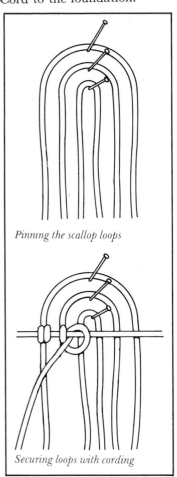

Pinning the scallop loops

Securing loops with cording

Knotted picots. Place three doubled threads side by side behind the foundation cord with the centre thread slightly higher than those on either

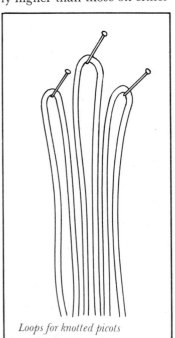

Loops for knotted picots

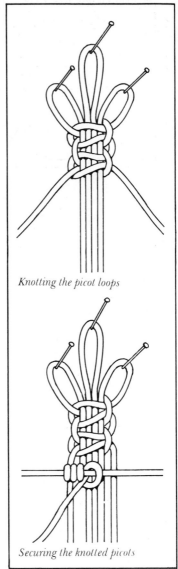

Knotting the picot loops

Securing the knotted picots

side. Work a flat knot using the four central threads as a core. Fix with a row of horizontal cording to foundation cord.

Knotted loops. Pin two doubled threads, one inside the other. Work two flat knots and attach scallops to foundation cord with cording.

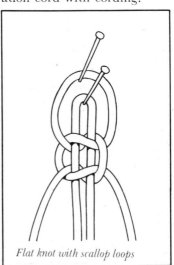

Flat knot with scallop loops

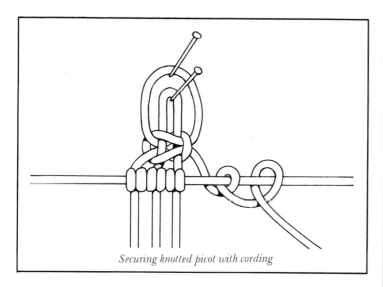

Securing knotted picot with cording

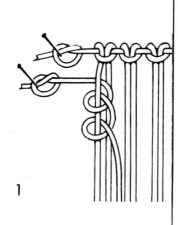

1

Joining in the pattern thread with a vertical knot

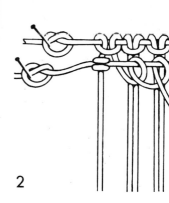

2

Using the pattern thread as horizontal cording leader

Knotted chain

Chains are made by alternating simple knots from left to right. A left and right hand knot make one knotted chain.

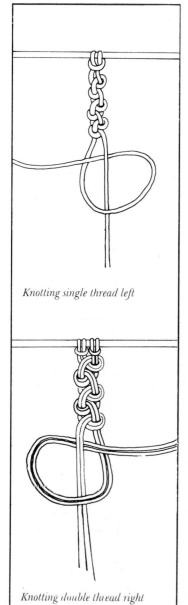

Knotting single thread left

Knotting double thread right

Cavandoli

In this technique only two colours and one knot are used. Traditionally, the horizontal knotting provides the background and the vertical knots form the pattern. The result is a smooth, tightly knotted fabric.

The horizontal knots are horizontal cording as given in the macramé crash course page 106.

The vertical cording knot is exactly the same but the hanging thread is used as leader and a second thread is knotted down the length of this leader. The knotting thread always starts by passing behind the leader so that when travelling across the work to the right the knots face to the right, and when returning across the work on the next row the knots point to the left.

The threads in the background colour are set on the foundation thread, and the ball of thread in the pattern colour is attached to the left hand corner of the work, from where it is used as a leader for the horizontal cording or used to make the vertical cording knots which form the pattern.

Designs are worked out on squared paper using crosses or shading for pattern. The resulting work, however, is elongated in comparison to the square shape of the original chart.

It is traditional to work the first and last threads in vertical cording with a little picot

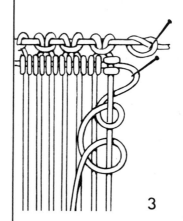

3

Pinning thread for picot; making first vertical knot

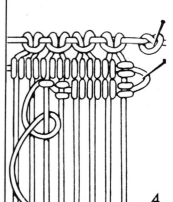

4

Working the pattern in vertical knots as required

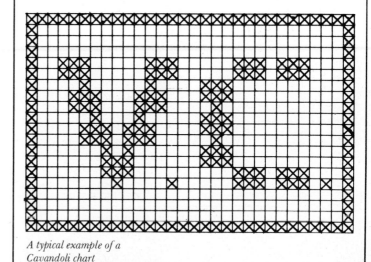

A typical example of a Cavandoli chart

when the thread is turned, thus forming a pretty border. Allow at least eight times the length of the finished article for the background colour threads. The pattern colour is all in one ball and is the same length as the total of all the background threads added together. Roll each thread into a ball to prevent tangling.

Persian Pattern Bag

A smart bag to wear with any outfit. It is worked in Persian pattern and decorated at the top with picots.

Cavandoli Watchstraps

These super Cavandoli watchstraps made in three sizes to fit a man, woman and child, are both practical and eye-catching. They can be worn for everyday or for special occasions.

Persian pattern shoulder bag

You will need
One 50grm ball each of tan, cream, light blue, dark blue in Sirdar Pullman Knitting Wool
Toning darning wool
¼yd cotton sateen lining
Sewing cotton to match lining

Measurements
8in square excluding heading and fringe
N.B. Make 2 squares of this size

How to make the bag
Cut 12 cream lengths each 90 inches, 6 lengths each of tan, light blue and dark blue, all 100 inches.
Set these threads with simple picots in the following order: *2 cream, one dark blue, one tan (cross the blue and tan picots and attach to the foundation thread alternately in the order blue, tan, blue, tan), 2 light blue, one tan, one dark blue (this time in the order tan, dark blue, tan, dark blue) 2 cream. Repeat from * 2 times more.
Fix with 2 rows of horizontal cording, using separate threads laid across.
The entire design is worked in diagonal cording, the rows being close together some sloping to the right and some to the left.
First row Using 2nd thread as leader, cord to left with first thread. Using 3rd thread as leader, cord to left over 2 threads. Using 4th thread as leader, cord to left over 3 threads. Leave these 4 cream threads to the left. Using 6th (tan) thread as leader, cord to left once. Using 8th (tan) thread as leader, cord to left over 2 threads. Using 10th (light blue) thread as leader, cord to left over 3 threads. Using 12th (light blue) thread as leader, cord to left over 4 threads. Using 14th (dark blue) thread as leader, cord to left over 5 threads. Using 16th (dark blue) thread as leader, cord to left over 6 threads. Using 18th (cream) thread as leader, cord to left over 7 threads. Using 20th (cream) thread as leader, cord to left over 8 threads. Using 22nd (cream) thread as leader, cord to left over 9 threads. Using 24th (cream) thread as leader, cord to left over 10 threads.
Leave these threads and repeat this use of alternate threads as leader so that work develops in triangular points. Repeat to end of row.
2nd row Cord first 4 (cream) threads to right over 6 threads. Repeat with next group of cream threads. At the end of the row cord the last 2 cream threads to left, then bring down next 6 coloured threads to the left over themselves, starting with outside (tan) thread, and using each of the others as leader in turn. Remember that the leader always goes over the knotting thread.
3rd row Cord first 6 threads to the right, using outside thread as leader in turn. In the groups of cream threads, cord the 4 on the right-hand side to the left. In the groups of tan and blue threads, cord left-hand groups to the right.
4th row Cord groups of 4 cream threads to left and right as they lie.
5th row Treat first 4 cream threads as in first row. Cord groups of tan and blue threads to left. Cord groups of cream threads to left. At end of row,

cord last 4 cream threads to left, using outside thread as leader in turn.
6th row Repeat as for the 4th row. Take care to continue the half patterns at the sides, as already explained. Work the pattern for 8 inches, ending with one row of horizontal cording.

To finish off
Trim the fringe to 3 inches.
Make a plait with 4 threads each of tan, light and dark blue, cut 90 inches. Tie a knot at each end of the plait.
With right sides together, stitch the 2 pieces of the bag up the sides, matching the pattern and using toning darning wool. Turn to the right side, part the fringe to each side and sew along the bottom of the bag.
Attach the knots of the plait level with the bottom row of horizontal cording on each side of the bag and stitch the plait up each side. Cut lining sateen to fit, sew up the sides and insert in the bag, turning in top and slip stitching to top row of horizontal cording.

Cavandoli watchstraps

Large watch
You will need
One ball each of damson and sungold in Twilley's Crysette
One buckle

Chart for man's watchstrap

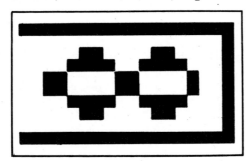

Measurements
Width, ¾in
Length to buckle, 3in
Length to tapered end, 4in

How to make the watchstrap
The instructions for how to work Cavandoli are shown in the Crash Course at the back of the book on page 112. Work from the charts given for each strap.
Length to buckle
Cut 5 lengths each 48 inches in damson, double and set onto bar of watch. Secure watch to working surface. Cut one length of sungold 144 inches and attach to left side of work. Use this thread as a leader throughout. Continue working horizontal and vertical cording following the pattern from the chart. Work picots at either side with sungold.
When the work measures 3 inches attach each of the threads to the buckle and sew in the loose ends on the wrong side. Trim closely.
Work the other end in the same way until 3½ inches have been completed. It will now be necessary to taper the ends. Work the first vertical knot on every row over 2 threads instead of one. Pin the outside

thread to one side until the article is finished. Turn under all the loose threads and sew in at the back.

Chart for child's watchstrap

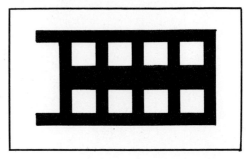

Lady's watch
You will need
One ball Twilley's Lysbet in champagne
One small card Briggs Nylon and Lurex in gold
One buckle

Measurements
Width, ¾in
Length to buckle, 2½in
Length to tapered end, 4in

How to make the watchstrap
Length to buckle
Cut 4 lengths each 36 inches in champagne, double and set onto bar of watch. Secure watch to working surface. Cut one length gold 144 inches and attach to left side of work. Use this thread as a leader throughout. Continue working horizontal and vertical cording following the pattern from the chart. Work picots at either side with gold. Attach threads to buckle as for the large watchstrap. Work the other end in the same way and taper at the end as for the large watchstrap.

Chart for lady's watchstrap

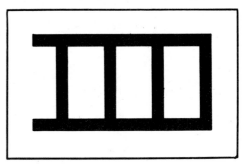

Child's watch
You will need
One ball each of brandy and light blue in Twilley's Lysbet
One buckle

Measurements
Width, ¾in
Length to buckle, 3in
Length to tapered end, 3½in

How to make the watchstrap
Length to buckle
Cut 4 lengths each 36 inches in light blue, double and set onto bar of watch. Secure watch to working surface. Cut one length brandy 120 inches and attach to left side of work. Use this thread as a leader throughout. Continue working horizontal and vertical cording following the pattern from the chart. Work picots at either side with brandy. Attach threads to buckle as for the large watchstrap. Work the other end in the same way and taper at the end as for the large watchstrap.

Chunky Ceramic Necklace

This chunky necklace with blue ceramic beads is worked in the basic macrame knots. It would make the perfect gift for any of your friends or for yourself!

Necklace with ceramic beads

You will need
One 4oz cone white Macramé Twine
5 large blue ceramic beads
One packet 100 small blue glass beads
Scissors
Glue
Tape measure

Measurements
Circumference of necklace, about 16in
Length of centre motif, about 8in

How to make the necklace
Cut 2 lengths each 96 inches and 2 lengths each 36 inches. Find the centres of the 2 36 inch lengths and of one of the 96 inch lengths. Positioning the centres level, lay the 3 lengths together and make an overhand knot 3 inches to the right of the centre, and another 3 inches to the left. These 3 threads form the foundation thread. Pin them to the working surface.
Cut 12 lengths each 48 inches and 10 lengths each 84 inches. Taking each thread separately, double it and set onto the foundation thread in the following order: 6 48 inch lengths, 10 84 inch lengths, and 6 48 inch lengths. These should fit comfortably between the 2 knots on the foundation thread.
Take the remaining 96 inch length, centre it on the work and make a knot 3 inches to the right of the centre and pin it beside the knot on the foundation thread. Using this thread as a leader, cord horizontally across all hanging threads to the left. Make another knot and pin this to the left-hand knot on the foundation thread.

Centre motif
This is worked with the 10 doubled 84 inch lengths. Pass the 2 centre threads through a small bead, then, taking the left-hand thread of these 2 and using it as a leader, cord diagonally to the left over the remaining 9 threads. In the same way cord diagonally to the right with the right-hand centre thread.
Pass 2 centre threads through a small bead and work a flat knot with 4 threads. Using the next thread on either side as a leader, cord diagonally to left and right, threading a small bead onto the next and each alternate knotting cord (3 beads each side).
Pass the centre 2 threads through a small bead. Work a flat knot in the centre with 8 threads, pass the centre 4 threads through a large bead and work another flat knot with 8 threads, pass centre 2 threads through a small bead and make a flat knot with 4 threads.
Work a flat knot with the group of 4 threads on each side of the large bead.
Using outside threads as leader, cord diagonally into the centre.
Using outside threads as a leader, cord diagonally into the centre, threading a small bead on next and alternate knotting cords (4 beads each side).
Pass centre 2 threads through a small bead and work a firm flat knot with 4 threads. This draws the motif into a convex shape. Pass centre 2 threads through a large bead and make a flat knot with 4 threads.
Draw all 7 threads on left side towards large bead and cord to the right with 8th thread. Repeat on right. Gather all threads together in an overhand knot. Leave 4 inches, pass each thread through a small bead, make an overhand knot, cut near the knot and secure with a touch of glue.

Side motifs
The motifs on either side are both the same, each using the group of 6 doubled 48 inch lengths.
Pass centre 2 threads through a small bead, cord to left and right over 5 threads. Work a flat knot with 8 threads. Pass centre 2 threads through a large bead, work a flat knot with 8 threads. Pass centre 2 threads through a small bead, work a flat knot with 4 threads.
Thread 3 beads on the outside leaders and cord them into the centre. Pass the centre 2 threads through a small bead. Draw the outside 4 threads on left towards the small bead, cord diagonally to the right with the 5th thread. Repeat on the right side.
Make an overhand knot with all threads. Leave about 3 inches of thread, put a small bead on each, make an overhand knot, cut near the knot and secure with a touch of glue.

To finish off
Undo the knots on the foundation threads. On each side * thread a small bead onto the 2 centre 36 inch lengths, and using these lengths as a core work 5 flat knots. Repeat from * until necklace is the desired length.
For a fastening, make a buttonhole loop at one end by working simple knots over one of the foundation threads with one thread, then work simple knots on an opposite foundation thread with the 4th thread and attach a large bead at the other end. Make a final overhand knot at each end and cut close to the knot, securing with a touch of glue.

Matching belt and wristband

You will need
1 hank each of pink, purple, green in Atlas Tubular Rayon Cord
Buckle
Small piece Velcro

Measurements
Belt. 26 in by 1¾in
Wristband. 8in by 1¾in
Each repeat measures 1½in

How to make the belt
Cut 2 pink lengths each 24 inches, 2 purple lengths each 24 inches and 4 green lengths each 15 inches. Set threads onto loop end of buckle as follows: 2 green, one pink, 2 purple, one pink and 2 green.
Using 2nd thread from left as leader, cord diagonally to the left over next thread. Using 15th thread from left, cord diagonally to the right over next thread.
Using 4th thread from left as leader, cord diagonally to the left over next 3 threads. Using 13th thread from left, cord diagonally to the right over next 3 threads.
Using each green thread in turn as leader, cord diagonally to the centre over next 8 threads, beginning with the inner green thread of each set.
*Using 4 centre green threads as core, make a flat knot with the 2 green threads on either side.
Using each green thread in turn as leader, cord diagonally out to the sides over next 8 threads, beginning with the outer green thread of each set.
Using 4 centre purple threads as core, make a flat knot with the 2 pink threads on either side.
Using each green thread in turn as leader, cord diagonally into centre as before.*
Repeat from * to * 14 times more.
N.B. Adjust length here, allowing 24 inches extra thread for each additional pattern repeat.
Using top right-hand green leaders to continue as leader cord to left over next 4 threads. Using inner left-hand green thread as leader cord diagonally to right over next 3 threads. Using next green thread from right-hand set as leader, cord diagonally to left over next 3 threads. Using next green thread from left-hand set as leader, cord diagonally to right over next 2 threads. Using next green thread from right-hand set as leader, cord diagonally to left over next 2 threads. Using next green thread from left-hand set as leader, cord diagonally to right over next thread. Using next green thread from right-hand set as leader, cord diagonally to left over next thread.
Using 2nd pink thread from left as leader, cord diagonally to right over next thread. Using outer pink thread at right-hand edge as leader, cord diagonally to left over next thread. Using outer pink thread at left-hand edge as leader, cord diagonally over next 2 threads. Sew in ends.

How to make the wristband
Cut 2 pink lengths each 9 inches, 2 purple lengths each 9 inches and 4 green lengths each 8 inches. Set on to green foundation thread as for belt. Work as for belt repeating from * to * 3 times more instead of 14.
Complete as for belt.

To finish off
Belt. Slot pointed end through buckle bar and stitch in place.
Wristband. Sew in ends of foundation thread. Stitch a small piece of Velcro under pointed end and on right side of square end.

Matching Belt and Wristband

Work this belt and waistband in different colours to match your favourite outfit. You can choose any buckle to fit in with the colour scheme.

Hanging Lampshade

This beautiful hanging lampshade worked in white cotton, is made up of three different panels. It would look equally effective hung over a table or used on a standard lamp.

Hanging lampshade

N.B. The lampshade has 8 panels. There are 3 patterns to choose from, so either take 2 and work them alternately round the shade, or take 3 and choose your favourite 2 to finish off with.

You will need (panels I, II, III)
White Cotton Cord No. 2
Lampshade frame, nylon coated with 8 panels

Measurements

Top diameter, 18in
Bottom diameter, 21½in
Depth, 9¾in excluding fringe
Fringe, 1½in

How to make panel I (see opposite)

[1]Cut lengths each 96 inches, double and set onto the frame in units of 20 per panel. Set a doubled length on the vertical struts. Using a separate thread as a leader, work one row of horizontal cording.[1] Take the 19th thread along a nd using it as a leader work double diagonal cording to the left.

Using the first thread along not yet worked as a leader, work double diagonal cording to the right. These rows should form the top half of a diamond.

Take the 4 centre threads and work a flat knot. Continue working alternating flat knots for the next 9 rows expanding the pattern at each row to form the first half of the diamond. Continue working rows of alternating flat knots down to the base of the diamond. There should be 17 rows of flat knots in all, the 9th row falling in the middle. Using the 2 outer threads on each side as leaders, work double diagonal cording to right and left so that the diamond shape is completed.

[2]Using the 2 threads set on the vertical strut, work 3 knotted chain to the left and 3 to the right, until you reach the bottom.[2] Cord all the ends over the frame and trim tassels to the desired length.

You will need (panel II)
Nylon coated ring 5in diameter

How to make panel II (see page 84)

Repeat from [1] to [1] as in pattern II.
Work a braid on each side of the panel on 8 threads. *Work a vertical knot from left to right, taking thread one over threads 2 and 3. Take thread 5 over thread 4 and work a vertical knot from right to left over threads 2 and 3. Take thread 8 and work a vertical knot from right to left over threads 6 and 7. Take thread 4 and work a vertical knot from left to right over threads 6 and 7.*
Repeat from * to * 14 times alternating threads 4 and 5 so that the braid is linked.
Take the ring and place it so that it is in the middle of the panel (see photograph). Cord the remaining 24 threads onto the ring. Using the 13th thread as a leader work double diagonal cording to the left. Repeat this to the right using the next thread along as a leader. Weave the doubled threads in and out to form a criss-cross pattern and then complete diamond shape by working double diagonal cording to the left and right (see diagram).
Using a separate thread as a leader work double horizontal cording with the 2nd row over the base of the frame. Repeat from [2] to [2] as in pattern I. Cord these ends over the base of the frame and trim tassels.

How to make panel III (see page 85)

Repeat from [1] to [1] as in pattern I.
Divide the threads into groups of 10. Using thread 5 as a leader cord diagonally to the left and then taking thread 6 as a leader cord diagonally to the right. Work a flat knot with these 10 threads. Complete the diamond. Continue across panel until 4 diamonds plus flat knots have been completed. In the next row make 4 diamond shapes again but work 4 alternating flat knots inside each shape. Repeat from * to *.
Repeat from [2] to [2] as in pattern I, cord all the ends onto the base of the frame and trim tassels to length required.

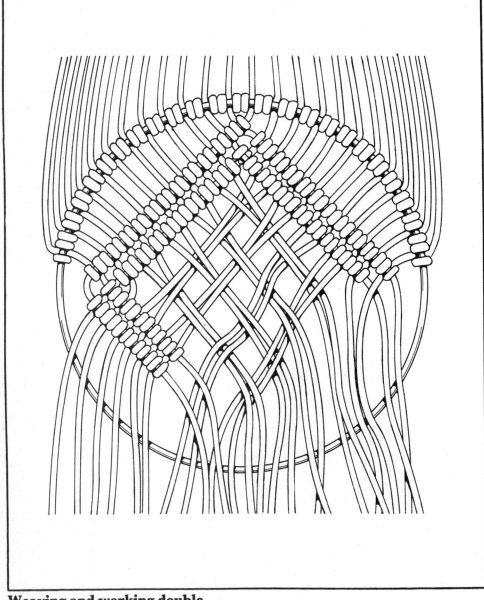

Weaving and working double diagonal cording

Panel I

Panel II

Panel III

Table Mats and Napkin Rings
This attractive set of table mats and napkin rings are worked in rayon stool twine to make them hard wearing and heat proof. The two-tone effect will go with a table cloth in any colour.

Beaded Cotton Jacket

Beaded cotton jacket

You will need
5 hanks Twilley's Vest Cotton No. 1
About 600 12mm beads
A blouse pattern one size smaller
than is usually worn
Crochet hook
Paper

How to make the jacket
The jacket is made in 5 pieces which are crocheted
or overcast together. If you find difficulty in
obtaining beads of the desired colour, use plain
wooden ones (coloured if plain are unobtainable),
string them up and spray with spray gloss paint,
taking care to protect the surface behind the beads
with a sheet of paper.

Preparing the pattern
Cut off the seam allowances on the blouse pieces.
Make a 2nd sleeve, reversing the shape. If the
blouse front is in one piece, cut it in half to give a
left and right front. If already in 2 pieces, trim to
the centre front line and make a 2nd, reversed
front.
Take the 5 pieces (right front, left front, back and
2 sleeves) and mark them off in one inch squares
on the right side. Start at the centre front line of
the fronts, the centre back of the back and the
centre of the sleeves.
Draw a coloured line across at armhole level of all
5 of the pattern pieces.

Setting up the board
The board should be slightly larger than the biggest
pattern piece.
Start with the right front and sellotape this onto
the board, making the centre front line parallel
with the edge of the board.
Crochet a length of chain to go round the sides and
top of the pattern piece plus 6 inches.
Pin the chain round the pattern, starting at the
bottom left hand corner and leaving 3 inches
hanging below the lower edge, thus allowing a
safety margin. Pin up the left side, round the
armhole, shoulder seam, neck edge and down the
centre front, again leaving 3 inches surplus.
Set on doubled threads at the shoulder line,
knotting them into the crochet chain. The threads
when doubled should be 4 times the finished length
of the jacket, including fringe. Knot one doubled
thread into the first chain, miss a chain, knot into
each of the next 2 chain, *miss one chain, knot into
each of the next 2 chain, repeat from * along neck
edge where another single thread is positioned.
Begin working in groups of alternating double flat
knots keeping the knots level with the horizontal
lines on the pattern paper and pinning each knot
in place as it is worked. The threads are slipped
through the crochet chain at the sides as the work
progresses.
Set on new doubled threads as required in the
crochet chain round the neck and armhole edges.
Continue in this way down to the coloured line at
armhole level.

Working the pattern
On all the pieces, the pattern begins at the bottom
of the armhole shaping where the coloured line is
drawn. The pattern is positioned outwards from the
centre front on the fronts, the centre back on the
back and from the centre line of each sleeve.
It is easier to see the pattern if the beads are first
pinned in position over the pattern piece on the
board and threaded in as the work progresses.
The pattern begins at the top with points, one bead
at the apex, then 2 beads and then a row of beads

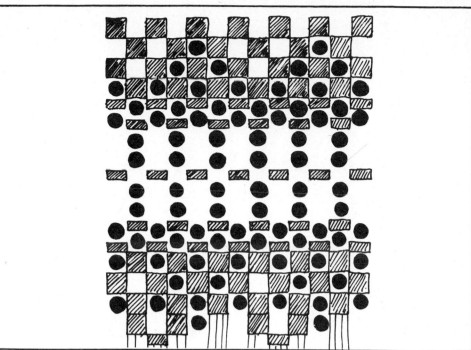

**Complete bead pattern, each full
square representing two flat
knots. (Below) How to thread
the beads horizontally.**

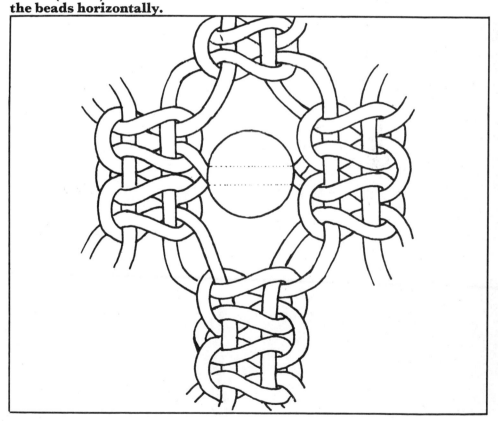

alternated with flat knots, and then a complete row
of beads only. The beads are threaded horizontally,
except on the row which is beads only, and these
are threaded alternately vertically and horizontally.
Under this there are 2 rows of double beading and
then the pattern is worked to form an uneven edge
before the fringe.

Completing the fronts
When the right front is completed, leave the threads
hanging and take the whole piece and the pattern
paper off the board. Sellotape the left front pattern
onto the board and work as before, making sure

both sides match.

Working the back
The back is worked on the same principle as the
fronts, sellotaping the pattern onto the board and
pinning a crochet chain round the side and top
edges with a 3 inch surplus at each end.
Set the doubled threads on at the shoulder seams
and work round the neck shaping, adding new
threads as required. Where the knotting meets at
the centre back it may be necessary to make slight
adjustments to the distance between the knots.
Begin patterning at armhole level as before.

The threads slipped through the crochet chain

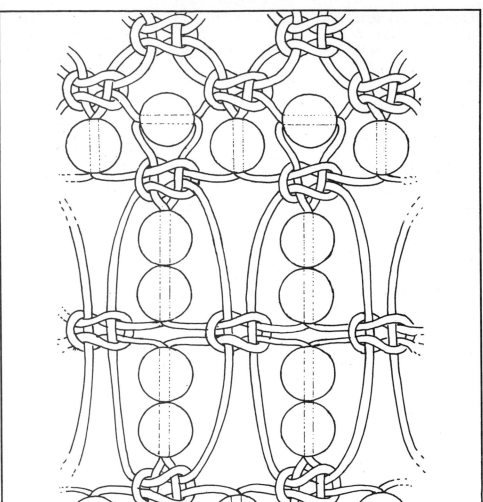

The completely beaded row is threaded horizontally and vertically

Setting on new threads to form the shaping

Working the sleeves
Work the sleeves from the top, increasing as before and placing the pattern centrally.

To finish off
Crochet or overcast the pieces together. Work double crochet all round the neck and front edges to strengthen, at the same time working chain loops down the right front edge for buttonholes. Stitch beads to correspond down the left front for buttons.

Finally trim the fringe and secure, fasten off crochet chain.

The formation of the uneven edge worked before the fringing

Dog Lead and Collar

Any dog would be more than delighted with this lead and collar! They are quick and cheap to make and worked in natural yarn look good against any coat.

Curtain Hanging

This beautiful curtain hanging can be put up over doors or used simply as a wall decoration. Work it to your own design or use the instructions as a guide.

Detail of the hanging

Curtain Fringe (instructions overleaf)

Dog lead and collar

You will need

26yds Atlas Cotton Seine Twine No. 18 medium
22yds Atlas Cotton Seine Twine No. 18 medium (collar)
One metal dog lead fastener
One gilt buckle, 1in by 1½in deep, with centre spike (collar)
One gilt D-ring (collar)
Adhesive

Measurements

Lead. Length, 30in excluding tassel
Width, ½in
Tassel, 7in
Collar. Length, 15in
Width, 1in

How to make the lead

Cut 2 lengths each 11 yards and one length 4 yards, double and set onto ring of fastener with the short lengths in the centre. Using these short lengths as a core work flat knots for 24 inches.
Divide the 6 threads into 2 groups of 3. Using the shorter thread in each group as a core work 6 inches of flat knots on each group.
Make an overhand knot with all 6 threads. Cut tassel to 7 inches and fray out ends.

How to make the collar

Cut 2 lengths each 120 inches, 2 lengths each 60 inches and 2 lengths each 216 inches. Double them, setting on across buckle bar in the following order: one 216 inch length, one 60 inch length, one 216 inch length, one 216 inch length, one 60 inch length and one 120 inch length, so that the spike comes between the 2 216 inch lengths in the centre. Divide threads into 2 groups of 6, and using the 2 centre threads as a core work 2 flat knots on each group. The flat knots on the left are made with the loop to the left (left threads over core threads first), and the flat knots on the right are made with the loop to the right (right threads over core threads first).
Make an overhand knot with the 4 centre threads (2 from each flat knot). Divide threads into 2 groups of 6. Work one flat knot with the loop to the left, and one flat knot with the loop to the right.
Repeat from * to * until there are 11 overhand knots in the centre.
In order to incorporate D-ring, loop the 4 centre threads over the flat side of the D-ring before making the next 3 overhand knots.
Repeat from * to * until the collar measures 15 inches.

To finish off

Work 2 flat knots each over 6 threads. Work a flat knot with 4 centre threads. Turn in threads and sew in at the back. Cut and secure with a touch of clear glue.

Curtain fringe

You will need

Atlas Stool Twine
(one reel for every 12in of fringe)

Measurements

Depth, 8in
Fringe, 7in

How to make the curtain fringe

The fringe is worked in patterns of 12 threads, each pattern measuring 2 inches across. Cut 34 lengths for every 12 inches of fringe each 72 inches and 8 lengths each about 4 inches longer than the finished fringe, one to act as foundation thread and 7 to act as horizontal cording leaders.
Set the required number of lengths onto the foundation thread. Using separate leader, work one row horizontal cording.

Divide the threads into groups of 4 and work 2 double knotted chain on each group. Work 2 rows of horizontal cording, each time introducing a leader.
Divide the threads into groups of 12 and * on each group work the top half of a double diagonal cross. Using both pairs of outside threads work 3 knotted chain and on the next pairs of threads work one knotted chain.
Complete the double diagonal cross*.
Cross the leaders of adjoining groups.
Divide the threads into groups of 2 and with the 2nd and 5th groups, counting from the left, work one knotted chain and with the centre 2 groups work 2 knotted chain.
Divide threads into groups of 12 and repeat from * to *
Work 2 rows of horizontal cording.
Repeat from ** to **.
Work another 2 rows of horizontal cording. Divide the threads into groups of 4 and make an overhand knot on each group.

To finish off

Trim the tassels to 7 inches and tease out the thread to form a fringe.
Sew in ends of foundation thread and leaders.

Curtain hanging

You will need

20 100grm balls Rug Wool
One skein Atlas Rayon Cord
½in dowelling 35in long
One 5in diameter ring
One 7in diameter ring
One 16in diameter ring
123 bamboo curtain beads

Measurements

27in by 67in

How to make the hanging

Cut 60 lengths each 15 yards and 8 lengths each 128 inches.
Set the longer lengths onto the dowelling.
Using the left-hand thread as leader, cord horizontally across all threads. Counting from the left, use threads 21 to 32. Divide them into 3 groups of 4 threads each and work 2 flat knots on each group, 7 inches below horizontal cording.
Next, use threads 17 to 32 and divide into 4 groups of 4 threads each. On the left hand group work 2 flat knots, on the other groups work one flat knot. Work a 3rd row of alternated flat knots, adding one group to each side. Continue in rows of alternating flat knots worked to the shape of a circle, making the widest point where the outer left-hand group is added in and leaving the centre 17 threads free.
Before working the lower half of the circle, place a bead on each of these free threads, tying an overhand knot under each bead to hold it in the required position. On threads 69 to 72 work the first half of a flat knot to form a spiral, beginning 4½ inches from horizontal cording and continuing for 8 inches.
On next group of 4 threads work a second spiral, 3 inches below the horizontal cording for 8 inches.
Work 8 more spirals in this way as follows: 6 inches down for 8 inches, one inch down for 11½ inches, 9½ inches down for 5½ inches, 5 inches down for 8 inches, 8 inches down for 7 inches, 4 inches down for 7 inches, 2½ inches down for 7 inches, 6½ inches down for 4 inches.

Cord the threads of the 3rd spiral onto the largest ring.
Set on 2 lengths rayon cord doubled as one to each side of the 3rd spiral and 2 doubled pairs between the 2nd and 3rd threads of the 3rd spiral. Cord on 33 threads to the left and 37 to the right of the 3rd spiral, introducing a pair of rayon cords as one between 2nd and 3rd threads of 6th spiral.
Using threads 1 to 40, work 11 spirals as before, as follows: 18 inches down for 5 inches, 21 inches down for 3 inches, 19 inches down for 5 inches, 21 inches down for 2 inches, 18 inches down for 9 inches, 23 inches down for 7 inches, 20 inches down for 14 inches, 22 inches down for 8 inches, 20½ inches for 7 inches, 17½ inches for 15½ inches, 24 inches down for 5 inches and first linking one thread to the ring. Under the first 4 spirals work 3 alternated spirals, the first for 4½ inches, the 2nd for 6½ inches and the 3rd for 13 inches. Under the first 2 of these work 2 further alternated spirals, the first for 2½ inches, the 2nd for 4½ inches. Using the 2 threads to the left of the 13 inch spiral and 2 threads from the spiral, work a one inch spiral.
Cord threads 15 to 55 onto the 7 inch ring, placing it immediately below the 14 and 15½ inch spirals.
Work the centre braid of the large ring on threads from 3rd spiral in rayon cord, using cord double throughout. Work 3 rows diagonal cording into the centre and link with a blackberry ball. Work 3 rows diagonal cording out again. Repeat this twice more then work 3 rows diagonal cording into the centre again. Cord onto lower part of ring. On the 3 groups of 4 threads to the left of the centre braid, work one flat knot on each group. Work 2 rows alternated flat knots under this*. Thread a bead onto the 4th, 5th, 8th and 9th threads and secure with one flat knot under each pair of beads. Work one flat knot on the outer 4 threads of this section and thread a bead onto the centre 2 threads. Secure with one flat knot under the pair of beads then work a row of 2 alternated flat knots, then a row of 3 alternated flat knots.* Repeat from * to * then work 2 rows more alternated flat knots. Cord onto lower part of ring.
On next groups of 4 threads to the left of this, work one flat knot on each group. Using the right-hand group as leaders each in turn, work 4 rows of diagonally cording to the left across the left-hand group. Divide threads into 2 groups of 4 and work one flat knot on each group. Work a diagonal cross. Repeat this 3 times, omitting lower half of last cross. Cord onto lower part of ring.
On the 8 threads to the left of this work 11 rows alternated flat knots, beginning with a single flat knot on centre 4 threads. Cord onto lower part of ring.
On the last group of threads work a zig-zag of diagonal cording at the same time cording over the side of the ring to cover it completely.
On the group of 8 threads to the right of the centre braid, work a spiral using the left-hand thread over the other 7 threads. After 4½ inches, divide into 2 spirals for 4 inches, work single spiral for 2 inches, 2 spirals for 3 inches and finish with single spiral before cording onto lower part of ring.
Working the rayon cord double, on the next group of 6 threads work diagonal cording to right and left for the required length. Cord onto the lower part of the ring.
On the next group of 4 threads work double knotted chain for 5 inches, 2 braids of single knotted chain for 3 inches and complete to the required length with double knotted chain. Cord onto the ring.
On the next group of 4 threads work a spiral for 5 inches, flat knot braid with picots after every 3rd knot for 4½ inches and complete to the required length with a spiral. Cord onto ring.
On the next group of 4 threads work flat knot braid with picots after every 3rd knot for the required length. Cord onto ring.

On the next group of 8 threads work 3 rows of diagonal cording to the right.
Using the 5th thread as leader, cord diagonally to the left across the next 4 threads. Work 2 more rows under this one. Thread a bead onto each of the 3 remaining threads. Work 2 rows diagonal cording to the right across all threads. Repeat the diagonal cording to the left as before, and thread a bead onto each of the next 2 threads. Cord onto the ring. Complete the last group of threads to correspond with the left-hand group.
Divide the right-hand 24 threads into 6 groups of 4 threads and work spirals from the left-hand group as follows: first spiral, from the ring for 14 inches; 2nd, from 3 inches below ring for 7½ inches; 3rd, from the ring for 17 inches; 4th, from the ring for 23 inches; 5th, from the ring for 16 inches; link the last group into the ring about half-way down the side edge and work a spiral for 14 inches.
Miss 8 threads to the left of these spirals, then cord the next 30 threads onto the 5 inch ring. Work one flat knot on each group of rayon threads and one knotted chain on the 2 wool threads between the 2 groups. *Thread a bead on each of the knotting threads of the flat knots and a bead on one of the wool threads. Work a flat knot and knotted chain on the same threads as before.* Repeat from * to * once more. On the remaining threads at either side, work alternating flat knots with 2 beads on the right-hand group and one bead on the left-hand group positioned centrally. Cord all threads onto the lower half of the ring.
On the left-hand group of 4 threads on the ring, work a spiral for 5 inches. On the next group of 4 threads to the left, work a spiral from 13 inches below the large ring for 5 inches. On the next group work a spiral from 9 inches below the large

ring for 11 inches. On the next group work a spiral from 15 inches below the large ring for 6 inches. From the first group from the next ring, make a spiral 4 inches from the ring for 4 inches. On the next group make a spiral from the ring for 11 inches. On the last 2 threads on this ring with 2 threads from the next group to the left, work a spiral for 2 inches.
Using the left-hand thread as leader, cord horizontally across all threads. Work overhand knots and place beads at random on the fringe. Trim to about 18 inches. Double 4 of the shorter lengths and work a spiral, leaving a one inch loop at the top and a one inch space in the spiral after 5 inches. Continue for 9 inches more. Tie a loop in the ends and loop in a 7 inch tassel. Make a 2nd hanging cord in the same way.

Table mat and napkin ring

You will need
2 70yd reels each of blue and green in Atlas Rayon Stool Twine

Measurements
Mat. 19in by 11in
Napkin ring. 7in round
Width, 1in

How to make the mat
Cut 16 lengths blue each 120 inches, one length blue 60 inches, 19 lengths green each 120 inches and one length green 60 inches. Cut 33 lengths blue each 60 inches and 39 lengths green each 60 inches. Pin the threads to the working surface 4 inches from the end, placing them in 9 groups

of 8 threads each, positioning the groups 1½ inches apart and with the following colour sequence: 1st group all blue; 2nd group 2 blue (one green, one blue) 3 times; 3rd group (one green, one blue) 3 times, 2 green; 4th, 5th and 6th groups all green; 7th group 3 green, one blue (one green, one blue) twice; 8th group (one-green, one blue) twice, 4 blue; 9th group all blue.
Work in rows of alternating flat knots for 14 inches. N.B. It is important to tie all the flat knots in the same sequence so that it always faces in the same direction.
Using a length of blue thread, tie a constrictor knot (see diagram) round each group of 8 threads and trim ends to 3½ inches from the knot.
Using a length of green thread, tie a constrictor knot ¾ inch below each blue knot and trim to match the blue ends. Ease up 2 threads on either side of each group between the 2 knots to make loops. Trim all ends to one inch below the green knot and glue ends to prevent fraying.

How to make the napkin ring
Cut 3 lengths blue each 48 inches and one length green 48 inches.
Place 2 pins in working surface and loop threads evenly round them and arranging the sequence to have the left-hand group 2 blue, one green and one blue and the right-hand group to have one blue, one green and 2 blue.
Work in rows of alternating flat knots for 5 inches. Draw the ends through the starting loop and double the ends over.
Using a length of blue thread, tie a constrictor knot round all 16 threads.
Tie a green constrictor knot immediately below the blue one. Trim all ends to one inch and glue ends to prevent fraying.

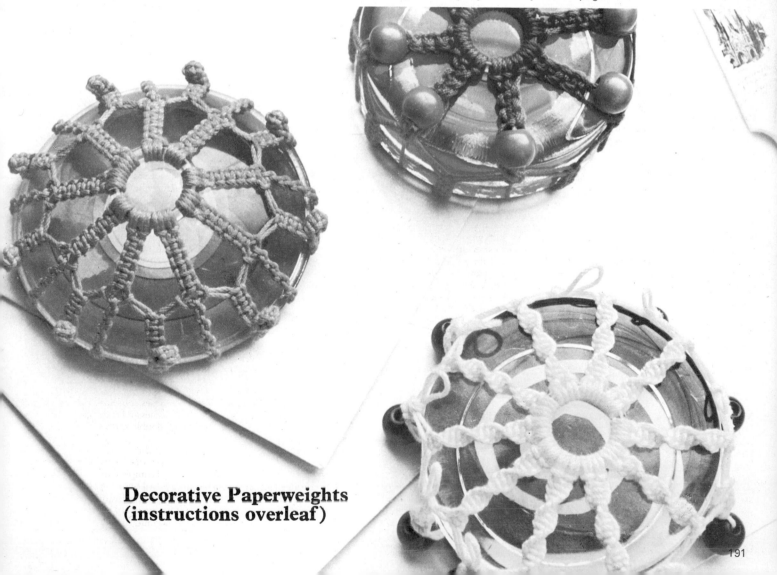

Decorative Paperweights (instructions overleaf)

Paper-weights

Paper-weight I, Kingfisher
You will need
*One ball Twilley's Crysette
One 3in bull's-eye glass paperweight
*Coloured paper
*Plastic curtain ring ¾in diameter
*Flocked Fablon
*Adhesive
*Required for all paper-weights

How to make the paper-weight
Glue coloured paper to base of paper-weight in design of your choice. Cut 18 lengths each 24 inches, double each length and set onto plastic ring.

Divide threads into groups of 4 and work 5 flat knots on each group.

Taking 2 threads of each group together with 2 threads of the next group to alternate the grouping, work 3 flat knots on each newly formed group, positioning the first knot ¾ inch below original groups (see diagram a).

Leave ¼ inch space before continuing for 5 flat knots more. Make a blackberry ball with these 5 flat knots, taking core into ¼ inch space. Secure with 3 flat knots. Cut 9 lengths, each 12 inches. Double each thread over-2 threads leading to alternated groupings, immediately under first 5 flat knots (see diagram a). On each group of 4 threads, work 10 knotted chain.

Remove macramé from working surface and position ring centrally over paper-weight. Holding macramé in position, turn paper-weight over and pin end of each group of knots to paper base. Cut a 48 inch length and double it. Lay the doubled length in a circle ¼ inch in from edge and knot each thread over this leader. Work 3 rows of cording in all (see diagram b). Cut Fablon into circle 2½ inches in diameter and position over ends.

Paper-weight II, yellow and brown
You will need
Paper-weight 2¾in diameter, ¾in deep
10 small wooden beads

How to make the paper-weight
Glue paper to base as for paper-weight I.
Cut 20 lengths each 28 inches and set onto plastic ring.

Divide into groups of 4 threads and work the first half of a flat knot 18 times to form a spiral.

Cut 10 lengths each 14 inches, double and pin top loop in position between spirals. Using these new lengths as cores, and 2 cords from either side as working cords to make the first half of a flat knot 6 times to form a spiral.

Thread a bead onto each core and secure with one flat knot.

Complete as for base of paper-weight I (see diagram b).

Paper-weight III, green and pink
You will need
Paper-weight 2¾in diameter, ¾in deep
8 small wooden beads

How to make the paper-weight
Stick Fablon to base of paper-weight.
Cut 20 lengths each 28 inches, double and set on ring.

Divide into groups of 5 threads and using centre thread as core, with 2 threads on either side as working threads, make 3 flat knots.

Thread bead onto core and secure with one flat knot immediately under bead.

Pin single core threads one inch below each flat knot.

Using the 4 threads between the secured threads, work 8 flat knots beginning ½ inch below bead.

Complete as for paper-weight I (see diagram b).

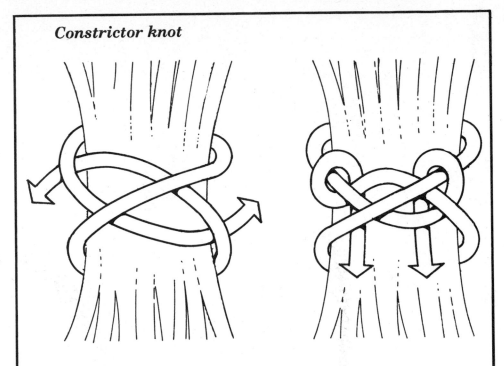

Constrictor knot

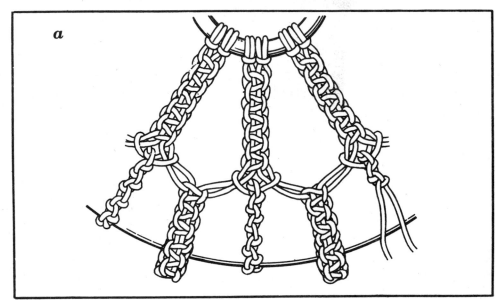

a

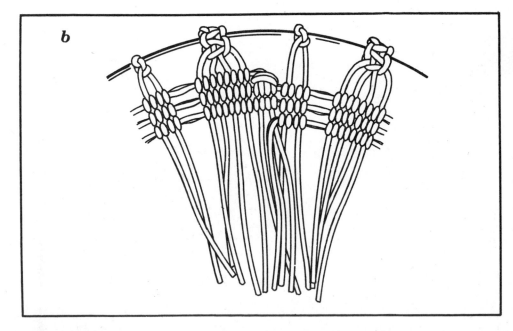

b